MW01633851

"No challenge is too great
for the motivated do-it-yourself
public land bowhunter.
Dream bigger. Achieve more."

—Cameron R. Hanes

Backcountry Bowhunting

A Guide to the Wild Side

Backcountry Bowhunting

A Guide to the Wild Side

Cameron R. Hanes

Eastmans' Publishing, Inc.

POWELL, WYOMING

CRH Publishing, Inc.
Eugene Oregon 97408
cameronhanes.com
Printed in Canada

Cover photograph by Roy Roth
Illustrations by Darcy Tate
Book and cover design by Scott Larsen

ISBN: 978-0-615-46485-5
Library of Congress Control Number: 2006822537

Disclaimer: Backcountry bowhunting and related training takes place in the outdoors. This environment is often remote, adverse and totally unpredictable. You will be involved in activities that include an inherent risk of serious injury or even death. While some situations may be beyond anyone's control, you are fully responsible for knowing your own capabilities, and remaining safely within those limits. Cameron R. Hanes and CRH Publishing, Inc. is in no way responsible in the event of any injury, death or loss suffered by you even if you choose to mimic Cameron's less than intelligent "Living Room Practice Round" maneuver. The publisher questions whether shooting a bow in your living room is sound advice.

Right, wrong or indifferent this book captures Cameron's backcountry bowhunting message, but we implore you, please use your best judgment. Enjoy the book, refine your skills, push your limits but above all else, be cautious and hunt hard. Life is precious.

To my wife Tracey, sons Tanner and Truett and daughter Taryn, who have given unwavering support for as long as I've chased my backcountry bowhunting dreams. When I am gone on those long, lonely, tough trips in the mountains, it is thoughts of my family that give me strength.

About the Author

With a passion for hunting the wild, pure backcountry and a love of the written word, Cameron is living a lifelong dream as the editor of Eastmans' Bowhunting Journal and hunting editor of Eastmans' Hunting Journal. Cameron is now proud to follow up his bestselling book, *Bowhunting Trophy Blacktail*, with this, his new release, *Backcountry Bowhunting, A Guide to the Wild Side*. Cameron has hunted all over the United States as well as Africa and Canada, but by far his greatest love is bowhunting the remote wildernesses of the West and Alaska.

For a glimpse into Cameron's passion for bowhunting, look no further than his training regimen for his backcountry bowhunts. To get ready for bow season, in addition to shooting every single day of the year, Cameron runs 31-mile ultra marathons in the mountains during the off-season. Setting this type of standard, raising the bar to this level, pushing his body to failure and beyond, inspires many. Inspiration...is basically what best defines Cameron Hanes.

Cameron has motivated thousands of hunters through his writing. "Hunters can be a tough crowd; they are savvy and can tell if what you write is real or if you're trying to sell them a bill of goods," says Cameron. He continues, "You can't pull the wool over their eyes. I practice what I preach and the readers know I am genuine because I do a lot of my hunts just like they do, on my own and on public land. It is because of this common thread that they seem to trust my advice." This type of hunting is tough, which is why Cameron's life is devoted year-round to preparing, mentally and physically, for that one, split-second chance to land an arrow on the mark.

More often than not, one chance is all he gets when bowhunting in front of the camera for *Eastmans' Hunting TV*, a nationally syndicated television show on The Outdoor Channel. "The pressure is undeniable, but it is all a challenge I have come to crave and love," says Cameron. "We have captured some great bowhunting footage in the face of very steep odds over the years, which is what I believe makes *Eastmans' Hunting TV* unique."

The motivation Cameron Hanes has is magnetic to hunters who read about and watch his undertakings. He has also been featured at widespread hunters' gatherings including being the keynote speaker at the 2005 Alaska Bowhunters Association banquet and has given seminars at many sportsmen's shows throughout the West.

Devoting himself to learning and honing hunting techniques for his fellow bowhunters has made for an exhilarating career for Cameron. Outdoorsmen have come to respect his knowledge and look forward to his stories. At only 38, Cameron has based his life and career around the things he loves...writing, photography and filming, his family and bowhunting the backcountry.

Contents

24-PAGE BONUS SECTION after page 192

Dwight Schuh feels he and Cameron are kindred spirits of sorts.

Foreword

Enthusiasm, drive, and know-how. These are intangible qualities that fuel and raise some bowhunters above the level of average. The fact that these qualities define Cameron Hanes probably explains, in part, his outstanding success and stature as a bowhunter.

To some extent, Cameron and I are kindred spirits. We both grew up in Oregon, and when we started bowhunting we were both short on money and long on desire. To satisfy our obsessions while keeping the costs down, we hunted on public lands, and we hunted Do-It-Yourself, without guides. We also frequently hunted alone, either because we couldn't find anyone else dumb enough to go along, or because we simply preferred to go alone. During our early years we hunted primarily by backpacking, but later we both acquired pack llamas to extend our mobility and range in the backcountry.

Today we both still love to hunt the backcountry, not only because wilderness and other roadless expanses generally harbor the best public hunting and some of the most beautiful country in North America, but also because they test a hunter's grit and push him to the limits.

Perhaps that's what sets Cameron Hanes apart from the average bowhunter – he pushes himself to the limits. He does everything possible to eliminate the variables and weaknesses in his own performance. He is what I call a "new generation" bowhunter, one of the guys who refines every aspect of his bowhunting equipment, knowledge, and ability. Back when I got into bowhunting – a generation ahead of Cameron – resources were limited. Compound bows were little more than a rumor, commercial tree stands were nonexistent, clothing consisted of WWII camo fatigues, hunting videos and DVDs weren't even in the dream stage... Back then, most of us just grabbed a bow and a quiver full of arrows and sneaked aimlessly through the woods, hoping for a shot at something. Success rate was low.

Oh, how times – and bowhunters – have changed. New generation bowhunters have tapped into all of the modern resources to become far more efficient and successful than in the past. Certainly Cameron Hanes ranks among those who have taken advantage of modern developments to perfect their craft. He does everything possible to get the most out of all the resources available today.

But getting the most out of modern equipment, technology, and educational materials is not what really sets him apart from other bowhunters. Lots of bowhunters do that. What sets Cameron apart is his drive to get the most out of himself as well.

That's probably most obvious in his physical conditioning. His efforts to stay in shape may have started modestly years ago, but over time they have escalated into long-distance running. The marathon, a race of 26.2 miles, will test anyone's physical and mental endurance, and Cameron has shown himself worthy by running marathons in times of less than three hours, a pace slightly faster than seven minutes per mile.

Not satisfied with that challenge, Cameron more recently has begun running ultra-marathons, distances greater than 26.2 miles. Unlike most marathons, which follow civilized courses on roads and streets, ultras generally follow backcountry trails—hunting conditions. Cameron has run 50-kilometer (31.1 miles) ultra-marathons in about 4 ½ hours.

His feats on the roads and trails clearly demonstrate his high level of physical condition, and his physical condition partially explains his success as a bowhunter. Hunting in the backcountry where high elevations, steep slopes, and long distances can wear out a person's body in a hurry, Cameron can hunt all day, every day, for weeks on end. In many cases, the outcome of a hunt depends on endurance alone, and Cameron Hanes makes sure that lack of endurance never hampers his chances.

Equally important, the total preparation Cameron preaches and practices builds confidence. Both confidence and doubt are self-fulfilling prophecies. A hunter who goes into the field half prepared will be filled with doubts about his stamina and ability, and he will find ways to fail. A guy like Cameron who prepares to the max removes all doubts. Sure he faces the same obstacles that any other hunter faces, but because of his confidence he will finds ways to win.

Perhaps above all, the ultra-marathon mentality of Cameron Hanes implies a never-quit attitude. Not that everyone has to run endurance races to succeed in the field, but the mentality that drives a person to run such races is a vital mentality in bowhunting success. It's the mentality that pushes Cameron to climb one more ridge, to explore one more canyon, to hunt one more hour, to endure one more storm, all in the hopes that he will gain one more opportunity at a big buck or a bugling bull.

Must you carry your efforts to the level of Cameron Hanes to qualify as a serious backcountry bowhunter? No, you do not. But the more you do to eliminate the variables in your own performance, the less influence the variables of all hunting – the actions of big game animals, the weather, other hunters – will have on your performance. To get the most out of yourself in the field, hook onto Cameron Hanes' vapor trail of enthusiasm, desire, and know-how. You'll be a better backcountry bowhunter for it.

Dwight Schuh
Editor, *Bowhunter Magazine* & *TV*

Preface

Twenty years ago when I started hunting the backcountry, there weren't any books that I knew of or resources like the Internet to help me learn the ropes. All of those tough backcountry lessons were learned the hard way and usually on my own on long solo hunts. Painful experiences? There've been a few...

I remember dropping to my knees in the bottom of a huge basin on the eighth day of an extremely brutal hunt after just blowing a 40-yard shot on the biggest bull I'd ever seen. He was a 6x6, 350-class Pope & Young bull anyone would have been proud to hang on their wall and he should have been mine. If I wasn't a tough, wilderness, mountain hunter I would admit that there were tears of frustration welling in my eyes as I looked skyward and asked, "Why?" The five mile, 3,000 foot climb out of that hole was long and dreary after that miss.

I remember easing through a stand of black, old growth timber toward a screaming bull as snow dropped silently from the late September sky. And then just as I'd seen in my dreams, there he was 45 yards away, broadside and looking the other way. Quick thoughts flashed through my mind. I thought about all my buddies at the bow shop back home and how proud I was going to be to tell them this story. I was finally going to kill a monster, on my own, in the wilderness. I thought about how cool the photos were going to look in the rugged country, with the snow and the bull's black antlers. With my bivy-camp-loaded pack hanging off of my shoulders, I eased my bow back and released. In horror I watched my arrow skip harmlessly off of the big 7x6's back. Not meaning any disrespect to any of my high school and college sweethearts, but if I've ever been truly brokenhearted in my life, it was then. The bull and his herd thundered off and my head and shoulders slowly dropped in a classic sign of defeat. I wondered if there was any bowhunting justice. I just knew no one was working as hard as I was for a big bull. It didn't matter though. Life is not fair and big bulls don't care much about bowhunting justice.

"Quod me nutrit me destruit"
— the ill-fated mantra of many no-limit adventure-seeking backcountry bowhunters.

The above examples were mental or execution errors, but don't think there haven't been gear and equipment failings along the way. I have had to sleep with all my clothes on, coat, boots and all because my sleeping bag was not built for the conditions I was subjected to. One time I accidentally cut my self-inflating sleeping pad, which meant for the remainder of the hunt I slept on little more than two thin pieces of canvas. Not good for body heat retention. Before I learned the positive attributes of synthetics, I wore two pairs of cotton socks for years while covering many miles in the mountains, which meant chronic blisters. After a long backcountry hunt back then, my feet looked liked they had been run through a meat grinder...and the list goes on.

I remember many nights spent alone on a lonely ridge, miles from any road asking myself, "Why am I doing this?" I could have had some pretty good hunting much closer to home while teaming up with friends or my brother, Pete, and slept in my own bed every night. Despite all this initial misery I couldn't let it go. Part of it was my pride. I couldn't be beat by the mountains, but another part was it felt like the backcountry called to me like an old friend. I was on my own usually because a 10-day bivouac hunt is a big chunk to bite off for a lot of guys. I simply had a hard time convincing others that like me, they too should love the backcountry. My sales pitch worked on a couple of guys, but only for one hunt. The expanse, remoteness and difficulty ensured that one hunt or scouting trip was enough for them. I have realized over the years that either you love the backcountry or you don't. There isn't much middle ground. This meant my choice was either to hunt alone or stay home. Well, I guess you know what I did.

Now I know all those tough experiences, from the hunting letdowns to the unwise backcountry gear choices, were all part of the deal. They were all part of the learning process and you might wonder, "Well, so how about now? Has your luck changed from all those close, but no cigar experiences?" Yes, it has. The missed shots on big bulls I concluded were lack of mental strength in crunch time or technique flaws. The gear problems have worked themselves out over time with constant refining. Because the feeling of failure is something that incessantly eats at me, I have devised a mental and physical training program. While not infallible, it has been amazingly effective. Consider the results of my last four years of bowhunting the backcountry. I have released 12 arrows and killed 10 Pope & Young animals, from mule deer to bear to caribou to elk. While there were those two shots, one on a big mule deer and one from this past caribou season I would like back, I am reasonably satisfied with these results. I say reasonably because like any psycho, compulsive perfectionist, nothing less than 100% is acceptable regardless of how unrealistic it might be.

As my book will reveal, I am proof positive that there are no shortcuts to backcountry bowhunting success, but if done right, you can definitely shorten up that learning curve. Believe me, you don't want to go through what I did and I don't want you to. I wouldn't wish that deep pain on anyone. If you follow the step-by-step advice I've compiled in this book, you too can have above average success on trophy animals in the backcountry.

Backcountry hunting can cost a little money, there is no doubt. A first-rate guided wilderness elk or mule deer hunt can run anywhere from $5,000 to $10,000. These are not the type of backcountry hunts this book is geared toward.

In the beginning of this personal journey, money or lack thereof meant that if I were to hunt deep in the mountains it would be on a "Do-It-Yourself" or *D-I-Y* hunt. *D-I-Y* is a reference that has really taken hold the last couple of years. What exactly does it mean? To me, plain and simple, it means the hunt starts and ends with you. You have done the research, bought the maps, tested the gear, scouted the country, found the animals and if it all works like it's supposed to, stalked or called your trophy to within bow range and finally, downed him with a razor sharp broadhead released from a well-tuned bow. Other than maybe your best hunting buddy with a sturdy back or a couple sure-footed pack animals, a D-I-Y bowhunt has everything to do with how hard you've worked to make your bowhunting dreams come true.

Bare bones D-I-Y backcountry hunting can still cause financial issues for the budget conscious bowhunter. Before he moved away to Alaska after our one short year of backcountry elk hunting together, I remember longtime hunting partner Roy Roth selling a mint condition .30-30 that his grandpa had given him as a gift, to help fund one of our road trips. We surmised that gas money was a noble cause for Roy's grandpa to bequeath his special offering. Plus, we had little choice; 500 miles separated us from elk country. Desperate times call for desperate measures. Roy's dad also bought us four llamas that I used for years, even after Roy moved, to get my gear in and bounty out of the wilderness. I couldn't afford to hire a packer, let alone buy a guided backcountry hunt in the mountains. As first a college student and then a newly married bowhunter with babies to feed and a wife depending on me, money woes meant if I wanted to experience and learn the ways of the mountains and the animals that called them home, it would be through my own sweat equity and on public land. And, while money might not limit me as much now as it did when I was in my early 20s and just learning the ropes as a backcountry hunter, tough D-I-Y hunts, ripe with adventure are still the most rewarding and are still my one true bowhunting love.

For a successful D-I-Y bowhunt to take place in the wild backcountry, there will typically be months of work involved. To those who have yet to experience a true Do-It-Yourself hunt, I encourage you to put it on your list of things to do. This type of high-octane hunting has had a huge impact on my personal growth and prepared me for nearly any challenge life throws my way, on the hunt or in everyday life. And, who knows, it might do the same for you.

It is my belief that all of the information you'll need to get started, if that is your goal, can be found in the pages of *Backcountry Bowhunting, A Guide to the Wild Side*. The greatest part of this challenge is because the level of commitment must be so high, when it does all finally come together and you've unraveled that blood trail and recovered your trophy, the feeling of accomplishment is unlike any other.

Success on your own in the backcountry is as sweet as it gets for a hard-core bowhunter.

C.R.H.

Mike Eastman interview from NWT Caribou Camp 2005
By Cameron R. Hanes

Well, here we are in the middle of some of the wildest country anywhere. Hundreds of miles from civilization—wolves, grizzlies, weather, the whole nine. Might be the perfect setting to talk a little about hunting the backcountry, which as you know, is my favored method of hunting the rugged mountains of the West and the primary focus of this book.

CRH: *When did you start hunting the backcountry?*

Mike Eastman: My first experience in the backcountry was when my dad, Gordon, came back from guiding sheep hunters in Alaska in 1957. I started serious backcountry hunting when I was 15 years old and a freshman in high school. The year was 1962 and I think what inspired me most was an article I read in Outdoor Life about hunting mule deer above timberline. My dad was given some of the best gear of the time from Eddie Bauer, who was outfitting Mt. Everest mountain climbers. I had access to down sleeping bags, backpacking stoves and so on. I grabbed some of this gear and headed out to an area near Jackson Hole, Wyoming called Cliff Creek. I remember it taking me all day to get up on top. Of course after the climb I was very tired, so I threw out my one-man tent and took a nap. When I woke up there were mule deer bucks feeding all around me. That is where it all started for me in the backcountry.

CRH: *The term "Coyoting Out," where did it originate? A lot of guys now call it bivouac hunting. I have always referred to my "bivy camp," but really it is all one in the same isn't it?*

Mike Eastman: Yes, everyone is pretty much on the same page. Essentially, what all the references allude to is a hunter packing necessary survival gear, shelter and food on their back to avoid having to travel back and forth to a base camp. When I started Coyoting Out, with all of my gear of course, I would set up and glass from high vantage points with a spotting scope much like my dad had been doing for years while sheep hunting in Alaska.

I didn't really refine the Coyoting Out strategy until after I was done outfitting, which was in the late '70s. That was when I got serious about hunting the backcountry and really hit it hard for about 10 years. The only guy who I could find to go with me was a fellow named Carl Oksanen. Carl loved Coyoting Out as much as I did, maybe even more as he did it all summer just because he liked backpacking.

CRH: *What is the biggest difference between Coyoting Out in your day and bivy hunting now?*

Mike Eastman: The major thing is guys now have better and lighter gear, higher quality food and much improved clothing. Back then five days worth of gear and food would weigh about 55-60 lbs. With today's gear it weighs around 35-40 lbs.

CRH: *Can it still be effective?*

Mike Eastman: In my opinion, bivy hunting the backcountry is the most effective way to kill any animal. Sheep, mule deer, elk, whatever, Coyoting Out is the #1 way to take a trophy. While everyone heads down the trail to camp in the creek bottom you are on top deeper into prime hunting time, which gives you an increased chance of getting that glimpse of a trophy animal that only comes out of cover at dark. The system can be used in any type of terrain. The most effective D-I-Y hunters on public land use this approach.

CRH: *Why don't more guys do it then?*

Mike Eastman: Most guys don't realize how effective it is but more so, there are quite a few hunters who are just too lazy. Backcountry bivy hunting takes discipline and patience and the bottom line is a lot of hunters just don't want to put out the effort. They want the results, but don't want to work for it.

The major media shows guys being successful other ways. The big name magazines are more interested in publicizing hunting the easy way because they know this is what is going to appeal to the masses. In my opinion another problem with today's hunter is that too many focus solely on the size of the trophy and not the way the animal was harvested.

To me, there is no comparison between a guy who goes on his own into the high country and kills a 175 mule deer as opposed to someone who kills a 195-buck on private land that can be accessed by vehicle. Some guys might not agree or may not understand why I say there is a difference between the two. To them all I will say is, "If I have to explain it to you, you wouldn't understand anyway."

Guys who hunt the high country on their own can appreciate and recognize that there is something very special about successfully hunting in the mountains. But, to answer your original question, "Why don't more guys do it?" Plain and simple, this type of hunting is physically and mentally very hard. It is more of a hunt than they want and more than they're ready for. As you are well aware Cam, because of the things I've talked about, the commitment and so on, this type of hunting is very rewarding and effective for hunters that are ready, willing and able to take on the backcountry.

Mike Eastman's thoughts on the book, *Backcountry Bowhunting*:
I think Cameron's *Backcountry Bowhunting* is really *the* guide for the next generation of hardcore bowhunters out West. Even if you don't want to take it to the extreme like Cameron does, this book has information that will help any bowhunter harvest big game trophies. But, if you truly want to be considered the real western deal, a guy that hunts public land, wilderness and national forest, this book is for you. I like how Cameron has called on his own experiences and those of other hardcore bowhunters to show the readers that his system works.

What I've learned from all my years in the magazine industry is the hardest thing for a writer to do is establish a connection with the reader. Throughout Cameron's long career here at *Eastmans'* he has always been able to do just that. The next most difficult thing is to earn the respect of your peers, especially in hunting circles, and Cameron has done that too by sharing his successes, failures and stories from nearly 20 years of backcountry adventures. Cameron has redefined what it means to be a truly hardcore mountain bowhunter. Now when readers see backcountry, D-I-Y, or bivy, they think serious hunter, intense passion and tough hunting. Cameron loves these assumptions because it is the toughest hunts that drive him the most. Consequently, to western hunters Cameron's writings hit home and as they naturally relate to his articles they can't help but become motivated and inspired by his message. It is because of this that I am convinced *Backcountry Bowhunting* is quick to skyrocket to the bestseller list.

If you implement the tactics and style of hunting portrayed in *Backcountry Bowhunting* you will be in an elite group of true outdoorsmen. Armed with the information in this book any bowhunter ready for the challenge will be on his way to pursuing the toughest and smartest big game animals on public land. Going one-on-one with trophy animals, using fair chase, Do-It-Yourself tactics in the backcountry is as good as it gets and that's the Eastman way.

Section 1

The Backcountry

Big Country

Big, remote, tough to get to, tougher to hunt…yup, there's a reason why the backcountry is a lonely place.

Bragging size backcountry bucks or sweeping antlered, ivory-tipped bulls are seldom killed in easy to get to spots on public land by regular guys like you and me. One thing is for certain; if you hunt areas that are reasonably easy to get to, you can count on seeing other hunters. If there are a multitude of hunters traipsing up and down the mountain, you can also plan on not seeing many trophy bucks or bulls. Those are just the cold hard facts. A lot of guys spend many years trying to disprove this theory. Don't be one of them.

Hunting deeper than anyone else is willing to hunt is a prerequisite in my opinion. Most of the trophy bucks and bulls I have killed not only had no idea I was in the country, but I don't think they had even seen a human since the previous hunting season. I don't have to explain to you how huge of a factor this is.

Some might not believe there is any place you could go to hunt 100% unpressured animals and I probably wouldn't either if I hadn't experienced this phenomenon firsthand on many occasions. As a lot of guys who have had some success, I have always been ultra-paranoid about someone else stumbling into "my" area. Even my best buddies used to call me Mac (Cam

I snapped this photo on an incredible D-I-Y backcountry sheep hunt where I filmed my father-in-law Larry Smith kill a trophy Rocky Mountain bighorn ram.

backwards) as a code word coined to poke fun at my secretiveness on everything in regard to hunting or where I hunted.

I was literally nauseous when the first Eastmans' video came out that highlighted my wilderness hunt. I just knew my area was going to be overrun with hunters the following season. On one hand I wanted to share my experiences with others who loved western hunting like I did, while on the other I didn't want to share anything as my #1 goal was to protect what I had worked so hard to find. But, guess what? Surprisingly, after the release of the video and my magazine article telling of my success I still didn't see anyone in the backcountry that next year. I told myself, "Well, it will just take a year for them to figure out where I am. This will probably be the last season I will have it to myself. After this season I am screwed."

Guess what happened the next season? Nothing; still no one. Fact is I still haven't seen one person off the trail in the country I have hunted for almost 15 years now. The first Eastman video (1999) and that first article highlighting my wilderness hunt (1996) came out years and years ago and the area is still as unsullied as when I first stumbled upon it. The reason? It is *big*, remote, tough to get to and tough to hunt country, which turns off many would-be hunters. Also, the country simply doesn't hold a ton of animals. But the key is, it holds enough. This is the exact scenario you are after when looking for prime mule deer and elk hunting areas.

Backcountry Advice: *Make sure your goals are fueled by the love of the journey.* What does this mean? A good analogy is this: Don't set the goal of being a great marathoner unless you love running. Same goes with high country mule deer or backcountry elk hunting. Unless you love everything about the backcountry—the challenge, the gear, the misery, the bouts of homesickness and the solitude—don't set a goal of arrowing a big buck or bull in the rugged backcountry. Without love of the former, you'll likely never have the chance to love the latter. Arrowing a trophy animal in deep is tough to do if you're not romanticized by the lonely backcountry.

Even given my overwhelming drive to succeed on my own in the wild, at times I have thought, "I will never kill another trophy buck. This is ridiculous—I must have used up all my luck." Or in the more frustrating of times a simple self-loathing "I suck" pretty much summed up my bowhunting performance as I watched a bull-for-the-wall crash down the hill with his herd, clouds of dust and rolling rocks marking their trail long after they had barreled out of sight.

The fact is hunting the backcountry is never going to be easy. By the time a mule deer or bull reaches trophy class he has lived about five years in the mountains. And for those of us who have spent time in the backcountry, you know how tough it is even just for a few days at a stretch. These animals live there day in and day out being subjected to all that the high country can throw at them. A five-year-old animal has been hunted not only by humans but also by the most efficient predator of all time, the mountain lion. This tends to make them a wee bit edgy.

When considering all of this I am not shocking anyone by saying that a trophy, high country bow kill is one of the absolute toughest challenges you'll face. Arrowing one big one is tough, and if you're like me and long for repeated and regular success, well now we are talking long and steep odds. Despite this less than rosy prognosis, I have bucked the odds and so can you.

Bowhunting Justice

WHY I LOVE THE BACKCOUNTRY

We all have heard stories about guys who lucked into great bucks or bulls. Regardless of the exaggerated stories they tell, in our eyes these hunters were undeserving. You know you've heard the one that goes like this – The guy and his buddy were done hunting for the day and driving up the road. On the way out to the store, they saw a big deer off in the timber. They didn't care how big it was in the least. They just wanted to kill it. As his buddy kept driving, the shooter slid out of the truck and put a little sneak on the deer, shot it and lo and behold it is a monster buck.

In my nightmares it is 190 inches. Yes, this does happen, but thankfully not very often. However, this is one of the reasons I started hunting the backcountry. I liked the fact that if anyone was, aghast, hunting the same country I was and did end up killing a bomber buck or trophy bull, well at least they earned the damn thing. If I see someone busting their tail, camp on their back in my neck of the woods, honestly, more credit to them. I simply head off to find more remote country. Life seems real fair back in the backcountry. No one gets lucky like the guy who eased out of the truck real careful like. In the backcountry, you earn every bit of luck you get; the way it should be.

Your next move determines whether you have what it takes to hunt the backcountry. This is a critical point in time where all successful backcountry hunters have found themselves at one point or another. The easy choice? Head back to the rig, pop open a cold Mountain Dew, turn on the tunes and go home shut out just like almost everyone else you know will. Quitting is easy and much more comfortable. The tough choice? Throw that pack back up on your shoulders, flex your stiff back, take a swig of water, grab your bow and head into the high country without another thought toward heading back to the trailhead. From this moment on, you just took a monumental step to becoming a hardcore backcountry hunter.

Believe me when I tell you *everyone* wants to pull stakes and quit at some point during a backcountry hunt. It is truly only the most determined and passionate that don't. If you are one of my backcountry brothers that have toughed it out in deep or haven't yet, but know in your heart that you want to, I tip my camo hat to you and welcome you into the pages of my book. You are going to love it.

Backcountry Myths

There is no way I could afford a wilderness or backcountry hunt.
Fact: *On a number of occasions, I have teamed up with three buddies and paid $2,000 total or $500 each, for a horse pack-in, drop camp elk hunt in Oregon's largest wilderness area. This fee includes four pack mules, which will haul 120 lbs. each, supplies and meat hauls. The meat haul deal is key, especially when we are talking big bulls. I've killed bulls in places where I would have paid double the $500 with a smile on my face. My packer leading a couple of pack horses to my boned out bull is a sight that warms my heart. Seriously.*

I have to be in supreme physical condition to hunt rugged country at high elevation.
Fact: *It sure wouldn't hurt anything to be in stellar shape, but if you pace yourself and hunt the entire trip, anything is possible. I like the saying, "You don't know if you don't go." My advice? Suck it up. You gotta try it to see where you're at. Everyone learns something every time out. But, you also must be realistic. Many guys go way too hard the first day or two, simply can't sustain it, and end up essentially quitting on the hunt. In the backcountry, once the desire is gone you may as well just call what you're doing a camping trip.*

Hunting the backcountry will be the most enjoyable time of my life.
Fact: *The hunt might not be enjoyable 100% of the time, but I guarantee, it will be one of the most memorable weeks or 10 days you've experienced. There is no feeling of accomplishment like successfully arrowing a big bull in the backcountry. And conversely, when times are tough, they can be real tough. The question is can you handle the day after day of lows and come back for more? After missing the bull or buck of your dreams or worse yet, not being able to even find an animal to loose an arrow at is when bowhunters are at their weakest. It is here that many throw in the towel because it is too hot, there's no water, the bulls aren't lighting up, bow is screwed up, I'm homesick, they ain't here, and even if they were here, I couldn't hit them.*

Trial by Fire

Scouting...beyond the obvious

In this book you will read a number of times the importance of scouting. The backcountry hunter must learn the country they'll be roaming, verify hunches, test new gear, as well as find those "pockets" that animals are seemingly always drawn to. But, those are pat answers, the answers you expect to read or hear when the topic is scouting. For me, "scouting" has always had a deeper meaning.

From way back when, I have always used my scouting trips as a test of sorts. Yes, I wanted to find animals. Nothing gets you more fired up to shoot that bow or work out harder than finding a bunch of big bucks during the summer, but more importantly, I head to the high country to find out more about myself. I use my "scouting" trips more as personal growth recon missions if you want to know the truth.

Hunting the backcountry on your own is a different type of challenge for a lot of guys and it was for me too. My lifelong hunting partner Roy Roth and I discovered the wilderness together, and while we didn't hunt side by side very much, we packed in together and hooked up every couple of days. There was a certain sense of reassurance just knowing he was in the same country.

The problem was, after that first season hunting the backcountry, Alaska called to Roy and he moved with his family to the North Country. So, now what to do? No one else I knew was interested in hunting as remote as Roy and I wanted to or for as long as Roy and I wanted to. Finding a hunting partner like Roy, someone I could trust and that shared the same "no obstacle is too great" attitude seemed impossible. That meant either I quit hunting deep or I ventured out on my own. I guess you know which option I went with.

At first, I had a hard time believing in myself enough to bomb off into the middle of a wilderness. I think a lot of guys share this same reservation. This is where short scouting trips fit the bill. The fact of the matter is hunting solo in the backcountry for 10 days is too much for a lot of guys, me included at first, but I kind of learned the ropes so to speak on two or three day overnight backcountry scouting trips. After Roy moved, I started my own little scouting trip tradition by heading over to the high country for the July 4th weekend. By this time of the summer, the snow was usually cleared out enough to get back to the "honey holes" we had found on that first trip. Then in the years that followed I would venture further and check out other potential hot spots I'd found. Then I would head over again the first part of August to get a better feel for how many bucks I could expect to find come opening day and get a good bead on their size.

My scouting trips were always of the "Banzai" variety, which meant they were anywhere from two to four days in length. I say *banzai*, which is fully defined later in this chapter in my EBJ classic, "Heart & Soul."

A typical weekend bomb over the hill scouting trip usually meant I'd take off from work late in the afternoon on Friday, drive the eight hours over to the Eagle Cap Wilderness of northeastern Oregon, which would put me at the trailhead at about 1:00 a.m. Then I would strap on my pack frame, and by the light of a headlamp, I'd start the long hike deep into the wilderness. It would usually take me the rest of the night to cover the 12 miles of pack trail all the way back to the country I hunt. Getting in there at about first light, I would glass and hike the ridges seeing what I could see for a few hours. By this time I was obviously getting pretty tired so I would bed down for a couple hours before getting up, hiking farther (my usual circuit would take me right at 18 miles from the trailhead at the farthest point) before finding a spot to set up my bivouac camp for the night. At first light on Sunday, I would get up, gather up my bivy, do some more glassing and then head back to the trailhead. On a normal trip I would get back to my truck at about 2:00 p.m. Sunday afternoon, which would put me at home in the driveway at about 10:00 p.m. Suffice it to say that Monday morning at work I was not fresh as a daisy, but mentally I had gained so much.

It was scouting trips like I've described, which I've done countless times

I've always used my scouting trips as mental and physical tests. This photo was taken after a late summer high country storm moved through one morning.

over the years, that gave me the confidence to do the long solo hunts. My point is regardless of what your goal is, you have to work up to it. Test yourself first before going all the way. I won't lie to you, many times I dreaded those long drives to the mountains, those long hikes in the dark and those even longer nights by myself.

My wife, Tracey, used to ask me why I had to put myself through all that. She'd say, "Cam, you're going to end up falling asleep and crashing and for what? All you do is go back to the same place you always go? Can't you just stay home?" She was right, but as I mentioned earlier, for me it was a test and as a backcountry hunter I was earning my wings. I would usually respond to her, "Trace, I learn something more about the country every time I go (which was true) and besides I want to do it to see if I can." The second part of that sentence was the key for me.

Pulling up to that pitch-dark trailhead at one in the morning, miles from the nearest paved road was a lonely feeling. The drive over was bad enough, but during that time I would be jamming to the radio, eating sunflower seeds and drinking Mountain Dew. It was when those headlights went out and I was engulfed in darkness at the trailhead that my wife's words would ring clear, "Can't you just stay home?"

Home is so safe and comfortable. But, home doesn't test you now does it? With red ringed eyes as the tiredness was beginning to set in, I would open up the door to my truck, strap on the headlamp, head to the back of the truck, put down the tailgate, stand up my pack frame and slip into the shoulder straps. Adjusting the waist belt as I headed over to the registration box, my normal routine was to check for people accessing "my" trailhead.

See, you are supposed to fill out a registration card so in case something happens, someone knows where you're headed and when you're expected to be coming out. I'd never fill one out because I was too paranoid another hunter would do what I did and check all the other cards in there to see who had been in the wilderness and what they were doing. The Forest Service would usually only pick up the cards once a month or so, so under the amber glow of the headlamp and with the cool night air starting to seep in, I would pull out the false bottom of the drop box and thumb through the cards. There were usually only a few as the trailheads I use are the most remote and least popular, but the ones in there would usually say something like, "Steve and Bill Johnson, heading to Eagle Meadow on the 12th with four horses and a dog to fish. Out on the 14th.

"Good," I would think, "Eagle is only about halfway in. No one has violated my country." After my P.I. work, I'd finally be on my way.

Lots of time to think; walking through the black timber in the middle of the night for hours gives you lots of time to think. Again, questioning whether all this was really necessary would usually come up in those long conversations with myself at about 3:30 a.m., especially when an owl would fly through my light beam and scare the hell out of me; or the time when I popped over the crest of a ridge to come face to face with a bear which was as shocked as I was.

Then there was the time when I got off the trail somehow on one of these midnight vigils, miles from the trailhead in a pounding thunder and lightning storm. All I wanted to do was get back on the trail, and believe me, it can be tough to keep track of in those mountaintop meadows where the ground is hard and the trails are not real pronounced. After wandering around for a while, getting soaked and with lightning striking all around me, I figured I should probably get in my bivy and wait out the storm. I was at about 7,000 feet and I remember being in a panic about getting struck by lightning as I could actually see it hitting. I decided to head out to the middle of a big meadow, as far as I could from any tree, and break out the bivy. The lightning was so bad and so close that I took out the little metal rods that are supposed to hold the bivy sack off of your face and threw them as far as I could as I thought they might attract the lightning. I had my bow

Finding the perfect spot to set up and glass is key during summer scouting forays. *Let your glass do the walking* is a good phrase to live by.

because it was bear season, which opens on August 1st in Oregon, and did the same thing with it for the same reason. It was a miserable couple of hours getting rocked by unbelievably loud thunder firing off seemingly a mere foot or two above my head and/or waiting to get struck by lightning. I couldn't tell you when it was at its worst or how close the lightning actually struck because I was huddled in my bivy like a kid under the covers hiding from the monsters under their bed. If you can't see it, it can't get you, right?

Once the storm finally passed I was spent just enough that I really needed to get something to eat before heading out again. I wanted a quick replenishment before hammering out the last of my 12-mile hike. I was still good for time because it wasn't even quite 3:00 a.m. so I broke out the cook pot and utensils. Since this was a "scouting" trip, it meant it was the perfect time to test out new gear in an actual hunting setting.

For this trip, I brought a white gas or Wisper Lite or hell, maybe it was some other kind of stove. The type of stove it was escapes me right now, which was the biggest part of the problem. I didn't know enough about the stove I was trusting to feed me in the backcountry. The moral to the story is it was a stove I had never used before and I couldn't get it lit. This was before my MRE days and I had always been an old school propane guy, but

I brought this new stove on a suggestion from a friend. He said, "Dude, this stove is so much smaller and lighter than your stove." My reply was something along the lines of, "Yeah, but I know my gear in and out and it works." My plan had been to quickly whip up one of the two Mountain House meals I had packed up the hill before hitting the trail again.

Backcountry Blunder: *I didn't know enough about the stove I was trusting to feed me in the backcountry.*

In the inky darkness, on that lonely ridge, I messed with that darn stove for plenty long enough before packing it back up and breaking out a granola bar and some jerky and getting back on the trail in a sour mood. Despite the personal growth opportunities, these short scouting trips are ideal times for giving gear a test run. If I would have tried to do the new stove thing on an actual weeklong elk or deer hunt I'd have been in a bad way.

It's conceivable, if the stove fiasco was something I couldn't figure out or get fixed, it could have cost me a day, two or three off of my hunt, if I would've had to pack all the way out to get a new one. Not good. This is a perfect example of how valuable times like this before season can be.

It seems that self-inflicted torture has always been my motif. Even when I hunted back home I would take something that didn't need to be that bad and make it miserable.

When scouting by way of mountain bike for Roosevelt elk and blacktail not too far from the house in Springfield, I would sometimes get to the motorized-vehicle-restricting gate that blocked the logging road at 3:00 a.m. Why? Who knows? I could have taken off an hour before sunrise instead of three and still been where I could start scouting, but I wanted to go farther.

In my mind, farther has always been better. Then, on top of the early morning departure, I would many times take off on my bike, headlamp beam leading the way through the crisp morning air wearing nothing more than camo shorts and a tank top. In short order, I would be miserably cold and would ride like this until I warmed up internally thanks to those long steep hills. If there were an award for suffering, I would have been on top of the podium accepting the gold. Why did I do this? Again, who knows? But in my mind I wanted to make the challenge as tough as possible as I reasoned this would make me that much tougher and that much less likely to quit when the hunting was hard.

I have gone from being the greenest guy out there in terms of wilderness experience to now feeling confident to hunt anywhere for anything. It has been a long, sometimes painful learning process the likes of which I hope to help you avoid with this book.

> **"No pain, no gain." The reality is that if you want to be successful in the backcountry you must push past your comfort zone.**
>
> *—Cameron R. Hanes*

So you see, to me scouting has always had a deeper meaning. To some of you, these stories might have a hint of craziness or leave you thinking, "That boy ain't right in the head." And, honestly, even when writing these accounts I am kind of wondering the same thing, but I will say all of the banzai scouting trips and the miserable mountain bike rides in the hills helped to get me ready for life on my own in the backcountry.

Is going through all that necessary? Heck no! But if nothing else, take from this chapter the value of short, high intensity scouting trips with a purpose beyond simply finding animals.

Before that first wilderness foray with Roy, I was the greenest guy out there in terms of this type of pure hunting, but thanks to those over-the-top experiences I learned a lot about myself and the backcountry in very short order. And, in a reoccurring theme to this book, remember these words, "If I can do it, so can you."

Straightforward Scouting Tips

- ***Gaining intimate knowledge of your hunting area is huge.*** *Get out into the country you will be hunting and verify hunches and investigate any leads you picked up from studying your topographical maps. I always note saddles or funnels and, of course, water on my topo map prior to heading out. During my summer forays, I will dedicate myself to checking out these areas. I don't necessarily need to see animals on these trips to know whether or not my map work will pay off. Obviously, if there are trails beat into the hard ground thru a saddle or funnel or if the water hole is secluded and has old elk rubs in the vicinity, well now I am on to something.*

- ***Carry a note pad and take notes.*** *I have filled up the back of many a topo map over the years because I didn't want to pack anything more than a pen. However you do it—be it in a small spiral note pad or on your topo map like me—make sure to keep a journal of any and all pertinent information. Over time you can pattern the animals by picking up daily travel tendencies, escape routes, favored funnels, likely bedding areas, waterholes, etc. I have also penned many of my thoughts in the backcountry that I have later used in articles. Like anyone else, I think very clearly in the mountains. During a hunt is the perfect time to write. For me it can be down right therapeutic. Try it out for yourself.*

WILDERNESS ELK '99

9-9-99 THURSDAY DAY 7 — SUCCESS! - GLASSED UP A GOOD HERD AT FIRST LIGHT - 6:00 A.M. PLANNED A STALK, WHICH INCLUDED A 3,000 FOOT DESCENT FOLLOWED BY A 1,300 FOOT CLIMB UP TO WHERE THE HERD WAS BEDDED. AT 4:00 P.M. CLAD IN FULL CAMO AND FACE PAINT AND AFTER SHEDDING BOOTS, I FOUND MYSELF 52-YARDS DIRECTLY ABOVE BEDDED HERD BULL - WHICH TURNED OUT TO BE A GOOD 5X5.
ON THE RELEASE I KNEW I HAD SHOT A 'GOOD ARROW' WHICH WAS CONFIRMED BY THE HEAVY 125-YARD BLOOD TRAIL TO MY BULL - THIS WAS A TOUGH HUNT.
MY ARROW ENTERED THE TOP OF THE BACK AND EXITED THE BOTTOM OF HIS CHEST, TAKING OUT HIS HEART!

- ***Make a call or two to local Game & Fish Department personnel.*** *They can be a fantastic resource and are generally more than willing to help if they can. I talked to the G&F sheep guy here in Oregon many times prior to my father-in-law's sheep hunt. I can't tell you how much help he was. They know the country and most of the biologists I've talked to have worked their areas for years. They can tell you in one conversation what otherwise would take you years to learn.*

- ***There is no better time than during scouting trips or overnight outings to test new gear*** *or learn things you may not have thought of from the comforts of your living room. This is a perfect time to break in boots. On many of my banzai* *scouting trips, I log many hard and fast miles. If I am going to have boot issues, I will know after a weekend-long, butt-busting scouting trip. It's also a perfect time to try out some potential backcountry food. You can take something new on a two day scouting trip. Worst case you're back to burgers and fries in 48 hours.*

- ***Talk to hunters who have hunted the area.*** *Hunters can be tough when it comes to sharing information, but I learned of my best elk area by visiting with a bowhunter who had hunted the country for years but deemed the spot too big, too rugged and too steep. My buddy Roy and I were having breakfast in a restaurant near elk country on our first—and very slow—wilderness elk hunt. We had never hunted the area and packed out of the wilderness to lick our wounds after four long days of nothing. We were in over our heads, but a chance conversation with a local turned our luck around and changed my future as a backcountry hunter.*

- ***Most importantly, when scouting, do so from afar.*** *Use your glass, stay back and just observe—especially when the quarry is trophy mule deer. These cagey old bucks will stand for little, if any, human interaction. If you screw up one time and blow the buck out, it might be the last time he is seen. I try to find a vantage point that offers me a commanding view of a number of different basins and as the ol' saying goes, "Let my glass do the walking." My favorite mule deer glassing spot back home is at the top of a peak where by just slinking around in the shadows from the one side of the hill to the other I can glass five different basins by traveling only about 150 yards.*

- ***When looking for a spot to bed down for the night, find an out of the way place.*** *I made a mistake of sleeping in the middle of a high country bench one year that, as it turns out, was an [illegible]s old elk travel route. I didn't notice the hundreds of elk tracks in my headlamp beam when I rolled out my bivy, as it was already dark. I figured it out in a hurry though after just slipping into deep R.E.M. sleep. The elk began feeding thru the area at about 2:00 in the morning and were relaxed until they winded me. That is when the stampede started and honestly, I thought I was going to get run over. With my heart pounding, I scurried out of my bivy and started waving my headlamp to at least let them know where I was. Now I carefully select a bedding spot tucked in or surrounded by large rocks or in the middle of a bunch of tightly grown trees. I would suggest you do the same.*

Banzai : *bon-'sI,*
When referencing a bowhunt for elk this term helps to describe a trip that besides killing a bull, little else matters. Typically it involves putting much stress on the human body in the form of sleep deprivation and rugged miles traveled at a quickened pace while loaded down with the weight of a bivouac rig. It very often includes bouts of extreme mental anguish brought on by days upon days of pursuing an animal that is built to survive against even the fiercest of predators and calls the mountains "home."

Heart & Soul

By Cameron R. Hanes

Originally appeared in Eastmans' Bowhunting Journal *Issue 14.*

For longtime readers of EBJ, it will come as no surprise to read more of my D-I-Y wilderness bowhunting exploits. For me, like many of you, I am most content when I have my pack and camp hanging off of my shoulders, bow in hand and binoculars bouncing rhythmically as I stride down the trail. Personally, I love hunting solo and deep, away from the crowds. I don't want to see anyone, even my buddies. If I see one fresh boot track, I feel deflated.

Based on all of the comments, questions and positive feedback I receive, there is little doubt that this is the type of hunting a majority of our readers either do or want to do in the near future. I can relate as nearly all of the highlights of my bowhunting career come from the wilds of the backcountry. D-I-Y hunting is my gig and whether I am successful or not, my wilderness hunts always seem to produce unforgettable memories and life defining experiences.

The 2002 season was no different. My good buddy, Shay Mann, who would be packing a camera instead of a bow, would join me on my D-I-Y public land drop camp hunt. Our plan was to capture the entire 11-day adventure on film for *Eastmans' Hunting TV.*

Our trip began the morning before opening day here in Oregon, which was on August 23rd. We met our packer at the trailhead bright and early that Friday morning. After getting loaded and saddled up, we got started on the four-hour pack into a remote lake deep within the wilderness boundaries. This site would serve as a base camp of sorts, if you could call six 18-gallon Rubbermaid containers a base camp. We ended up only staying at "base camp" one night during the hunt and pretty much just used the site as a cache of food, gear, a broadhead target and a backup bow.

Getting into the lake at about noon we loaded our pack frames with five days worth of food,

took a couple of practice shots and headed out in search of bucks and bulls. The fact that Shay was with me had me in sort of a quandary as it was. Nothing personal, but as I mentioned, I don't like seeing anyone or hunting with anyone for all of the obvious reasons. Double the noise, double the scent, double the movement, etc.

I don't like having to explain to someone why I am doing something or not doing something and it goes without saying that when you want to hunt by yourself and anyone is with you, even Chuck Adams, they make much more noise, roll more rocks and break more branches than you. I know there is the whole camaraderie thing and that is fine, but I can camp with my buddies anytime. When I am in deep, I am there for one thing, to produce the results I have worked all off-season for and envisioned all year.

When you hunt solo, you make decisions faster. If it doesn't work out, it doesn't work out and you'll just move on. Problem is, trying to video a hunt for television on a solo hunt is a tough proposition that is not going to work out. That being said, if I had to have someone with me, Shay would be as good a candidate as any. He was 100% dedicated to the mission. He is in great shape, has all the right gear, is mentally tough and good with the camera. We had all the ingredients for one of the most unique and tough bowhunts to be filmed in some of the most spectacular country in the West. Our number one goal was to get a good bull elk or trophy mule deer on the ground, captured on film. We wanted more than anything to share this hunt with all of the Eastmans' viewers.

We spotted a good herd and a decent five-point the night before the opener. This bull was not trophy caliber so come morning, Shay and I worked our way out a long, high ridge that had prime deer and elk habitat spilling off of both sides. To say it was an amazing day probably wouldn't do it justice.

We videoed a handful of bighorns, six or seven mule deer bucks of varying sizes that we couldn't put anything together on, elk and mountain goats. One big herd of elk had quite a number of bulls but nothing worth closing on and then as daylight waned, I was able to ease within bow range of an average five-point. I came to full draw on this young bull and contemplated releasing momentarily as Shay filmed over my shoulder. Too early in the hunt and too young of a bull. That night we bivouacked on a small bench overlooking one of the grandest creek drainages in the wilderness.

Day two dawned and we quickly put our camp together, and loaded it on our backs. We had no sooner climbed the ridge from where we had bedded when I spotted a herd of six bulls. There was nothing monstrous in this bachelor group, but since they were only a few hundred yards away, it was definitely worth a closer look. A fickle wind put the skids on this stalk as the bulls fed steadily at a caribou-like pace before we blew them out.

From here we moved on down the ridge and got into the middle of another big herd of elk that had at least nine bulls. Again, the best bull was a run-of-the-mill five-point, which I again opted to pass on after nestling one of my fiber optics tight behind his shoulder. It wasn't quite late enough in the season to settle for a five. I still had visions of a monster, and given that we had videoed 15 bulls this morning, passing was easy.

That evening we worked down the ridge a number of miles to a hidden basin I had discovered years earlier. The '99 season was the last time I had made it to this tucked away oasis and that time I stalked a good four-point buck that eluded me.

The evening hunt produced nothing, but first thing in the morning, we rolled out of our bivouac and threw the glasses up. Immediately I spotted a cow and calf, which were on a beeline toward a bull Shay had glassed. I studied the bull, and even though I knew it was a young bull, I opted to ease down and get a closer look.

After sliding down about a half-mile off of the top, Shay and I found ourselves looking over a great little bench that you could not see from the top. We were still at least a quarter of a mile above the bull, which was now bedded. I threw the Swarovskis up and quickly scanned the bench. Almost immediately the glass was filled with images of two big bucks. Now, what I call a big buck in Oregon probably wouldn't raise an eyebrow in Utah or Colorado, but for me, these dudes were trophy animals. One appeared to be a good, wide 4x4 with eyeguards; the other was a very tall 5x4. Either one would work as they both appeared to be a fair amount over 160 Pope & Young and in full velvet.

The wide buck bedded down in a great position for a stalk. After noting a couple of good landmarks within his close proximity, off we went, camera rollin'. We closed to within a couple hundred yards fairly quickly and then switched into ultra stealth mode. I am not sure if there is any greater challenge than getting within bow range of two bedded mature mule deer bucks, except trying to do it on film. We had a number of things going our way, namely the wind as the sun was up and hitting the hillside, which sent wind currents wafting upward. The bucks were also in country that was broken enough to assist us in a close quarters approach. In fact, until we were within 30 or 40 yards we had been completely out of their line of sight.

At this point I got conservative. Instead of keeping Shay right over my shoulder, which would require both of us to get inside the "Red Zone," I signaled him to stay put while I tiptoed forward in an effort to get a bead on the bucks. One step, scan and glass. Another step, scan and glass. With Shay filming from about ten yards off my shoulder, I was now within 20 yards of where I believed the upper most buck, the wide one, to be bedded.

Ruled White

Index Cards

100 4" x 6" (10.2x 15.2cm)

www.pendaflex.com

There was no sign of him, and thoughts raced, "Did the wind give us up? Did he move his bed? Did they hear us? Am I in the right spot?" Then I saw movement. The sun bounced off of velvet-encased antlers as his head swiveled. He was bedded behind a small tree and when not moving, blended in perfectly. As he rose, unaware of my presence, I came to full draw while Shay filmed. He stepped from behind the tree broadside at what I figured to be 25 yards. No need for the rangefinder; I was on autopilot and he was oblivious. I anchored steady, locked the top fiber optic on high lungs and fingered the trigger of my release. The sound of the arrow impacting solidly is unmistakable, and after a short and frenzied burst by the buck, all was quiet. I heard the buck slowly expel his last breaths and had no doubt of his fate. Shay filmed while I quickly followed blood, and after only 50 yards, I spotted him piled up. On a hunt that is more geared around elk than deer, I had arrowed one of my best bucks ever and had done it while the camera rolled. Unbelievable!

He is a rocking-chair-wide buck, with four good tines per side, great eyeguards, and what had been an unnoticed bonus up until I recovered the deer was his cute little dropper off of the left main beam. I excitedly gave my buck the tongue-in-cheek moniker, "Ol' Dropper."

We got busy with butchering and photos as the morning warmed quickly. In no time, we had the quarters, backstraps, neck meat, rib meat, and tenderloins separated into four evenly proportioned game bags, which we hung in a very cool and secluded spot within some mature timber. The meat would be fine here until the packer could provide a mule and we could yard the meat out of the backcountry.

Now we could fully concentrate on elk. To make a very long story a little bit shorter, I will give a brief account of the remainder of our "uneventful" hunt. I say uneventful because in the magazine and video business, "eventful" means filled tags and photos/video of posing with your trophy. Uneventful means everything else that happens that doesn't include a kill. Despite all of the indelible memories that can define a hunt, there would be no more butchering chores, blood trails or photo sessions.

The timeline went something like this: Remainder of day three—dealing with meat. Half of day four—dealing with meat. We then bombed back to "base camp" four miles and restocked our packs for one last five-day effort.

Despite our considerable efforts the last five long, hard days could be summarized with just a random handful of words -- Glassing, rain, frigid wind, many elk, no elk, blown stalks, cougar, thunderstorms, swirling winds, no shots, big bucks, bighorns, lightning, snow, small bulls, big bulls, bivouac, no food, desperation, blistering sun and then finally after 11 days and 10 nights of sleeping on rocks and living off our backs, we were headed home. We met the packer at base camp and were in serious need of a shower and something other than an MRE and a granola bar to eat.

I am not a big fan of the ol' tag intact syndrome I had been afflicted with and no matter how many times I told myself, "Hey, you should be happy. You didn't kill a bull, but you did arrow a good buck. A trophy!" And, then there is the always popular, "At least we got some incredible film, which means the hunt was a success." Who was I trying to kid? My goals are seldom considered reasonable and this was no different. I wanted it all. I wanted my buck *and* I wanted a good bull. But, the

hunt had ended and with it my elk season.

Tapped out of vacation and with work waiting, I only had weekends left to hunt. Being that the elk woods near home were closed because of "fire danger," realistically, I was done.

Or was I? My only hope was to bomb back over, across the entire state, to the wilderness on a weekend banzai trip. And, this is exactly what I did the last weekend of season. This last gasp effort for elk required me to leave the house at 2:00 a.m. on Friday morning, drive nine hours and pack in over ten miles to get into my elk country. I contemplated hunting a closer or more easily accessible area, but in the end decided to go with what I knew. I had no doubt that if I could put all of the logistical pieces of the puzzle together and get back into the wilderness I am so familiar with, I would have opportunities at bulls, even given the severely abbreviated schedule. Really, all a guy can ask for is opportunity. What you do with that opportunity is another story.

Immersed in full banzai mode, I was some ten miles into the wilderness with red-ringed eyes and a fatigued body before I knew it. Pausing on the pack trail for a moment I heard a bugle, and then another and another. No surprises here, it was just as I knew it would be.

I dove off the trail toward the bulls, through the creek and up the side of the canyon. I traveled close to a mile. After pulling myself over cliffs and bouncing across creeks, I finally was in a position to ease over a handful of boulders and spy the elk I had long ago heard.

The first elk I saw were two bulls sparring. I came to full draw on the larger of the two, but deemed the quartering away angle too steep and he was out of "slam dunk" range. I did not want to force a shot now. They moved up the hill, trailing the main herd and I went wide and followed. Perfect wind. Neither of these guys were the herd bull. He was up the hill, trying to bugle, but was either too old or simply too bugled out to elicit even a halfway decent bellow. I closed and bumped two cows.

Things were on the verge of blowing up when I saw the herd master. He was a big six-point that I figured would go over 330 P&Y. The cows stared intently and I moved forward, desperate to capitalize before they'd had enough. The big bull was slowly ambling through the timber away from me at 50 yards. I ducked and strained trying to manufacture a shot. There were simply too many limbs and branches. Just then I noticed another elk coming my way. It was a bull, and not a bad one, especially for the last weekend.

I had already told myself that any five was in trouble. Mud covered, he kept coming. At 40, I came to full draw and sidestepped behind a tree. His pace was such that I felt if I hadn't drawn then, he might be on top of me before I could have. At 20 yards he stopped, completely unaware. I felt so confident the shot was almost like a formality. My arrow blew through him causing much and quick trauma. The bull didn't even make it 30 yards before I watched him go down. It wasn't even 5:00 p.m. and I had left the trailhead at 11:30 a.m. That was a long day that didn't end until much later after breaking down my bull.

I still can't believe it worked. A D-I-Y wilderness double in "perfect game" fashion as I released two arrows all season and tagged two animals, which traveled a total of about 80 yards. My bull is a pretty good five-point and as beat up and raggedy as his rack is, right now he is one of my most prized bowhunting accomplishments.

Getting this dude out was quite an endeavor in itself. There is no way it was going to happen on my back by Monday morning when I had to be back at work by 7:00 a.m. I hung the meat in some big timber and flagged back to the main trail with surveyor's ribbon. It really pays to have a good packer available and I sure do in Barry Cox. I hired him for $300 to run in Monday to haul the meat out while I was all the way back at work. He spent the better part of a day, took a couple of horses and grabbed my meat. Barry again performed admirably for me and without a hitch, hauled it down to the meat shop where they cut and wrapped 191 lbs. of prime and pure elk meat.

I have to thank Nate Simmons, who is as game and tough as anyone I know and really helped me garner some great photos of my bull. He bombed into the wilderness without so much as a second thought, and after securing the meat stash and our photo shoot Saturday morning, we had a couple of great hunts before packing out on Sunday. He was a hair from getting opportunities at two different six-point bulls and I guarantee you we didn't go more than about an hour the entire time back there that we didn't hear a bugle, day or night. He had not hunted the wilderness before, but took to it like a fish to water.

Despite his young age, 21, Nate is already a consummate trophy hunter (see his feature in EBJ 13). At one point we were right on top of two spike bulls that like most spikes had no idea…about anything. It was basically the hunt s last hour and I wanted him to kill one. What a great story and I could see the title, "The Banzai Double." However, Nate would have none of it. Said he would rather go home empty than kill something he wouldn't be fired up about. You have to respect that.

What a year it was in the backcountry. I captured a lifetime worth of memories in the 14 days I spent bivouacking deep. The best part was I didn't have to share my country with anyone other than Shay or Nate. Fact is, we never saw another hunter in the woods. Ran into a few guys on the trail, but never while hunting. Sound intriguing? Start now with the research and find your own backcountry bowhunting area for next season. Believe me, hunts like this will get in your heart and the wilderness provides a venue that grows your soul like perhaps nothing else can.

Hunt Report Card – Hindsight is always 20/20

What I learned on this hunt: The #1 thing I learned had to do with filming. Do not shoot the animal unless the camera is on it. And believe me, Mike Eastman reminds me of this nearly every time we get together. As I mentioned, I sneaked up on that buck and shot him while leaving Shay behind as I was concerned we would blow the bucks out. In Mike's opinion, it would have been better to not shoot him than to shoot him and not capture it on film. Simply put, at that stage in my career I hadn't killed enough Pope & Young mule deer to let a slam-dunk walk. I think it still worked out for us as we still got some good mileage from the kill and more importantly, I was ecstatic to arrow such a great buck. I still get pumped thinking back on it now. Look no further than the cover of this book for an example of this mileage. Yup, that's the buck. Mike's still not buying it though—on film or nothing so far as he is concerned.

The elk hunt? Not much to say there. I learned a lot about never saying never. As soon as you limit yourself, you are lost. Despite the overwhelming odds against me given the distance, the effort and the time available to get a bull on the ground, I didn't care. And, while I was exhausted afterward, it felt great. Who cares if I was tired? I had all off-season to rest up.

What I did wrong: Other than the filming scenario and losing my patience with Shay (no fault of his own as when you're used to and want to hunt solo, any mandatory hunting partner is in a no-win situation), I can't think of anything I would have done differently.

Grade: For a D-I-Y wilderness hunt, I don't know if I could have asked for more. Of course there is always the hope of a bigger buck or bull, but given the country I was in and its trophy producing potential I was satisfied, as anyone who hunts the Eagle Cap would have been. ***A***

BACKCOUNTRY CHALLENGES

Rugged country, thin air, primitive weapon, hard ground, wary animals - and that is the *easy* part!

In addition to the normal tough stuff (i.e. getting within bow range of a trophy class animal that calls the rugged backcountry home), the big country hunter will face a number of other challenges that can sabotage the hunt. While these factors might seem overly dramatic to guys that do mostly backyard type hunts and sleep in their own bed every night and/or can drive to their camp spots, believe me, these issues are real. I do think though, that only guys who have lived in the backcountry for extended periods will understand and appreciate the true challenge that thirst, temperature extremes, fatigue, loneliness and boredom, and fear can present.

I will discuss each topic in detail here in this chapter except for fear, which deserves an entire chapter dedicated to the subject, because in my opinion, it is the ultimate backcountry challenge.

THIRST

The challenges of finding water in the backcountry can be daunting. Many people fail to realize that our bodies use water as a coolant all the time, not just during warm weather. In the backcountry, dehydration can be debilitating. It can creep up on you without you ever really knowing that it is there.

Regardless of how pure the water looks as it bubbles over rocks, savvy backcountry guys know it still must be treated.

Symptoms include a nasty headache, unusual fatigue, dark urine, irritability, and dizziness.

Even with seemingly minor fluid loss, say two percent or so, the results are pale, clammy skin, nausea, general discomfort, a lack of coordination, a lack of physical strength, an elevated heart rate, sleepiness, and decreased appetite. The key to fluid replacement is quite simple: Drink water and plenty of it. I drink at least one full water bladder that holds 96 oz., which I purify with Potable Aqua (active ingredient iodine) and supplement with Emer'gen-C powdered drink mix. Sports drinks such as Gatorade are fine for the replacement of electrolytes, but it should be diluted to reduce the sugar level so that the body can easily absorb the water from the stomach. Sugar slows down the absorption rate.

Sometimes in the high country, water can be tough to find. This is why I carry what many would consider a large water bladder as well as a supplemental 16 oz bladder that can be used for cooking or when I run low with my primary supply. When water is scarce, look for seeps and of course snow banks. Even the smallest of drips can be used to fill your water bladder. Remember, back here you have nothing but time, so build a funnel with a granola bar wrapper if you need to and fill your container while you nap, eat, glass or write in your journal.

If you find a good water source, make sure you note it with your GPS or on your topo map as this is very valuable information. Big stands of black timber are also a likely spot to find water. The only problem with this is it usually requires a substantial drop in elevation. If you do drop down, fill up everything you have that will hold water. Reap all the benefits you can off all that work. And know if there are elk in the country, there is water somewhere. Elk need water at least twice a day, especially those big bulls during the peak of the rut.

Without water, you're weaker mentally and besides the health risks, thirst can be one more reason to throw in the towel on a tough hunt. If you're looking for reasons when in the "any excuse will do mode," being thirsty is a good one.

BACKCOUNTRY WATER TREATMENT

The fact of the matter is no matter how clean, cool and refreshing the icy water tumbling down a secluded mountain stream looks, you simply never know. And, regardless of what the backcountry "experts" tell you they've done in the past, you can't trust the water is safe to drink, ever. I have heard many guys say, "I've been drinking out of those high country creeks for years and never got sick." That may be, but all that really means is they've been lucky and aren't very smart. The coldest, purest looking mountain water may carry a stray microscopic pest that, if it finds its way into your intestines, could leave you weak, nauseous, cramped, bloated or vulnerable to diarrhea and vomiting for weeks.

Treating water is a must in the backcountry. The treatment used in this photo is Potable Aqua tablets with a little Emer'gen-C powdered drink mix to mask the taste and to supplement.

Experienced backcountry bowhunters recognize the need to play it safe with backcountry water and thus treat every drop before

Packing out a heavy load, like meat and the head from this wilderness bull, can easily lead to over exertion and heat related illness.

they drink. You have three options for treating "raw" water found in the backcountry: Boiling, chemical treatment (iodine) and filtration. I have tried them all and have found using iodine, the active ingredient in Potable Aqua tablets, to be the best and most efficient for what I do.

The boiling was too much of a hassle. The pump made clean water, but meant that I had to pack something extra in my pack that weighed around a pound and took up ever precious space. Iodine weighs next to nothing and takes up even less. I have used it on every backcountry trip over the last 15 years and returned home 100% healthy. Love the iodine. Some complain of the taste, which has never been a big deal to me. I cover it with Emer'gen-C and drink away. The point is that with a little iodine in there, there might be some taste, but it is wet. And when you're on the verge of dehydration at the tail end of a long, hot day, I guarantee you the slight taste won't matter in the least.

KEYS FOR MAKING CLEAN WATER

Avoid filtering water in areas where animal activity is obvious. Have there been cattle in the area or big bull elk making an awesome urine-soaked wallow in your clean and refreshing water?

Try to select water from still, clear water sources above the wallow you hope to catch that big bull in later that afternoon. Many microorganisms, particularly giardia, tend to sink in still water due to the weight of their shells; turbulence keeps them suspended.

If your only water option is melting snow or ice, choose ice. Ice supplies more water after it's all melted, but keep in mind bacteria is impervious to freezing. Thus, while boiling can kill pathogens in water, freezing cannot. Clean snow, though, is still a good source for water. Beware of pinkish "watermelon snow," however This coloring is from a toxic algae that filtering will not remove. If you see it, look elsewhere for ice or clean snow.

TEMPERATURE EXTREMES

I don't know about the country you hunt, but where I run around, the elk season especially early on is *hot*. And regardless of where you think humankind hails from, one fact remains undeniable: Man is a tropical animal. This means you can't survive naked year-round unless you live in the tropics. The problem there is not many big bull elk are being killed on that end of the hemisphere these days.

Given this, the backcountry hunter must take temperature extremes very seriously. Not only the cold, mind you, but the heat as well. Add to that wind, humidity, and precipitation. In other words, every facet of the weather has to be carefully considered in your survival plan. The part you forget will almost always be the part that comes back to bite you.

Underestimating the weather might get you dead in a hurry. Even seemingly mild temperatures can and have become fatal for hunters who failed to take precautions. Hypothermia (a sustained cooling of the body's core temperature) and heat illness (where the body's core temperature raises to and stays above 100 degrees Fahrenheit) are two of the most serious common problems, and they are preventable in nearly all circumstances. This is one reason why I always preach the importance of good first layer gear. A high quality, wicking first layer can make all the difference in the world when combined with a synthetic insulating layer and a waterproof outer shell.

Symptoms of hypothermia include uncontrollable shivering, slowed reactions, weak motor skills, lethargy, reduced ability to make decisions, irritability, and speech that has become slurred and possibly incomprehensible. If you start to feel any of these symptoms, especially the shivering and shaking, do something immediately. This is a sign that the body needs to either become more active to increase heat production, reduce heat loss by putting on additional clothing or get into a warmer environment. Without acting in time, you might be too far gone to start a fire, which as we know is something that can make a bad situation better in a hurry. But, you know how hard it can be to do anything with your hands when it's freezing. The reason why it gets tougher to work with your hands is because as you get colder, blood is routed from the extremities to core areas of the body, including organs.

I have made some mistakes in this regard myself. Hunting too long without my raingear on and getting soaked to the bone comes to mind. Then I remember getting caught in one of those nasty high country thunderstorms with hail raining down instead of water, which with the stiff wind, dropped the temperature 20 degrees almost immediately. Given that I was wet and cold before the storm moved in, I knew full well I'd have a hard time starting a fire. I took off all my wet clothes, pulled out my bivy and sleeping bag, got inside, activated a hand warmer (remember this tip) and burrowed as deep as I could, pulling everything tight over my head. Within a half an hour I was warm enough to start a fire and dry out all my clothes. And soon after the rain had stopped, the hunt was on again.

However, it doesn't always work out so well. If I had stayed out hunting in the rain another hour longer over which time the temperature dropped at least another ten degrees, I believe my body temperature would have been knocked down dangerously low. At that point, it would have been tough getting warm enough in my sleeping bag given where my body temperature could have dropped to.

Treatment for hypothermia includes getting to a warm dry environment (inside your sleeping bag), putting on additional clothing (not really an option for most bivy hunters as you don't typically pack a bunch of extra clothes), and taking in warm fluids.

Hypothermia can be avoided by maintaining a constant level of body temperature. If you are humping it uphill, take off some clothes before you start to sweat too much. If you stop for more than a few minutes, put on some clothing before you start to chill. And, hey, I know as much as anyone what a pain this is because of your pack and everything else, but when you're on your own in the backcountry, you have to be smart. Remember that hypothermia can occur in all seasons, even at air temperatures in the 50s or 60s, if there is accompanying wind and rain.

This is when we have to be smart. I mean guys die every year by not making good decisions in this situation. If you know where your rig is and you can walk out, get out even if it means a four-hour walk. At least you'll be moving and creating warmth. Get to your pickup, get that gear dried out, get warmed up, eat, load your pack and head back up the hill to hunt some more or decide to cut your losses and regroup at home. The bottom line is to make the right choices.

As I mentioned, it can get very warm during elk season. Combine heat with packing all your gear every step of the way during a long hunt in seriously rugged terrain, and you could have a problem with heat-induced illness. Here are a few quick tips for preventing heat-related issues:

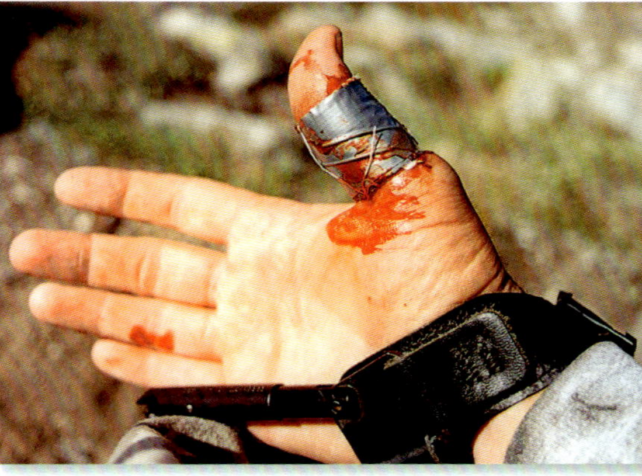

Pushing to fatigue can contribute to backcountry accidents. A sharp broadhead will cut to the bone if used improperly.

Dress for the heat – *Wear lightweight clothing. This last season I wore Mossy Oak Apparel's Trek-Lite shirt and pants (which have a zipper to transform them to shorts) with great results. It is also a good idea to always wear a hat.*

Drink water – *I think we covered this in the H_2O section—the key is to carry water with you at all times and drink continuously even if you do not feel thirsty. Avoid alcohol and caffeine, which dehydrate the body.*

Eat small meals and eat more often – *Avoid foods that are high in protein during the heat of the day if it is extreme, which increase metabolic heat.*

Slow down – *It's kind of tough to avoid strenuous activity in the mountains, but if you have a hole to climb out of or a big ridge to hump, try to do it during the coolest part of the day, which is usually in the morning between 4:00 a.m. and 7:00 a.m.*

Take regular breaks – *When hunting hard on warm days, take time out to find a cool place and rest as often as possible. Remember, you're not on a strict time schedule back there. Take your time and stay healthy.*

FATIGUE

Fatigue is one of the most preventable threats to the success of your hunt. When not recognized and dealt with, it can even be fatal. A tired backcountry hunter breaking up some firewood is more likely to injure himself than a guy who is well rested. The exhausted bowhunter will not cope with the other dangers of the backcountry as readily as the one who has been taking short "cat naps" and getting the right amount of sleep at night. This is also a big reason why you must take on the challenges of the backcountry in the very best physical condition you can.

Your physical condition is very likely to be the best it is going to be at the beginning of the hunt. In other words, as time drags on, your physical (and mental) condition is likely to deteriorate because of your imperfect handling of your body, in regard to sleep, fatigue, loneliness and so on. A slip of the knife or broadhead that makes a deep cut in your finger makes camp chores more difficult. Forgetting or not bothering to purify the water you drank in that stream could give your stomach fits, which can further contribute to dehydration.

Under such circumstances, you are not on your game mentally. Obviously, this can make releasing a precisely aimed arrow all but impossible. I stay sharp by always keeping my eye on the prize. During the tough times, I think back on all the work I did during the off-season to hopefully have even just one chance at a trophy. I'll admit, it is easy to forget how much backcountry hunting means to you when you're fatigued.

WHAT TO DO TO OVERCOME FATIGUE

- *Truthfully, most of the work needs to be done out front. Go into your hunt in shape physically. Backcountry hunting takes commitment.*

- *Take frequent breaks. No need to push it; most guys go too hard out of the gate and get burned out. Pace yourself.*

- *Keep your eye on the prize. Think back on all the hard work you did in preparation for the hunt. All you need is one chance.*

LONELINESS AND BOREDOM

For the backcountry hunter, loneliness is very common and honestly one of the #1 challenges you'll face. Man is by nature a social animal—we crave human companionship, and in this day and age, we are so distracted by life, phone calls, kids, TV, etc. we never really learn what truly makes us tick.

Days and days on your own, deep in the backcountry, I promise you will find out who you really are. For many this can be an uncomfortable acquaintance as it is simply too real and too raw. When you feel lonely, issues at home or work that aren't really problems become problems. Guys over analyze this or over analyze that, wonder what their wife or girlfriend is doing and pretty soon, they are packing up and heading out.

Just because you are alone doesn't mean you must be lonely. For me, this was always one of the most difficult parts of my backcountry adventures. Similarly, it has stopped many of my would-be, long-term backcountry partners from ever coming back.

The worst or most lonely time in my opinion is the first couple of days of the hunt. Then it seems that, while not forgetting about the loved ones back home, I get into a survival type mode and focus more on what I need to do instead of the comforts of home. It is a challenge every time out, but now I am ready for it and know it is just part of the deal. Besides, this is one of the big reasons the backcountry is not overrun with other hunters. They simply aren't strong enough mentally.

Days and days on your own, deep in the backcountry, I promise you will find out who you really are. For many this can be an uncomfortable acquaintance as it is simply too real and too raw.

What can help when you're homesick is to stay preoccupied with a useful activity. The busier you are, the less bored and lonely you will feel. When you think that nothing else can be done to increase the chances of arrowing a trophy bull or buck, reevaluate and think again. There is always something practical to be done. Always. Go get water or pack over to a better spot to glass from that evening. Or write in your journal, which is the main time-consuming thing I do. I have filled up many topo maps or notebooks with my chicken scratch memoirs. I document everything I've learned that day or assumptions I've made in regard to the animals. By noting movement of game you can start to develop trends or animal tendencies. I jot down the weather conditions and what areas I am finding animals in given these conditions.

After a few years of this, it started to get easier to figure where I'd stand a good chance of finding those trophy bulls and bucks. Now, I can go back to those areas and because the wilderness never changes in regard to logging, new roads, etc. and animal movements rarely change, what was hot years ago is still hot now. Reading back on my notes I also notice that I write quite a lot about my kids and thoughts I have on them, missing them and my wife, as well as simply my general view on life. Someday my kids will love to look back and read my journals and get a little insight as to what I went through in the backcountry.

In regard to middle of the day activities, whether it is napping, writing in your journal, eating and so on, do it in a place that might just lead to success. Instead of waiting out the non-peak hunting hours on a lonely ridgetop in the beating sun or a windswept ridge, do it in a spot where something might work its way by you or in a place you can glass a bunch of good country. Animals get up and eat a little, change bedding locations, head to water and so on all day. If you're always working hard, glassing, sitting on saddles or by water there is at least a chance at success. The reason I love the backcountry is because anything can happen at any time.

I arrowed a beautiful cinnamon/blond black bear at about 1:00 in the afternoon on opening day in 1997 as I was sitting eating lunch with my boots off. By making the decision to spend the midday in a low saddle riddled with trails that connected a lush basin with a good water source, I was able to capitalize on this "bonus bear."

Another time, I set up shop to ride out the five hours between 11:00 a.m. to 4:00 p.m. near a small pond I could tell was being visited by a number of animals. A couple of hours into my vigil a nice little four-point buck came in. With a deer, elk, bear and cougar tag in my pocket, I could have taken a poke at him if I wanted to, but he wasn't quite what I was after. I did snap a few photos of him, which is always fun. Later a 6x5 bull came in and I missed him, twice. That hurt, but you get my point about making the most of each and every minute you're in the backcountry.

Big, rugged and remote country is intimidating for a lot of hunters—me included when I first started hunting the backcountry. Now, the mountains are where I feel most alive.

Fear

The Ultimate & Unspoken Backcountry Challenge

Although you have no doubt read of the dramatic rise in mountain lion attacks throughout the West or grizzly attacks in Montana, Wyoming, Idaho and Alaska, the chance of becoming the victim of such animals is extremely remote—almost too remote to even give a single thought. You stand almost as much of a chance of being struck by lightning as being torn up by a bear or cougar. But I think the typical backcountry hunter fears much more than the rogue grizzly or cat even if they don't want to admit it. I have corresponded with many would-be backcountry hunters and predictably, fear never comes up. Regardless, for most, fear, either of the known or the unknown, will be part of the equation.

Fear is a defense mechanism, which kicks in naturally because above all else the human body wants to survive. When fear hits as a big fat dose of adrenaline rushing through your veins, it leaves those who aren't mentally strong enough shaking, panicky and not in position to make the best decisions. Outside of the backcountry, our normal life seems secure and comfortable, but in deep that will change. We will definitely be separated from all the other conditions that make us feel safe—our home, our family, our circle of friends, the money in our bank account, our physical health. Uncomfortable thoughts racing through the minds of new wilderness hunters can be debilitating.

So, how do you use fear or anxiety as an advantage? As we know, fear is normal, so the big question is, "How will you react?"

Using Fear To Your Advantage

Once we are equipped to handle and control fear, we can start using it to our advantage.

In its positive sense, fear can drive us—it can spur us to become bigger and better, wiser and more tolerant, more awake and therefore more responsive. In particular, once we learn to place fear into perspective, we can use it as a useful and positive catalyst for change.

"Only those who risk going too far can possibly find out how far they can go."
—T.S. Eliot

Fear hits us mostly as a result of a major crisis in our lives, whether through an accident, illness, a sudden job loss or getting lost in the wilderness or dealing with an aggressive bear. Such a crisis will often signify a big turning point. How we respond to the crisis will influence whether this turning point will turn out to be a tragedy, a nightmare, or a triumphant statement of human spirit.

Many have used the traumatic experience of losing their job as a springboard into a brand-new and successful career. Although their initial experience was filled with fear, they focused on the opportunities that they could gain, took the risk of branching into unknown and new fields, and just kept going.

We can see how this would work in regard to hunting the backcountry. I know and plan on at least a little fear on all my big hunts. I imagine in my mind's eye how I think my hunt will play out. I know it will be tough and I am ready for it. I know I will be uncomfortable and I may even want to quit and go home and I am ready to overcome such feelings. When hunting Alaska I know I will have bear issues. I know these fears and while I don't welcome them, I have no problem dealing with them. By using my fear positively, I find it keeps me sharp and alert. If the hunts take on an unanticipated twist, I will not panic, but will be wide awake and quick to respond.

I am not too proud to admit that when I first started doing the solo thing deep in the Oregon wilderness or Alaska's Kodiak Island, I was intimidated beyond belief. No, not just intimidated. At times I can admit now, I was

Learn to control your fear or your fear will control *you*.

—Cameron R. Hanes

afraid. Of what, I couldn't really tell you. Everything I guess—the vastness, getting lost, the brown bears, the long nights, the solitude and so on.

I remember one time as clear as a bell. I was laid out in my bivy sack on a sidehill on Kodiak. Roy was miles away, likely doing and thinking the same thing I was. The rain was pounding down and it was sometime during the middle of a long 16- or 17-hour black November night, but I was not anywhere close to sleep. My eyes were probably saucer-like as the bivy sack lay on my face while being pummeled by the storm, which meant I also couldn't hear anything but the pop of raindrops on the Gore-Tex shell. I had killed a buck that day and had it stashed about 100 yards away but knew I had blood all over my pants, boots, etc. The thought of a big brown bear grabbing my head through my bivy sack and shaking me around like a dog chew toy was unsettling to say the least; not a lot of sleep to be had as I tossed and turned in my cramped quarters all night.

Despite my fears I made it through the night, and got my boned-out buck down to the meat pole and hung up. That next day I was feeling confident, and while still a little intimidated, I made it and was getting stronger with each passing minute. There were a few times on the island that the fog was so thick, I could only see about 30 yards at the most. I can't tell you how many times I spied hulky brown bears ghosting through that white shroud. As it turned out, no bear closed on me in the fog but a nice little buck did, and through the heavy wet air I hammered him with a good arrow. I was afraid, but I at least stayed sharp enough to move into killing mode. I was making headway.

So, all in all, despite the intimidating situations, I did all the hunts, survived and killed during all those adventures and eventually I overcame my fears, which ranged from getting eaten on Kodiak to getting lost in Oregon. I faced them all head on and while it was not fun, it was necessary and I think fairly normal. Regardless of admitting your fears, here are a few things that I found helped me.

For me, it was fear of the unknown. The future, and whether or not I'd have one, was the primary fear I experienced. I think that most serious backcountry hunters who push the envelope searching for the most rugged, out of the way places like I do probably share some of these same worries.

Since working through my fears, I have hunted the backcountry with guys who simply were uncertain or didn't have faith that we'd be able to find a way out of the mess we'd got ourselves into, but then again, they didn't have a manual like this book to help prepare them for the challenges of the backcountry.

There were times when I wondered if I was cut out for wilderness hunting

Bivy hunting on Kodiak Island by myself in 1999 was a huge personal test. Sleeping with my boned out buck, in a thin bivy sack with hulking brown bears roaming during the long 17-hour nights of November was almost too much.

myself. During my first couple of years by myself in the backcountry, I would only hunt from or near a pack trail. I was simply too afraid of getting lost to risk diving into uncharted territory. I remember sitting and staring for hours at one far-off basin in particular, longing to go check it out.

The problem was it was miles from any trail and I didn't have confidence in myself to navigate over there and hunt it. Finally, after more time in the wilderness and more experience reading topo maps, I made my way to the area I'd longed to explore and found out that many others must have had the same reservations I did because the hunting was incredible. That remote basin holds some very special memories. It is where I've killed my two best wilderness bulls and two of my best wilderness bucks, and I've never even seen other boot track let alone another hunter to this day.

A few other frightening situations come to mind as I write this. One, dangerous skiff rides on the angry ocean waters off of Kodiak in November; two, circling grizzlies at dark in the rain while sheep hunting Alaska with only a two-man tent for shelter; and three, scaling a sheer cliff while wearing a pack and holding my bow only to get stuck.

It is a sickening feeling when you can't go forward, you can't go back and your stomach is seemingly stuck in your throat. You just know, "I am going to fall." After being in this position a number of times, I can tell you with confidence that if you panic and let the adrenaline take over, which often results in shaking and making poor and too quick of decisions, you will fall. Hunting deep has its risks no doubt, but if you face your fears and come out

It took me years to work up enough courage to get over to this basin. I had my eye on it, scoured the country on my topo, but because there were no marked trails, I was too afraid to go cross-country. Finally I gained enough confidence and made it happen. The results have been incredible.

on top, you'll be a better man, I promise.

This fear, which is experienced to one degree or another by all hardcore big country hunters, can be just as much a healthy thing as a debilitating one. Fear has a way of forcing you to act, and action is what survival is all about.

These actions include building a quick and worthy shelter, starting and maintaining a fire in the rain, finding and preparing something to eat, fixing yourself when you are injured or sick, getting water, becoming focused to a higher degree than you ever thought possible or setting up a signal system if things get too out of whack.

Fear is natural, but we should not allow it to overwhelm us. By learning to handle our fears and by using it to look for opportunities, we can take the same path that other successful hunters have also taken in their lives. It all depends on our ability to channel this vital force constructively, and turn it to our advantage.

I know it sounds dramatic, but even the most experienced and savvy outdoorsmen get in bad situations each and every year. I thought by mentioning it here, it might plant a seed of awareness or at least make a positive impact on how you act and react when you find yourself in your next backcountry "jackpot."

Random Bear Thought: Back in the 1990s, my buddy South Cox was torn up by a black bear where we hunt blacktail in the Marble Mountains Wilderness. Since that time a canister of Bear Assault is on his pack frame waist belt virtually 100% of the time. You might say, "I am not packing that can around; what are the odds I'll be attacked?" Well, you might be surprised. The more that humans infringe on their country, bears might feel forced or feel more inclined to protect their country, their kill or just wreak a little havoc on you just on principle. The point is, you never know, but let me tell you, a can of bear spray may just be the best investment you ever make for backcountry gear. Be careful.

Moments like this keep that flame of desire burning bright. *"No guts, no story." —Quote taken from the back of an Easton Archery t-shirt.*

Desire

How bad do you want to be a backcountry hunter?

Commitment, drive, passion, desire—whatever you call it, this attribute paves the way for all the other required components that make up an accomplished backcountry hunter. Ivan Crews of Washington puts it in rather simple terms, "I eat, live, breathe and sleep bowhunting." For Ivan and most other backcountry hunters who succeed as often as he does, bowhunting is not just a hobby. It's a way of life.

In my case, it seems as though I am forever reading hunting magazines, writing something pertaining to the hunt or exchanging e-mails with hardcore bowhunters. Or I may be taking photos with a hunting theme, shooting 3D tournaments or Techno-Hunt at our local pro-shop. If not the former or the latter, I am probably mulling over new equipment, reminiscing about prior hunts, envisioning future hunts or watching a hunting show on TV or video. Archery in itself is a compelling sport, but for me, the need to achieve my bowhunting vision is overwhelming and all encompassing.

My best hunting buddy, Roy Roth, and I coined what has come to be essentially our bowhunting mission statement, "We may not be the best shot and we may not be the best hunters, but we will outwork anyone." Whether this is true or not, I don't know, as I am sure there are plenty of bowhunters out

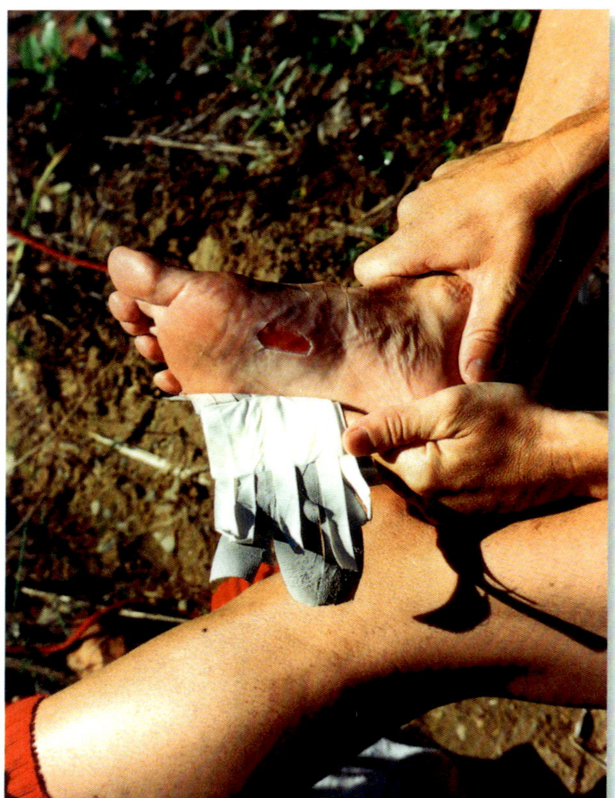

A nasty blister could never stop me from chasing my dream. It might hurt every step I take for a week in the mountains, but it will eventually heal. You can recover from a tough hunt, but you can't recover from quitting.

there who hunt their butts off. Besides this, I guess the most important realization we grasped together is bowhunting in general and backcountry hunting in particular may not be fun all of the time.

Take for example my annual wilderness elk and mule deer hunt here in Oregon. I have lugged a pack with all of my camp, food and gear for over 20 miles, with feet blistered and bleeding, shoulders and back aching, hot, sweaty, tired and dirty. Despite that misery, I have tasted the thrill of victory enough to not only draw me back every year, but my desire to succeed consumes me. A big stumbling block for most guys is that even if you are successful, 99% of the time spent in the wilderness on this kind of hunt is not technically "fun."

Bottom line, the country is big, rugged and unforgiving. On my hunts, even if I killed an animal right in camp, it would still be one very tough hunt. There is a lot of work that is involved in getting a dead bull from the ground to the meat locker when you're 10+ miles back on one of those typically warm September days.

Here's the thing about tough hunts. How hard are they really? Even in the most remote setting, under the most unenviable conditions, you are probably only one long day from the nearest supermarket and a shower;

when one minute you have convinced yourself you are living hell on earth and could care less whether or not you have a successful hunt, and a few hours later there you are, cruising down the highway with the radio and cruise control on, sipping a Mountain Dew.

It is then that you realize, "Well, I guess it wasn't all that bad." But guess what? You have already pulled stakes and headed home, ending all chances of tagging out. Remember, you can recover from a tough hunt, but you can't recover from quitting. When I think about what "hard" really is, I don't think of backcountry hunting.

THE ESSENCE OF DESTINY

Watch your thoughts, for they become words. Choose your words, for they become actions. Understand your actions, for they become your habits. Study your habits, for they become your character. Develop your character, for it becomes your destiny.

Author Unknown

Hard times in my mind would be living in poverty, deaths of loved ones, serious health problems, your kids getting seriously ill, etc. Being tired, missing your favorite chair and wanting to watch SportsCenter does not exactly compare.

I realize not everyone will share my desire to succeed, but try to keep in mind a quote on one of my favorite T-shirts from Easton Inc. The backside depicts the silhouette of a successful archer with a caption underneath that reads, "No guts, no story."

That pretty much sums it up. What Roy and I talk about is the fact that the elk or mule deer hunt itself may not be fun, but the other 350 days of the year usually are. For us, the off-season after a successful season is often spent reliving hunts and sharing harvest photos with family and friends, which in general gives us an overall feeling of accomplishment. These experiences are not only fun and enjoyable, but in my opinion, life defining.

Section 2

Backcountry Conditioning

Survival of the fittest

The Intangibles

To set the tone *for this conditioning section, I want to focus on what I call "The Intangibles." To the backcountry bowhunter, the intangibles, which by definition means indescribable or indefinable, are qualities hard to put a thumb on. The intangibles as they relate to mountain hunting might be even tougher to quantify precisely. I mean, how can I explain in black and white the incredible importance of getting your body in shape and your mind in the right frame for hardcore bivouac hunting? How do you know when you're there? The intangibles aren't like shooting, where if you can put four arrows out of five in a three-inch spot at 50 yards, chances are your shooting is up to snuff. The age-old phrase, "Words can't do it justice," probably sums it up best. What is not up for debate is that backcountry hunting will tax even the most able bodied and mentally capable bowhunter.*

More than hunting strategy, knowledge of animal tendencies, specific trophy areas, shooting skills and so on, I believe the intangibles can have more impact on public land, D-I-Y backcountry hunters than any other factor, period.

Physical conditioning for the hunter is a topic that many writers have covered. However, I don't think any of them have covered this topic as in depth as I will here. Of equal importance to "being in shape" is being strong mentally, or mental conditioning. This is why I give getting the "mental edge" its fair share of coverage too. Truth be known, physical fitness equals mental fitness. A strong body, built for any challenge, gives you confidence and more appropriately gives the mind strength.

Physical Conditioning

Getting Ready for the Mountains

"As humans we are best suited for endurance, and I think we have a desire to find our limits."

Scott Jurek, seven-time winner of the Western States 100-Miler endurance race.

Make no mistake, backcountry hunting is and will always be an extremely physical challenge, especially in the backcountry. There are exceptions. Some guys can afford to pay to get onto private ranches and conceivably kill a great bull or monster buck in a less demanding venue than most of us. However most guys, myself included, have a very tough time coming up with $5,000–$10,000 for a trophy elk or deer hunt. As a result, we are left with bust-your-butt public land free-for-alls, where I believe the hardest hunters are the guys that will bring the bulls home.

The wilderness areas I typically hunt are open to anyone willing to get back there. That said, I have never seen another bowhunter off the pack trails during the 15 plus years I've been hunting the backcountry. The reason? The country is too tough, too steep and too big for most guys. There are many who could hunt back here and be successful, if they put the time into preparing their bodies prior to the hunt. More often than not though, bow-toting hunters learn of their physical shortcomings one or two days into the hunt, and by then it is too late. The more concentration you can put on the hunt itself, and not your lack of stamina (which adversely affects desire), the greater the likelihood you will experience success.

When hitting the weights, keep in mind that for the most part, everything you do in the woods starts and ends with your legs.

I could sum up my process of achieving physical fitness in one word, variety. I will go into this in more detail later. When hunting the mountains, you will be subjecting your body to a multitude of challenges. This is why I don't rely on any one exercise to prepare for the hunt. Throughout the spring and summer I will do something physical everyday. This could include any of the following: Mountain biking, lifting, running, hiking with a weighted pack, abs and stationary biking. The bottom line is to do something everyday.

Everyone complains of not having enough time in the day, as do I with a wife, two boys, a little girl and a full-time job piled onto the time commitment bowhunting requires. But not too many guys could convince me they don't have a half-hour to an hour at some point during the day to exercise. I routinely sacrifice sleep to exercise, getting up at 3:30 a.m. to go on a 20-mile mountain bike excursion or running at night while most sleep.

My workouts break down like this: I try to do cardiovascular exercise four or five times a week, for 45 minutes or more per session. Whether it is long distance running, hill work or an intense "Spin" class (stationary bike) at the local gym, I try to push my body to its limit and beyond each and every time. Your body will reach new levels and become stronger to accommodate the stress you put on it. If you do not continually push yourself, your gains will plateau.

There is a difference between interest and commitment. When you are interested in something you do it only when it is convenient. When you are committed to something you accept no excuses and produce only results.

—Anonymous

Weight training is invaluable—providing your goal is overall hunting prowess. When hitting the weights, keep in mind that for the most part, everything you do in the woods starts and ends with your legs. Big biceps will not make an ounce of difference if your objective is to get an arrow into the vitals of a trophy bull, but strong legs might.

That being said, don't think that I don't do any upper body, as I believe in total body conditioning. One day I will concentrate on squats and lunges, with curls following this grueling leg workout. The next lift session will include chest, shoulders and back. I can do all of the weight training at home with a surprisingly small amount of equipment. All I have is a bench, squat rack, 325 lbs of Olympic weight and a couple sets of dumbbells. All of it ran me under $300.

Exercise can be hard to get up for all of the time. This might require you to get creative with your workouts. Running on the road can be very boring, which is why I enter local road races throughout the summers. It is amazing what simply getting the competitive juices flowing can do for enhancing your workout regimen.

I find myself taking on more and greater challenges each and every year in an attempt to see how far I can push myself. Recently I've done a couple of 31-mile-plus ultra marathons with the goal of preparing my body for the battle that is bowhunting the backcountry. I have never put limits on what I am capable of physically and neither should you. My ultimate goal is to redefine the term "hardcore" as it relates to hunting. In my sights this coming off-season, a 100-mile endurance run.

This wide variety of exercise and intensity gets me close to adequate backcountry hunting condition. Believe me when I say that there has been more than one instance in my hunting career when, if not for the fact that I was in perhaps above average physical condition, I would not have successfully arrowed my quarry.

When first reading this phrase some 15 or more years ago, it immediately held special meaning to me. These few sentences perfectly sum up what I live to do—bowhunt the West's most rugged and remote backcountry for trophy class animals.

The challenge of getting within bow range of big mature bulls or bucks is immense. Here in my home state, the success rate on elk hovers around 10% and for deer the average is 20%. That equates to about one elk every 10 years and a deer every five. That average includes any elk and any deer, not just the mature animals I focus on. If we had the numbers on only record book animals, most guys would probably throw in the towel thinking, "What's the point?"

While these numbers don't look real good, they are just numbers. This is an average. Most of us bowhunt because we want a challenge. Like many of you, I love having the odds stacked against me as it just makes me work that much harder. To get above-average bowhunting results, a guy must put out above-average effort. For me, average success won't cut it. I want more, which is why I eat, live, breath, and sleep bowhunting. Like my favorite phrase states, "I will accept no excuses and produce only results."

I think to successfully hunt the backcountry of the West and focus solely on trophy animals you must be in excellent physical condition. If this is your goal, hitting the Stairmaster a couple times a week isn't gonna get you there. This is the type of effort a lot of guys put out. Remember, we are talking next level, which requires pushing the envelope type preparation. I run, lift, do adventure races, etc. If it involves pain and endurance, sign me up. I will do it just because it might help in making me harder, tougher and leaner, or in other words, a more successful bowhunter. Everything I do is almost like a personal Frankenstein-like science project to try and become a virtual hunting machine.

The Hanes Exercise Regimen for Elk and Mule Deer Hunting

Now I will say, "I love working out." To me, there is nothing like the feeling of being in top shape and ready for anything the backcountry can throw at you. When I have a goal, like punching my tag on a big buck/big bull wilderness combo, I get fanatical about physical conditioning. My wife, Tracey, mentions something about being "overboard" or "obsessive" but whatever the case, I hit it hard.

I know many of you don't have time to workout everyday, or bodies (knees) that will allow long runs on asphalt, and the truth is that exercising hard six or seven times a week probably is not really all that necessary. While it is true you can never be in too good of shape, moderation is the key for most of us.

Throughout the spring and summer I will do something physical everyday. This could include any of the following: Mountain biking, lifting, running, hiking with a weighted pack, abs, and stationary biking.

I came up with a schedule that guys interested in backcountry hunting might want to reference. Now, I know, for many of you a 10-day or more wilderness hunt is simply not realistic. The good news is you can still be successful on three- to five-day jaunts, but like those long hunts, you can greatly increase your odds by doing some moderate conditioning before heading to the mountains.

If you go too hard right out of the gate, you'll probably either get burned out, be too sore to continue your regimen or cause injury. Granted, I do think you need to do more than long walks two or three times a week in preparation for a backcountry hunt. Inadequate physical condition sabotages more "big hunts" than anything and believe me I have learned this the hard way. This is a lesson I don't want to "re-learn."

The minimum amount you should workout in the months prior to bow season is 30 minutes a day, four times a week. Hour-long workouts obviously give you more benefit and help in the weight loss category as well if

Hanes Exercise Regimen

Running mile after mile everyday is not necessary to get in shape to hunt the backcountry. While moderation is the key, don't expect overnight results. Give yourself time to prepare your body for the mountains.

- ***Work out 30 minutes a day*** *(increase this time incrementally up to an optimum amount of one hour), four days a week beginning three months before your backcountry hunt.*

- ***Cross train***. *Mountain bike, lift weights, run, jog, hike with your pack on or walk. Do it all. Cross training is the key for the backcountry bowhunter, plus you won't get burned out as fast by "keeping it fresh."*

- ***We all have favorite exercises.*** *Whatever yours is, just get out there and do it. Remember, something is always better than nothing.*

- ***Push yourself.*** *Without striving for new goals, gains will plateau.*

- ***Running for 30 minutes or an hour straight isn't necessary.*** *Jog for 20, walk for 10, jog for 20, walk for 10. If and when you can jog the entire time, fine, but it is not 100% necessary.*

- ***A smart, balanced diet*** *will accentuate your conditioning gains. When working hard, your body needs good, high quality fuel. Don't sabotage your effort by piling on the high-fat foods. Reward yourself, but be smart about it.*

- ***Remember, if success is your goal, there is no substitute for hard work.***

- ***When you're just*** *sitting there watching TV, try doing push-ups and sit-ups during the commercials. Doing the "commercial workout" can make a big difference.*

- ***Every day that you spend in inactivity, you are getting weaker.*** *Every day the elk and deer move through the high country, they are getting stronger. The longer you wait, the wider the gap grows. Today is a good day to start preparing for the backcountry.*

that is a concern. Experts say that it takes an hour of exercise a day to lose weight without going on a diet. A half an hour will do for weight loss if you both diet and exercise.

I am not saying you need to get out there and run for an hour solid. If you are starting off at ground zero, you will need to walk before you can run, so to speak. I suggest walking for 10 minutes and slowly jogging for five. Do this back-to-back for a half hour, say four times a week to begin with for a couple of weeks time.

Slowly begin to lengthen the workout until you are walking for 20 minutes, jogging for 10, and repeating it. Now you are at an hour. Work on cutting back the walking and increasing the jogging time. Eventually you will get to a point where you can maybe not run for an hour solid, but hopefully run for 25 minutes, walk for 10, then wrap up your hour running for 25 again.

If running isn't your thing or even if it is, I do suggest variety or cross-training. I like to throw on the pack and either climb hills or the bleachers at a nearby stadium with a little weight, once or twice a week. Throw in a day of mountain biking and you are set. Personally I don't like the biking as much because it seems like I need to ride forever to get a decent workout. If you have the time, that is great. But a 25-minute run challenges me more and increases my heart rate more than an hour and a half bike ride on moderate terrain. If you have nearby hills to ride, well, that is a different story. Hit those, which will hammer your quads and now we are talking.

Now we come to the most important pre-season question. Do you just want to hunt the backcountry, or are you committed to hauling a trophy out of the mountains? If success is your goal, there is simply no substitute for hard work. Remember, the bigger your goal, the harder the work required to get there.

Long Hunts

WHERE THE HARD WORK PAYS OFF

Prior to the beginning of the 2003 bow season I was running at least 10 miles a day, five days a week for months in an effort to get my body ready for life in the mountains pursing elk and deer that, we must remember, call this country home. They live in this harsh country day in and day out and will never get fatigued or frustrated or desperate. They are concerned with one thing—staying alive, and they are good at it. What it comes down to in my mind is survival of the fittest.

Note from CRH – My good friend and hunting partner Ben Maki is as well versed on the topic of conditioning for the hunter as anyone I know. He grew up hunting the backcountry of Alaska, killing everything from brown bear to mountain goats. Additionally, Ben was a world-class athlete in the biathlon, having finished 4th in the 1994 U.S. Olympic Trials and was on the U.S. military national team, the military national championship team and the military world team. Because of all this I think his insight is valuable.

Cam,
You have titled this section "Survival of the Fittest" which I think is an awesome way to look at fitness for hunters. To get them to think of themselves on the same terms as the animals they pursue is very cool. I am a huge fan of anything that gets people thinking of themselves as part of something larger than just themselves. To get motivated enough to commit to fitness, people need some connection bigger than just tagging animals. It has to be fundamental to the way they look at the pursuit of hunting.

Physical fitness = mental fitness = good shooting.
Ben Maki

Something I learned from competing at the international level was that the better physical shape I was in, the better mental state I found myself in. Not just because I was faster, but that there are honest chemical changes that occur with solid fitness. I am convinced that better physical fitness brings about better decision making abilities in the field and will also keep your mind sharp when unplanned opportunities present themselves.

A perfect example of this is that mulie you arrowed after the miss a half hour earlier. I watched the video of that hunt the other day and noticed the events unfolded in a pretty quick fashion. You shot with a pretty sizable pack on your back and at a fairly long range. If you weren't fit, first the miss would have dropped you into the pit of, "I blew my chance" despair and your senses would have been deadened a bit by that. Secondly you wouldn't have been able to make a clean shot with a big pack on and thirdly, you likely would not have even seen that encounter as a shot opportunity.

The more I hunt, the more I realize that there is a huge difference between people who are regularly successful and those that aren't. That difference is not because they are lucky, it's that they find opportunity where others find obstacle. In my opinion, that is a state of mind built from physical and mental fitness. I truly believe that physical fitness = mental fitness = good shooting. Ben Maki

Rain, sleet, snow, hail, heat...if you're looking for an excuse not to exercise there are many. The hardcore backcountry hunter must be committed to preparing mind, body and spirit for the challenges that await.

The recipe for success is a fairly simple one. This isn't brain surgery, but at the same time there are no sure-fire shortcuts that will guarantee success. The way I see it, if I can hunt my absolute hardest over a 10-day period in good, remote elk and deer habitat, I will be successful. This can be easier said than done though. Where all the preparation and superior conditioning pays off is at the tail end of a long hunt. By this time, most guys are beat down, and depending on what has happened in the days prior, are probably feeling a little desperate as the days pass by. That was the case for me on a memorable Oregon wilderness hunt.

It was the sixth day of the hunt and I had just missed a good 4x4 Pope & Young mule deer. I was depressed as it had been very warm and the opportunities few, which made missing that deer very hard to stomach. I thought I was above such things after going the previous two seasons without missing an animal. But, as we know, there is nothing more humbling than bowhunting. It mattered little to that buck that I had been on a roll. In bowhunting you have to prove yourself each and every time out. No resting on laurels here. This can be draining and I will tell you, after that arrow ricocheted off the rocks and that hard-earned opportunity slipped through my grasp, I was feeling a little pressure. Shrugging off the miss, I had confidence that if given a shred of opportunity again, I would undoubtedly capitalize. I truly believed that I had worked too hard to get shut out.

A half-hour after that miss I jumped a buck that I had glassed that morning. When the big 4x4 hesitated for a moment in bow range, I dotted him with a perfectly placed arrow. The P&Y buck went about 100 yards before piling up. The next day, day seven, I arrowed a good five-point bull, which topped off my best wilderness double ever. It went from the worst hunt to the best just like that. But, the key was staying focused and being ready when opportunity knocks.

When hunting the backcountry, miles from any road, I typically bivouac out for up to 10 days at a time. This means packing gear and camp on my back every step of the way. Packing a 40 to 50 pound pack during a long hunt like this can be difficult, but in my opinion it is the most effective way to hunt remote areas. Because of the training and a diligent shooting regimen, in addition to that Oregon wilderness buck and bull, I filled the rest of my tags that memorable season on eight trophy big game animals in five states and Canada. Is success like this possible for anyone?

It sure is. As I stated at the beginning of the chapter, the key is a guy can't go into backcountry unprepared physically. If you do, you'll be miserable. Commit yourself to excellence and the sky is the limit.

**The best bowhunters have two things:
Specific goals and a burning desire to achieve them.**
Cameron R. Hanes

Mental Conditioning

Get in the Zone

There are many backcountry hunters who come back from their big hunting trip spinning fables to cover foibles. They will spend the entire off-season mulling over the woulda, shoulda and couldas, then tell themselves, “Next year will be different.” Next year will not be different for these guys, unless they stop just hoping it will be different and commit themselves to making it different.

As I mentioned, mental conditioning is an intangible, but the truth is having confidence in your abilities might be the single most important factor contributing to a successful hunt.

Why is having confidence so necessary? Because, to build confidence, you must first attain complete confidence in everything, beginning with your equipment and proficient use of said equipment, on down the line to basic hunting ability.

I myself have straddled the confidence fence many times in my bowhunting career. Emphatically, I can tell you how frustrating the unenviable side of that fence is and conversely, the feeling of complete control that confidence brings. Confidence is a hard fought accomplishment, which hardly seems fair since it can so easily wane. Each of us may take different routes in an attempt to gain the self-confidence needed to be an accomplished backcountry hunter.

Personally, the confidence embryo is born in the faith I put into my equipment and my body. The confidence is nurtured and grows as my shooting becomes more proficient and as I become stronger physically, or in my mind, more predator like. As in hunting, tournament 3D shooting success is dictated by your ability to deal with an ungodly amount of pressure. In this arena, you must "pick a spot" while being cognizant of the fact that the thin line of success and failure is measured in inches or fractions of inches, not yards! For me, when my confidence reaches the boiling point, it becomes the driving force behind my desire to scout more during the pre-season. As the hunting season begins I find myself hunting longer and harder, because I believe if given a shred of opportunity I will exploit it, with the end result being a big bull or buck for the wall.

The important theme here is to use whatever means necessary to achieve a high level of confidence. If intense scouting and the increased faith in your hunting area that comes from patterning wall-hanger bucks bolsters your confidence and pushes you to shoot or prepare more, that's fantastic. Or perhaps you have more heart or fortitude than most, continually pushing yourself far past the point where most bowhunters would quit? This in itself plants a seed of confidence that spreads to the rest of your skills. Find what makes you tick and use it as a vehicle to strive for perfection in the process of preparing yourself mentally as well as physically.

I believe an individual prepares differently when confident of success. You will strive for perfection in preparing for the chance at a trophy animal—from the razor sharpness of your broadheads to your own mental toughness and everything in between. Believing success is inevitable may never be more important that when chasing a big bull elk, because nothing will challenge one's mental strength like a bugle-screaming 6x6 at 20 yards.

You can recover from a tough hunt, but you can't recover from quitting.
Cameron R. Hanes

By giving credence to these "Intangibles" of backcountry hunting, I have had the fortune of arrowing many trophy bulls, bucks and bears during my backcountry bowhunting tenure. And like me, new and old bowhunters alike can experience similar success by being cognizant of these sometimes indescribable and oftentimes overlooked attributes of the successful bowhunter.

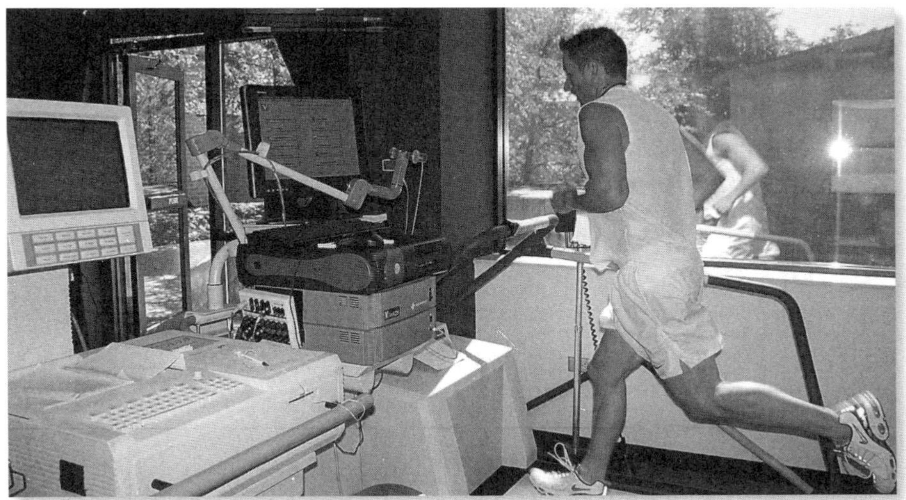

This photo was captured at the Boulde- Human Performance Lab where they ran me through a gamut of tests. From lactic acid profiles to body fat analysis to VO2 Max, I learned some great information that could help anyone preparing for the mountains.

The Next Level

Becoming a Bowhunting Machine

Blue Collar Bowhunter Becomes Lab Rat

Because I put so much emphasis on and attribute most of my backcountry success to being in good shape physically, I took very keen interest in an article by Christie Aschwanden that ran in *Backpacker* Magazine, August 2003, called "Body of a Backpacker."

For this piece, Backpacker funded an "ambitious study of eight hardcore hikers" at the Human Performance Lab at the Boulder Center for Sports Medicine. As the article states of the athletes they tested, "These folks are not like run of the mill joggers," said Neal Henderson, the center's coordinator of sports science, "They are serious endurance athletes." The piece also said that the backpacker bodies they tested were lean and strong with powerful, healthy hearts and had high-endurance capacities. Henderson admitted that he would be hard-pressed to distinguish their results from those of serious cyclists or runners.

I was surprised to learn that you don't need to kill yourself getting in shape for hunting. Even Olympians confess that most of their workouts are done at "conversation" pace.

To say I was intrigued with this article would be an understatement. I wondered as a blue-collar bowhunter how I would rate in such a test and better yet, what could I learn that might enhance my training.

BOULDER CENTER FOR SPORTS MEDICINE—HUMAN PERFORMANCE TESTING

After a few emails and phone calls, I flew to the Boulder Center for Sports Medicine in Boulder, Colorado and subjected myself to the exact same testing those eight elite athletes went through with Backpacker. Neal Henderson and fellow exercise physiologist, Paul Kammermeier put me through a battery of tests designed to measure aerobic capacity, cardiovascular health and body composition. When it was all said and done, not only did I have a killer workout, but also I learned a ton about the human body and endurance training.

The first test we did was the Lactic Acid Profile, which determines Lactate Threshold (LT), i.e. pretty much the point of no return when running.

LT is the one best predictors of endurance performance and can be improved greatly with proper training. The LT data gathered by examining blood samples taken every four minutes of an increasingly difficult treadmill run that lasted for nearly an hour suggested that I could run around 6:45 miles with a heart rate of 164 beats per minute for two to three hours—perfect marathon or ultra marathon pace. By speeding up to say, 6:10 miles with a heart rate of 170, I would be running on borrowed time. This pace could only be sustained for a 10K or maybe a half marathon, which was consistent with my history. This past summer I ran a 10K in 38:16, which is exactly 6:10s. Incidentally, at the end of the run, I was pretty well spent.

Me and my oldest son, Tanner, with our medals from Tillamook Burn Scramble. He won the youth division.

Many hunters unknowingly hit their LT very quickly when, for example, they're trying to cover more ground than normal in the thin mountain air when heading off a herd of elk. They go absolutely as hard as possible at first and then hit the wall, which forces a severely slowed pace as the elk get farther and farther away. Once you blow past your LT all that will help is recovery time. The best strategy is to stay just below your threshold, which just as in my running test, can usually be sustained for quite some time if you're fit. Don't go out full bore to cut off the elk; steady is the key.

The best way to improve your LT is to train at your LT or slightly above one to two times a week for a four to eight week period. A sample workout would be to run at or above your LT, or where it feels like you're really pushing it, for 20 minutes, rest for 10 and do another 20 minutes hard, rest for 10 more, then one final 20-minute interval. Whatever the interval is, rest for half of that time. So if you are running hills at or above LT and you run for 12 minutes, rest for six. Remember for this workout it has to hurt a little; faster than "conversation" pace.

We did a VO2 max test and a body fat composition analysis, which like the other tests, yielded very interesting results. Neal, a professional triathlete himself, agreed to test me because he grew up hunting and knows that working out and physical conditioning is a big part of being successful in the woods. He thinks hunters are a huge group of people that have very little information on what our bodies are physically capable of. He gave me some great advice on how the average guy can tailor his workouts to accommodate long, grueling hunts that require much endurance.

I was surprised to learn that you don't need to kill yourself getting in shape for hunting. Neal, who has tested some of the world's greatest athletes, says that most of their workouts are done at "conversation" pace. While jogging, go at a pace in which you can carry on a conversation. "Even many

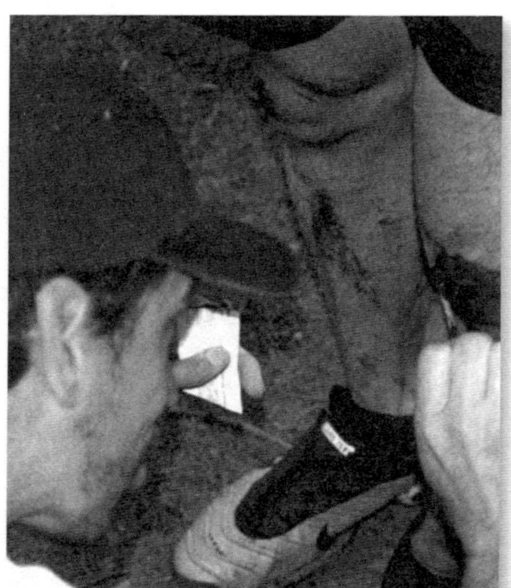

Doctoring up cuts earned during 2nd place finish in the Tillamook Burn Scramble, a no holds barred adventure race.

Olympians," says Neal, "workout at what might be considered a comfortable pace 90% of the time. Hard is not always better."

Just as the Backpacker test indicated, the fitness benefits of backpacking rival those of much more intense sports. You don't have to be a world-class athlete to build up amazing endurance. Many people underestimate what their bodies are capable of. Neal suggests doing long, comfortable workouts (45 or more minutes) three or four days a week and then one day of the week do a hard, faster-paced workout.

I supplement long runs with shorter, more demanding hill workouts, weights and mountain biking. For me, as I mentioned before, variety is the key. Granted, I run a lot and love the feeling I get during long treks, but sometimes these workouts leave me with aching knees because of all the pounding. I can't just not workout though, so I switch it up and lift or bike.

One key fact to consider before heading out for a quick 10-mile run to begin your exercise regimen is first and foremost, set realistic goals. If you've been doing nothing recently go for a brisk walk. There's no point jogging if you can't go for a brisk walk. But of course, many people do and I have made this mistake myself a number of times. The problem of going overboard right out of the gate is you get too sore, which hurts and could cause you to stop your workout routine before it gets started.

Remember, there is plenty of time before the next elk season. There is time to do it right.

Get in shape first, and then work out hard and work out smart. If plans call for a physically demanding hunt anywhere in the world, you'll be glad you put in the gym time and pounded the pavement. When running around the mountains, success is much more likely if you can concentrate on killing a buck or bull as opposed to killing yourself.

I had my wife, Tracey, snap this photo in response to a few e-mails I received after describing my practice routine in an issue of *Eastmans' Bowhunting Journal*.

In Closing

Do What is Right for You

A number of readers took issue with my suggestion of shooting every single day even if it is just a handful of arrows. They said there wasn't enough time to shoot everyday because they got home too late—after dark or didn't have a good place to shoot. I say get innovative. If darkness is an issue, I have a solution. If you are committed to the sport of bowhunting, committed to improving and mostly committed to gaining that edge mentally, I suggest bringing bowhunting into your living room the way I do.

I will say concentration is of the utmost importance, as you definitely don't want to punch the trigger on a "Living Room Round." In my opinion, this level of dedication will really help you keep that edge mentally and technically stay sharp. There isn't a day that goes by I don't shoot at least six arrows (takes five minutes) in the house if need be or outside. I should say some experts disagree with my approach as I've read articles that say daily practice is too much. Maybe they're right? I am just telling you what I do, and for me, it has worked. Similarly, I am at least as fanatical about

I ran with ultramarthon legend Scott Jurek in sight for about 12 miles during my first ever ultra, but in the end just didn't have the endurance to keep pace. Besides winning the WS 100 later in the year, Scott also won the 2005 135-mile Badwater Ultra, which is run in Death Valley. It took Scott 60 hours and it got up to 130 degrees during the race. I get a lot of motivation from endurance athletes like Scott.

exercise, maybe more. Sometimes I am equally neurotic about both.

I have run a 31-mile ultra marathon in the morning, drove home three hours from the mountains where the race was held and still forced myself to hobble out and shoot a couple groups before collapsing on the couch in a vegetable-like state. The need to succeed drives me. You see if I don't shoot and exercise every single day I can promise you, I'll be in a bad mood. Not only by design mind you, I just can't shake it; it's a mental thing.

Is this obsession healthy? I doubt it, but that is a completely separate subject I am guessing should be talked about with a professional! In fact, as I type this a couple days after Christmas, I can tell you it is real hard this time of year to want to go running, but I did today in the pouring rain. I also ran on Christmas Eve, the day after Christmas and a couple weeks ago when it was 20 degrees out.

Did I really want to? Not in the least. I put myself through all of this regimented exercise and shooting with the goal of becoming the best mountain bowhunter I can be. I want to "Tame the Mountains" and this is the only way I know how.

Above all else, remember in regard to exercise, anything is better than nothing. Don't think that with all this talk of extreme this and ultra that, I have always been so over the top. Truthfully, it has taken me years to work up to where I am now. There was a time, a number of years back and 20–25 pounds ago where my conditioning consisted of walking with the wife and kids or hiking while training the llamas a few times a week with my oldest, Tanner (when he was one or two) on my back in a baby backpack. And you know what? Even though it was relatively tame, it sure did help.

My attitude at that time was, at least I wasn't losing ground. I couldn't run 31 miles non-stop in the mountains, but I could still hunt pretty hard, and while I probably wouldn't have experienced much success in the later stages of a long hunt, I did pretty well early. Back in the day I would just tell myself, "One foot in front of the other. One step at a time." It is all a matter of perspective and understanding what you're capable of.

Ben Maki had some good insight for me in regard to this subject as well. He writes, "I am not trying to come from too far out in left field on this, but I remember in the movie *Dirty Harry*, Clint Eastwood was fond of saying, "A man has got to know his limitations." I think that quote applies here. This book is about helping people prepare so it should be motivational which it is, but in the same breath, most people haven't been put in position to find their own breaking point. I think you have the responsibility to help people focus on the fact that a clear understanding of what they are capable of will make them more effective. They don't need to be finding that point 15 miles into the backcountry; they need to understand their bodies and how much they can take before they get there. I think people get swept up in the hubris of good intention when it comes to getting fit. Like simply reading about it is enough. I would encourage people to try to find their own personal uncle-point in some safe setting so they know what it feels like coming on and can react in the field. As you said in *Eastmans' Bowhunting Volume 3* when you found the 'bou killed by the grizzly in NWT, 'Life on the Artic Tundra is Hard and Final.' I might add, as is life in most harsh backcountry settings that many big bucks and bulls call home. Thanks for helping to educate our hunting brothers on this topic." Ben Maki

The biggest factor is to make sure your goals match your level of physical conditioning. If you are hunting or plan on hunting in country that isn't all that rugged, or big, you don't need to run 10 miles a day for months before season. I do, but nowadays my goal is to be in shape to hunt the mountains—any mountains—successfully for 10 or more days and bring out a trophy every time. In 2004, I hunted the Wyoming backcountry for elk and killed a 6x7 bull on the tail end of a long hunt in country I had never even seen before. In 2005, I killed a big Nevada 4x4 in some of the most rugged mule deer mountains of the West, again in country I had never even stepped foot in prior to the hunt. If you don't plan on doing hunts like this, your training doesn't need to match mine. I just wanted to share what I've done and the measures I take to prepare for the ultimate challenge that is backcountry bowhunting. Mine is not the only way, it is my way, and it has worked for me, period. You might ask, "Cam, does your approach work every time? Is your method flawless?"

No. Bowhunting is never guaranteed, no matter what you do or how hard you work, but it is my hope that somehow bowhunting justice will be served and all the hard work will be rewarded. I have collapsed to my knees wracked with pain after screwing up a shot on the biggest bull I'd ever seen in the wilderness. I sat there and cussed the bowhunting gods for the deep hurt I felt. Which brings to mind another favorite phrase of mine, "Life is not fair."

EBJ 31 Dialed In by Cameron R. Hanes

> *"Well, it is Showtime! By the time this issue hits your mailboxes most of us will be deep in the backcountry or heading out trying to make our dreams become a reality. It will be time to find out if those lonely nights spent pounding the target with arrows and all those hours getting in hunting shape were enough? And, did we make the right equipment selections this year? Did we do enough to come out on top in the supreme challenge of bowhunting? Regardless of how our season unfolds, one thing that can never be taken from us is the unrivaled experience of living and hunting the West. I will never take for granted how lucky I am to be able to bed down in the middle of the wilderness, look up and be blessed with the most beautiful display of diamond-like stars sprinkled across a velvety black sky. This is truly God's country.*
>
> *Personally, at this time of year I feel like a fighter getting ready for a championship bout, or an NFL'er getting ready for the Super Bowl. It is like I am sitting in the locker room, headphones on, chilling out, in a zone. I am waiting for my name to be called as I've put in the time getting to this point and now it is time to hit the field. My skin tingles with anxious anticipation when I think that by the time this magazine goes to print, I will be deep in the Nevada backcountry doing everything in my power to arrow a majestic high country buck. This will be public land D-I-Y bowhunting in its purest form. Back there I will be doing the bivouac thing with my good friends South Cox and EBJ Managing Editor, Shon Simpson. We are going to do our absolute best to film the entire hunt, the highs and the lows, and bring it back home to share with all of you. Matching our skills as hunters versus the survival instincts of big country bucks. Now that should be some good, raw, and real television. Stay tuned.*
>
> *It is strange; while I am more psyched than ever to have a crack at those big Nevada bucks with the camera rolling and all the pressure that brings, I feel at peace. I know in my heart that regardless of whether I bring a buck home or not, I have done absolutely everything in my power to get ready for this hunt. If I don't kill, well that is bowhunting. I am not saying it won't hurt and hurt bad, but honestly, I'll have no regrets."*

On this run, like many of the others, the 20 milers, the ultras, I wonder, "Is there any other bowhunter doing what I am doing right now? Is there any other bowhunter willing to put their body through what I will – the pain, the fatigue?" I tell myself *no way* and what that means to me is that I am gaining on some or widening the gap on others. Who? My competition. You see, to the public land hunter, *everyone* is competition.

Update: January 1, 2006

Well, it just turned midnight of a new year and here I am hammering away on this book. Almost done now. Revisiting that Dialed In, *which ran just prior to my Nevada mule deer hunt with South, gets me fired up as you might guess. As you know, we had an incredible hunt. Proof positive that hard work can and does sometimes pay off. That one hunt will motivate me for years. On that backcountry adventure, bowhunting justice was served.*

I was thinking about bowhunting justice tonight, New Year's Eve, as I was running through the mountains in the miserable cold rain. I parked just before dark, about 4:45 p.m., in an empty gravel parking lot. The mountain that I run is not too far from Eugene, which for those who don't know is a fairly large college town. On a sunny day, there might be 150 rigs parked in the exact lot where tonight sits not a one. I run this 3.5-mile up and down mountain loop on Mt. Pisgah everyday of the week at least once (2x to 5x in the summer) and today, a day of merriment for most was no different. It was no surprise that I was the only person there to run the hill. I got my iPod fired up, put on my stocking hat, pulled over my hood and took off running through the muddy muck up the hill. It would take me about 45 minutes tonight. By the time I got back to the truck in the dark I was soaking wet, but felt great. I worked up a good sweat despite the frigid conditions, which is my goal every day. On this run, like many of the others, the 20-milers, the ultras, I wonder, "Is there any other bowhunter doing what I am doing right now? Is there any other bowhunter willing to put their body through what I will – the pain, the fatigue?" I tell myself no way and what that means to me is that I am gaining on some or widening the gap on others. Who you ask? My competition. You see, to the public land hunter, everyone is competition.

Section 3

Equipment

Backcountry Gear A–Z

Gear for the Bivouac Hunter

Some four years ago in *Eastmans' Bowhunting Journal* Issue #13 I wrote an epic (not because of quality but because of interest) piece entitled, "EBJ's Guide to D-I-Y Bowhunting." It seems since that first D-I-Y manual, which at that time not many were familiar with the D-I-Y reference or what it meant, EBJ has become known as the number one resource for the backcountry bowhunter.

In the last four years, there has been advancement in regard to backcountry gear, which I will cover as well as share a few more tricks and tactics I've learned since that first D-I-Y article that might help make you more efficient and successful on your next or first wilderness hunt. But, much of what I wrote then is still good, sound advice now.

To set the stage properly, I will start with a few ground rules. Like any other budget-conscious bowhunter, I simply cannot pull off big expensive guided hunts for trophy western big game annually. This means I set up my own hunts, which is what almost everyone now calls, Do-It-Yourself, or D-I-Y bowhunting. There are other differences besides the obvious monetary consideration when comparing guided to D-I-Y hunts. The thing I like about hunting on my own is that if I kill it, it's because of me and if I don't kill it, it's because of me. In the field, making all the decisions in the heat of the

This image shows the perfect relationship between the hunter and his well fitted pack. This pack is a high quality internal-framed pack all loaded down.

battle is how many of us like it. Plus, the feeling of accomplishment after a successful D-I-Y outing is indescribable.

A classic D-I-Y hunt is exactly what I experienced in September 2004 in the backcountry of Wyoming. I was on my own other than having my cameraman Trevon Stoltzfus in tow after trophy bull elk. I would have to buck the odds given the fact that I had never even laid eyes on the country I'd be hunting and because of a slight snafu I wouldn't even have a topo map of the area.

We had all the maps we needed on Trevon's handy dandy laptop, which did nothing for us some 10 miles from the rig. Nothing like making something very hard even harder. Oh well, we were there, and there for only one reason, to hunt—maps or no maps. We quickly threw our bivouac gear together, tossed in a few days worth of food, shouldered our packs and headed out. The deeper the better was our approach and you could say it worked. At the tail end of a dreadfully long hunt I was able to arrow a good 6x7 bull. If you've seen the video you know how relieved, happy and caught up in the moment I was. It was a very special time for this ol' bowhunter, and all on film to boot!

I will share the gear I have used and the lessons I have learned on that Wyoming elk hunt, a D-I-Y bighorn sheep hunt with my father-in-law in 2004 and over nearly 20 years of backcountry hunting. Since my first time back in the wilderness, I have made many gear upgrades.

On my maiden trip in "deep," I had one of those sleeping bags with flannel lining that had deer and pheasant on it. My tent was one we used to use when sleeping in the backyard when I was a kid. Believe me when I tell you, this is not the gear you want when bowhunting at about 7,000 feet the third week of September with the temperature in single digits. I was miserably cold at night and vividly remember trying to sleep with all of my clothes on, including my boots in that "little kid's" sleeping bag. Amazingly, I did arrow a spike bull on that trip and subsequently was hooked on backcountry hunting.

As I mentioned, I am always learning new tips, tricks and strategies that allow me to hone my approach, but for now I am feeling pretty confident in my system and the gear I've listed below as it has never let me down. Keep in mind that much of my hunting has been solo, so the gear listed is what I carry on my back to go remote after bulls or bucks for four or more days at a time. So, without further ado, in referencing that original write-up let's get into the gear you'll need to live life in the high country.

Equipment

BACKCOUNTRY CREED: WHEN IN DOUBT, GO WITH QUALITY.

- **Pack** – *This is hands down, the #1 question I get on e-mail or after speaking at seminars. For shorter hunts (under five days), I like the Ultimate Hardcore external frame pack by Adventure Outfitters, as it is 3,500 cubic inches, which seems just about right for four days worth of food and gear. It will be jam-packed, but it will work. This pack will run you about $320. For hunts over five days, I would go with the internal framed Badlands at 4,500 cubic inches, $350. For a week-long hunt, it too will be packed and fairly heavy (you'd better be in good shape to hunt the mountains for a week). I've heard Kifaru makes a good pack; I simply don't have any firsthand experience with them but I need to get it. I hear a lot of buzz about their product. Comfort with these things is the key. That was the biggest difference I*

This photo was from a couple years back—I was using a Peak-1 external frame pack and Nike Gore-Tex cross trainers. To answer your question, yes it all worked fine. However, I did upgrade.

noticed after switching from my old Peak-1 external frame pack to the Badlands. I was carrying pretty much the same weight (45 lbs. loaded down with five days worth of food and a full allotment of water) only doing it much easier because the internal framed pack was so much more comfortable. The difference was amazing. I was able to stay fresher, thusly hunting harder and longer. Make sure whatever pack you choose has a good waist belt and thick padded shoulder straps. There is nothing worse than buying a new pack, getting it loaded down ready for your bivouac hunt only to find out the shoulder straps cut into your collar bones like baling wire after a few miles of humping up the trail. Always err on the side of comfort. A waist belt that won't tighten properly (it simply must go tight enough) is also something to watch out for. You'll need a good waist belt to distribute the weight of your pack. If you're like me, I switch it around during long hunts. When my shoulders need a break, I tighten the waist belt taking some weight off the top end. When this starts to get uncomfortable, or when I am doing a lot of uphill hiking which requires a higher stride, I loosen the waist belt a touch and cinch down those shoulder straps. Make certain the pack you decide on has a number of different shoulder strap adjustment points. You will use them all at some point during a 10-day hunt.

- **Sleeping bag** – *Can't sacrifice quality here. Must be lightweight; I use down which is not too bulky. I have a system in which I am able to put my entire camp (sleeping bag and bivy) into my sleeping bag stuff sack. I use a down Marmot Hydrogen +15 for the early season and a Cabela's XPG –10 (4 lbs.) if there is a threat of serious weather. A good rule of thumb, the lighter it is, the more expensive it will be. My Hydrogen bag weighs less than two pounds and will run you about $350. You can get a four-pound bag for about $280. While the money/ratio is a little skewed in these examples, a fairly accurate rule of thumb in regard to bivouac gear is, one pound equals $100. There are many good bags out there. Get on the Internet and do some research before you buy. A sleeping bag is not something you'll want to be spending money on every year. My entire camp consists of my bag and my...*
- **Bivy Sack** – *For true bivouacking, I don't think you can do better than an all Gore-Tex bivy sack. I have had mine (from Outdoor Research it is an Advanced Bivy Sack, $280) for over six years and it's still going strong. It weighs less than 2 lbs.*

When mulling over the tent vs. bivy question, keep in mind, in regard to room to operate and room to store your gear, bivys have zero extra. Which is why a tarp is almost mandatory when there is a real threat of weather.

and with my sleeping bag inside, as I mentioned, will fit in one stuff sack. For hunts where the threat of anything more than a thunderstorm is unlikely, try Cabela's XPG Bivy. It weighs less than a pound and runs about $100. I used one in Nevada and had great success. For hunts where long-term nasty weather is likely, say on Kodiak in November, I wouldn't take the Cabela's bivy. I don't like the way the opening is on the top side of the bag. I think with extended periods of rain, you'd eventually get wet. To protect my gear when hunting with a bivy, I use an Oware 8' x 10' Flat Silnylon Tarp for shelter, which weighs less than two pounds with stakes and rope, and is completely waterproof. Find out more at www.owareusa.com. *At about $100, I think this is a must have for the serious bivy hunter. Some guys don't like the bivy setup, as there is simply no extra room in these things whatsoever. A tent will at least let you sit up and gives a little room to cook, change clothes, etc. Tents can be very appealing when hunting in rain or snow, as it is nice to have some room to take wet clothes off and get gear situated while out of the weather. Just because many ultra light travelers like myself end up using bivy sacks doesn't mean this is the only way to travel ultra light. In deciding whether to tent or bivy, you can approach the problem from a "pounds per person sheltered" perspective. In general, a solo hunter won't be able to beat a bivy sack for weight, but for those guys who don't like hunting alone there is another very appealing option. When you can start sharing the load amongst hunting partners, the weight numbers can change to make the tent option much more enticing.*

For true bivouacking, I don't think you can do better than a Gore-Tex bivy sack.

- **Pack Cover** – *This will protect your pack and its contents from the elements. I have always used black plastic GLAD bags but think it might be time to upgrade. Integral Designs makes the Silcoat Pack Cover, which runs between 30 and 35 dollars.*
- **Compression bag** – *This will compress your sleeping bag and bivy sack into virtually half the size. When it is lashed to your pack frame, size is almost as important as weight. You can get them from Cabela's.*
- **Headlamp** – *Must have a good headlamp. My Cyclops is a LED/Krypton headlamp*

powered by three AAA batteries and goes for about $20. This is a very long lasting headlamp.

- **Sleeping Pad** – *I used to recommend a self-inflating pad, but after having one pop on a recent backcountry hunt I am back to the old foam standby. Folding foam pads are indestructible, lighter, cheaper and do their job as well as the air pad. After popping the one, for the rest of the hunt it was like sleeping on two thin pieces of canvas. Not much insulating quality, which is not good. I use the Therm-a-Rest Z-Lite Short, 11 oz., $30.*
- **MSR Pocket Rocket** *(unless you're using Meals-Ready-to-Eat in which case you won't need a stove) and titanium cook set. See it at* msrcorp.com. *Includes stove and titanium pot that can be used as a cup or mug and holds everything for ideal backcountry travel. Weight 7.5 oz. – awesome product.*
- **Snow Peak Titanium Spork**
- **Rangefinder**
- **Binoculars** – *The old cliché, "Get the best pair you can afford," still holds true. I honestly don't know how you could do any better than a 10X pair of Swarovskis or Leicas. Remember, you can't harvest what you can't find. Quality optics are responsible for increased opportunities. Paramount item.*

To stove or not to stove? Nate Simmons is pictured here lighting his Giga Stove to heat up dinner.

- **Bino-System**
- **Platypus or Camelback water system** – *Must have item for the guy who will be working hard and covering lots of ground. You have to keep yourself hydrated and this deal will make that task much more doable. It will hold 2 liters of fluid and the tube that comes from the container and attaches to your pack's shoulder strap makes drinking very easy, which lends itself to more fluid consumption. This is a good thing.*
- **Water Purifier** – *Potable Aqua, active ingredient iodine.*
- **Knife and sharpener**
- **Topo Map** – *7.5 minute topographical map.*
- **Suunto Wristop Computer (watch)** – *These things will do about anything, tell you your elevation, heart rate, global position, compass bearing, depth, speed and barometric pressure. This is one awesome and valuable piece of equipment for the backcountry hunter. Gotta love technology.* www.suunto.com.

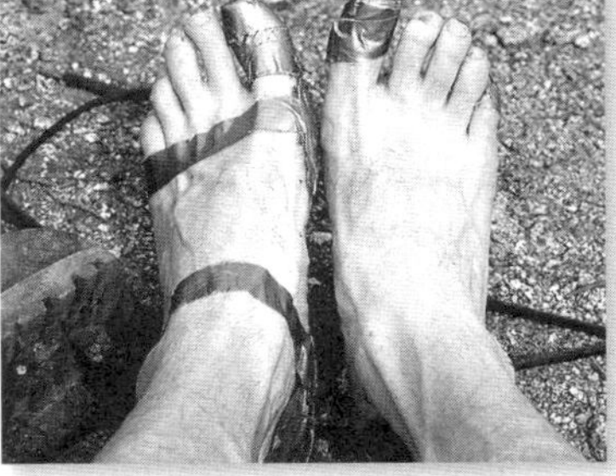

Duct Tape: For years, at the tail end of all my long hunts, my feet looked like they had just been pulled out of a meat grinder. The culprit? Not bad boots—I was using *great* boots—what caused the problems were cotton socks. Don't make this same mistake.

- **Duct Tape** – *This might be the best first-aid kit ever.*
- **First-Aid Kit** – *You should have some stuff to clean up cuts etc., as a nice complement to the duct tape.*
- **Nylon cord** – *100' of small diameter, braided, nylon rope.*
- **Extra release**
- **Extra serving** *(dental floss will work).*
- **Oversized, durable cotton game bags**. *Alaska Game Bags are some of the best.*
- **Camera** – *I use a Canon Digital Rebel. At the least, shoot with a good 35mm camera with flash and self-timer and small tripod. Carry a minimum of two rolls of 100 or 200 speed film, take a number of different set up shots with your trophy. Be sure to throw in an extra battery.*
- **Allen wrenches** – *You should pack a couple of the key sizes. If a rest or sight comes loose, your hunt could be over unless you have your Allens.*
- **Disposable lighter**
- **Leatherman**
- **Mini-Flashlight**
- **Windproof/waterproof matches**
- **Throw in an extra nock or two, and a field point**
- **Surveyor's ribbon for bloodtrails, etc**
- **Game calls**
- **Fire starter**
- **Compass**

Three key pieces of backcountry gear pictured here: A topo map, GPS unit and good quality head lamp.

Miscellaneous

- **Chapstick**
- **Ibuprofen.**
- **Unscented moistened body wipes.**
- **Small bar of unscented soap and small washcloth.**
- **Sportsmen's Edge** *Multi-Vitamin by Robinson Labs,* www.sportsmensedge.com.
- **Moleskin** - *Gotta have a little bit of this in your pack for blisters or hot spots.*

Held in place by duct tape, it works pretty well. On its own it usually ends up sliding off from where it is supposed to be and ends up rolled up in your sock somewhere.

- **Cut your toenails.**
- **Cell phone** – *I have used one to call my packer for meat hauls and directions to the kill site. Very important during those warm and getting warmer Septembers. Obviously, the battery will only last for a few days, but that is the precise time you'll need it. For instance, if I kill a bull early, I can still hunt for deer or bear and vice versa, but before I am free to do that I have to get the meat taken care of off the first kill. Verify coverage before you pack this thing all around the wilderness.*
- **Satellite phone** – *not a bad idea if you're hunting on your own in big, very remote country. The fact is you could lay there and die from a broken leg if you don't have any way to get hold of someone, not to mention medical issues like appendicitis. Also, great tool to have at the ready when you need to call your packer and there is no cell reception. Rent an Iridium brand satellite phone for $9 a day at* www.mobalrental.com.

Clothing and Footwear

Do you sleep with your camo on at night? Nope, no camo PJs at night in the backcountry. If it is dry, my camo is usually laid out on my sleeping pad to add loft. If my camo is wet, it's in my sleeping bag with me to dry out from my body heat during the night. I will put it down at the bottom of my bag so it doesn't chill me while I am trying to sleep if in fact it is damp. At most, I will sleep with just my first layer gear on.

This Silvis boot is one I wore for a season in the Eagle Cap and came away impressed. Might be worth checking into as they are very affordable. Good value for the money.

- **Boots** – *All about timing of your hunt and comfort. I have hunted during times of unpredictable weather in mountaineering type boots, which can be tough on the feet after many miles and days, but are very necessary. I have also hunted during the September elk season, where chances of any substantial weather are nil, in Gore-Tex trail running shoes which are much more* *comfortable. Some guys might not feel as though the trail shoes or anything less than a heavy leather boot would give enough support to ankles, feet, etc. and they would be right. This is a personal preference and knowing what your body needs structurally to stay operable is imperative. A couple of good bets in regard to boots: Cabela's Alaska Hunters by Meindl, $270, and Lowa Tibet's by Schnee's, $260. I have used them both in the nastiest and most rugged country of the West. Both are awesome boots, and for me, not too hot for those early-season hunts. Remember, sweaty feet can cause blisters.*

- **Two changes of high quality socks (no cotton)** – *Some of the best out there are Thorlos available from Cabela's for $12 - $15 a pair or SmartWool for about $20 a pair. Definitely, they are both worth every penny. I had blisters for years despite wearing high quality boots because I thought two pairs of cotton socks was the ticket. This might have worked for high school basketball, but for the backcountry, synthetic socks are a must.*
- **Lightweight high performance first layer gear** – *This is worn against the skin to wick away moisture. So far as first layer gear, Under Armour and Mossy Oak Apparel are tough garments to beat.*
- **Lightweight waterproof/windproof jacket and pants** – *Even late summer storms can be brutal in the high country. One great option is the gear available from Mossy Oak Apparel. Their APX (Advanced Performance for Extremes) line of clothing pretty much sets the standard for the hardcore hunter. Another good bet is the new lightweight raingear by Rivers West, www.riverswest.com. I have heard some good things about Browning packable raingear but have no firsthand experience.*
- **Cheap raingear** – *I bought a $9 set of cheap-o raingear at Wal-Mart prior to my father-in-law's sheep hunt and I truly believe it had a huge impact on the outcome of the trip. The four-hour horseback ride in pouring rain/snow and gusting wind would have soaked us clear through, even with the best outerwear. This may very well have put us in a hole we couldn't have climbed out of on an already very difficult adventure. The plastic Wal-Mart special pants and jacket shed the rain and snow and got us to camp dry. If in a similar situation you might want to consider such a move.*
- **Plastic garbage sack.**
- **EBJ baseball hat.**
- **Stocking hat.**
- **Gloves.**

Nate Simmons shows the ideal way to incorporate a good tarp into the bivy hunter's bag of backcountry tricks. The added coverage of a tarp makes a huge difference.

Nasty Weather Bivouac Gear

In regard to clothing, I take pretty much the same approach whether it is an early September elk hunt in Oregon or a rut hunt on Kodiak for Sitka blacktails. I say pretty much because there are differences. What stays the same is I always have an ultra high quality first layer like I mentioned. I also always have the great outer layer I mentioned. The key difference is in between these layers. On that note, layering is always the key in nasty weather.

For the late-season stuff or say, chasing Dall sheep in the mountains of Alaska, I use the same tight first layer against your skin philosophy as always, although I will upgrade from Under Armour Heat Gear (the thin stuff) to their Cold Gear (the thicker, heavier stuff), followed by one of UA's quarter zip, high neck pieces, then a synthetic fleece or wool garment with a little wind stopping action, then my jacket with a hood.

I will upgrade to a heavier stocking hat and gloves and throw in a balaclava that will protect the back of my neck from the chill. On the lower

In conditions like this where temps were hovering right around zero degrees, I use a tent. More room to operate is hugely beneficial to staying warm. For one, it allows you to use your small cook stove to create some instant heat.

With the threat of snow and being that we were hunting at 8,000 feet, my father-in-law Larry and I decided to leave the bivy sacks home for this adventure. A small canvas tepee provided plenty of room to get out of the snow and stay alive until Larry could kill his ram.

extremities, I will again change out the thin UA for the heavier stuff and add a layer of Mossy Oak Apparel's fleece.

Lastly, on the boots, I like the Lowa Sheep Hunters instead of the Tibets because they are a little higher and have more insulation. Both of course are available from Schnee's in Montana.

A couple of hand warmers are nice; I always throw those in my pack when hunting in cold weather. I have used them to, of course, warm my hands, but I've also put them in my boots when hunting from a quickly thrown together ground blind like I sometimes do on Kodiak. I've also activated them and put them in my sleeping bag after particularly frigid days. It is amazing how much difference those little things can make when I am all hunkered down in my sleeping bag and bivy with top pulled and closed tight. I get down right hot, which could be a lifesaver in certain conditions.

Topo Mapology

Breaking the Code

One huge piece of my elk hunting puzzle comes in the form of the painstaking attention I pay to topographical maps. I use these great tools to accentuate the knowledge I learn while hunting or on the scouting trips I take. By scrutinizing topo maps, I can locate water sources, saddles (low spots in a ridge) or likely bedding areas to check out. A good topo map is the serious backcountry hunter's most useful tool.

When heading to a new area, the first order of business is to get a 7.5-minute topo map of the area. For me, the next order of business is to find the most remote, hard to get to spot that has a water source (spring, seep, creek, swamp, etc.) nearby and invariably, that is where I will head.

In regard to maps in general, no ifs, ands or buts, you *must* get a 7.5-minute quadrangle topography map of the area you're planning on hunting like the one I am studying here.

Also, check out your hunting area at *www.googleearth.com*, which offers free satellite imagery right down to the tree, waterhole or boulder.

Once the initial topo deciphering is done and

In country as big and rugged as this is here in the Eagle Cap, a guy would be lost without a good topo map and just as important, the ability to read it. Luckily Tanner Hanes is well-schooled in topo mapology.

I have located a remote area that looks hot, I break it down even further. I focus on saddles or any land contours that will concentrate the movement of animals. North slopes will serve as your typical elk bedding area. I will pick apart my topo looking for a bench on a cool, north-facing canyon wall. This bench will draw elk, as obviously it is easier for them to lie on flat ground than to lay on more vertical landscape.

I also look for at least five or six likely feeding areas within a radius of a few miles. The reason being is that one, elk are nomadic by nature and two, a herd of elk can hammer the prime feed in high country meadow in short order. So, they have what many guys refer to as a "circuit." They will move, usually at night as they browse or in the morning while lining about to bed, from one area to the next. I seldom see elk in the same meadow two mornings or two evenings in a row. I have put them to bed at night in one area and then rolled out of my bivy in the morning to glass them up again near the same spot, but in my experience elk rarely stay for a full day in the same spot during the rut.

Finding your trophy in 7.5 minutes

A few years back, I received a great suggestion for an EBJ article from Bert Mattis out of Missouri. Bert wrote, "Cameron, this idea for an article is purely selfish, but hear me out. I live in the Kansas City, Missouri area, and of late have been able to get out West for one week a year to try for new

Make certain to set aside time each day (middle of the day is perfect) to map where you've been and where you're planning to head to. In big backcountry, it can be very easy to get turned around if you don't make a conscious effort to stay up on your mountain travel.

hunting areas. I love the mountains and backpacking, so any trip is a good trip no matter what the final outcome. It is a challenge to find a good area with a good population of mature animals, especially when you don't live anywhere near where you want to hunt. I would like to see an article that gives sound advice on how to pick out a good area to hunt elk.

What sort of things should I look for on a topo map that will lend itself to holding elk? I am well aware of all the other variables (healthy animal population, etc.) and tools available that make up researching an area, but maps hold a special interest to me. Maybe this is too narrow of a subject, but I think it could be broadened to make for a very helpful article.

I am by no means an expert mountain hunter, but I have researched an area in Idaho I am going to backpack hunt with my brother. We got a good tip from a veteran elk and deer hunter about the specific drainage for starters. There is one basin I am drooling over that is about six miles from the nearest road, and a mile away from the nearest shown trail, and more than 600–1000 feet down off of the adjoining ridges. It has several springs at the bottom of the main slope. The basin itself is mostly north facing, near timberline at the top, steeply rimmed, and has several white areas interspersed with the green on the map that is not timberline.

Does this area sound good to you? It does to me, but I would like to know if there are other things to consider when just looking at a piece of paper with a bunch of lines on it." Thanks for your time, *Bert Mattis*

In regard to maps in general, no ifs, ands or buts, you *must* get a 7.5-

minute quadrangle topography map of the area you're planning on hunting. There are many maps that will show more area than a 7.5-minute map will, but how much do you really need to see? The typical 7.5-minute topo map shows approximately a 40 to 70 square mile area, which should do for even the heartiest of hiking hunters. The key is these maps also show great detail.

I thought Bert's area sounded good. I look for food, water and cover, just as he did and of course, it has to be remote. The green on a topo map indicates timber and the white is either meadow or rock or more likely a little of both in a high alpine setting.

Typically, elk feed up out of the timber at night into the higher meadows and down again at daybreak. I also look for basins that are well away from likely travel routes that any other hunters might take. I never see anyone back where I hunt, but I know guys are hunting the same country or at least moving through. But, what I have found is that most hunters will not travel up and over a high ridge just to look in one secluded basin. They typically head to vantage points that offer the grandest view and pretty much figure the odds of something being in that one hard to reach basin is not great enough to offset the effort required to get in a position to glass it.

This is the exact scenario I took advantage of to kill a good backcountry buck a couple years back. I doubt if the buck I killed had even seen a human in almost a year. As a side note, there was also a herd of elk not 400 yards below where my buck was bedded when I arrowed him.

I also look for saddles or funnels that connect the head of a drainage to an adjacent basin or water source. Living in the rugged backcountry can be tough, even for animals, and I have found that elk will almost always take the path of least resistance when they are not pressured. A dip in a ridge creates a natural funnel that may very well connect a bedding area to a feeding area. Circle this spot on your map and make a point to check it out.

I have a place deep in the Eagle Cap Wilderness exactly like what I am describing which I have named, "The Funnel." I have watched bulls, bears, bucks and coyotes move back and forth through The Funnel and the best part—it is 12 miles from the nearest vehicle. It is one of the first places I head when hunting the Oregon backcountry. A diamond in the rough if you will.

A good way to hone your map reading skills, test gear and learn prospective country is by scouting your hunting area during the summer prior to the season. This can be difficult for a guy like Bert who lives in the Midwest, but one three or four-day banzai trip can make a huge difference.

Backpack Weight Reducing Tips

Lightening Up Your Load

Look for innovative ways to reduce backpack weight. Look at your gear with a critical eye. Before, during and after each hunt, give your gear a good once over and note packing habits with the goal of reducing the weight strapped to your back and hanging off your shoulders for days on end. You may be surprised at the gear that ends up suddenly not making the cut anymore and never being missed. Keep in mind, it is a process. To be effective and efficient in the backcountry requires a long-term commitment.

Make the most of multi-use equipment. Using one piece of backcountry equipment for more than one purpose saves space and weight. I encourage you to take the time to scrutinize the worthiness of each piece of gear that makes it into your pack and on your back.

Here are a few examples of good, multi-purpose gear: A Leatherman tool can be used as a knife, scissors, saw, screwdriver, etc. (I've even hacked deer antlers off with my Leatherman.) Duct tape is a good moleskin substitute, bandage wrap, gear repair (quiver, packs, boots, tents) and splint wrap among other many uses. Socks can double as hand warmers. Clothing can be turned into makeshift slings, a pillow or bedding. Zip-Loc freezer bags will aptly hold small items, serve as a bowl for preparing and eating food and make a functional carry-out container for garbage.

Here are a few backpack weight-reducing tidbits, which to experienced mountaineers are old hat, but to many backcountry hunters might be something new.

Use Titanium *Pots, stoves, backpack stays, tent pegs, anything metal, if made of titanium, will be significantly lighter than any other metal. I read a good quote on a mountaineering website addressed to those who lament the unreasonable cost of titanium equipment. Their pro-titanium poster noted in part, "Never mind the naysayers who scoff at those who purchase titanium products. If they could afford it, they'd get some too. You can't eat titanium, but for a lightweight packer, it's as good as sliced bread."*

Eliminate Map Edges *Cut off the large and unnecessary edges of your topo maps. To me, if it doesn't have at least one function, I don't want it in my pack. The prodigious edges of maps, sometimes as much as three inches, are useless. Of course you need to leave longitude and latitude markings and other important map attributes, but the rest can go in the burn barrel.*

No Pillows *Instead of carrying a pillow, stuff your clothes in one of your larger stuff sacks or a meat bag. Your clothes will be drier and maybe even a little warm in the morning from the heat of your head on them all night.*

Replace your Alkaline Batteries with Lithium *Replace the AA alkaline batteries in your flashlights with AA lithium batteries. Lithium AA batteries weigh 50% less than alkaline and last about three times longer. They only cost about $5.00 for two, so you actually come out ahead in the long run.*

Cut the Handle off your Toothbrush *Pretty self-explanatory, but you really*

Pack Frame Q & A

I am considering an internal frame and know you use the Badlands 4500. How do you like it? I currently have a Cabela's external frame and it has held up good but is not very comfortable. —Jason Eituts, Anchorage, Alaska

I am sold on the 4500 for long hunts of 5–7 days and will be using it again this coming season, *www.badlandspacks.com*. Didn't know how the internal frame would work for what I need it to do, but I've been very impressed. I have been able to pack everything I always have in years prior, only much more comfortably. I too have a Cabela's external, which has worked well for me in certain applications. I don't like how the frame sticks up above my head and it is not as comfortable as my Badlands, but it is great when its sole purpose is packing meat. If a guy wanted to keep it in the truck or at base camp and use it just when an animal was on the ground as opposed to wearing it the entire hunt 24/7, this pack frame is ideal. It is quite a bit less expensive too.

I was reading thru one of my old EBJs, and I noticed that you used the Badlands 4500 last year. I'm very curious to know how it performed? I have been bivy hunting for the last few years, and am in the process of updating packs. I think that I've pretty much narrowed it down to either the Badlands 2800, or the 4500, or the Dwight Schuh pack (I think it's rated at about 3500 cubic inches).

I average about three days in the field before returning to the truck to re-supply. But, I would like the option of having enough capacity to stay out for 5-7 days, if necessary. What do you suggest? —Travis Scott, Alma, Nebraska

If there is even the possibility of a 5–7 day hunt off of your pack I would go with either the 4500, a Hardcore Hunt Pack by Jeff Janssens Adventure Outfitters in Hillsboro, OR 1-888-935-HUNT (4868) or the Schuh pack. The 2800 is perfect for the shorter duration hunts. I should note that I have not used one of the newer Schuh packs. They look great and seem like quite a bargain in Cabela's but I haven't had my hands on one or given it an in-the-field run through so firsthand advice is limited, *www.cabelas.com*. Another pack I have heard a lot of great things about is the line available from Kifaru, *www.kifaru.net*. Many serious backcountry guys recommend Kifaru. Might be worth checking into?

only need the business end of your toothbrush and maybe an inch or two more. No need for the full-length handle as this is just more unnecessary weight.

Eat Heavy Foods First *I usually try to eat the heaviest foods first. I typically hit my MRE main entrees pretty hard from the get go, then the packages of peanuts, cashews, etc. Really all you are concerned with in the backcountry is counting calories anyway and so long as you get about the same amount everyday, you'll be fine. Well, you might not be fine, but you'll be the same level of miserable everyday throughout the hunt. Eat whatever weighs the most first to lighten your load.*

Backcountry Food

Fueling the Machine with High Octane

"**Taking the right food** and *enough* food can be the most challenging part of preparing," says my friend and hunting partner South Cox. "There really are some good options available, but after 10 days of eating backpacking food, the idea of a burger and a shake will about drive all but the most dedicated of hunters off of the mountain. For breakfast I will either eat instant oatmeal, granola with powdered milk or some kind of breakfast cereal bar. From breakfast through dinnertime, I snack all day on dried fruit, trail mix, jerky, granola bars, peanut butter and crackers, fruit leather, etc. Finding something substantial for lunch has always been a battle. One thing I've found to take the place of my usual sandwich is a jalapeno bagel, a few slices of dried salami and some pepper jack cheese in individually wrapped packages. The cheese can be found in the string cheese section of your local grocery store. My choice for dinners will depend on the duration of my stay from base camp."

South says, "My two main meal options are MREs or freeze-dried. MREs are convenient because they don't require any cooking, but are heavier than freeze-dried meals. The weight of five days worth of MREs is approximately 6.75 lbs.; the weight of a MSR Pocket Rocket with a full small fuel canister and a titanium pot and five days of freeze-dried is 3.6 lbs.

"I've found the cutoff for the weight-to-meal ratio for MRE as opposed to freeze-dried meals works out as such: MREs are better for three meals days. Any longer of a stay in the field and you'll be better off carrying freeze-dried and a stove from a pure weight standpoint. If you are eating oatmeal for breakfast then this can quickly tip the balance in favor of the stove and freeze-dried as the oatmeal weighs next to nothing compared to your other breakfast options. It should be noted however that you can lighten the MREs considerably by getting rid of the excess packaging, condiments and some of the "inedibles."

"Digging a little deeper, I averaged out the total carbs and calories each of the two options offered. I took three different meals each, MREs and freeze-dried, at random and compared the values of each. What I found surprised me. The MREs averaged 157 grams of carbohydrates and 1043 calories, while the freeze-dried averaged almost exactly half of that at 72 grams of carbs and 533 calories. It should be noted that one of the randomly selected MREs skewed the numbers with double the number of carbs and over 50% more calories than the lowest MRE measured. If you are counting calories then it is worth looking at labels as they vary widely.

"Adding a stove to your pack is about a pound of dead weight, but when coupled with the right food choices that pound of weight can be more than made up for. The downside is that at the end of the 4–5 days in the field, you are still going to be carrying that extra pound, less a little for burned fuel. With the MRE option your pack gets significantly lighter daily. If you couple freeze-dried with instant oatmeal and MREs with granola, the equation gets a little more interesting. The scale starts tipping more rapidly in favor of the stove and freeze-dried option.

"Whatever the case, make sure to pack plenty of food; this is not the time to go on your Jenny Craig starvation diet. You need a lot of energy and will be burning many more calories than you would back at home."

More on Hot Eats and Cool Treats

FOOD AND WATER

Average daily calorie requirements in the field are 2,800 to 3,600 calories for males and 2,000 to 2,800 for females. Not getting enough food and nutrients leads to rapid weight loss, which leads to: loss of strength, decreased endurance, loss of motivation and decreased mental alertness. Given this, it should be obvious how important packing the right foods are to bowhunting success. I am not even sure if a guy can haul enough food in his pack for an extended backcountry hunt, but you need to really pay special attention to exactly what you'll be hauling on your back for body fuel.

So far as food goes, it should contribute at least 100 calories per ounce of weight otherwise it's not worth packing. For instance, I pack a handful of Nature Valley 100% Natural Oat 'N Honey granola bars. They weigh 1.5 oz. and have 180 calories, 29 grams of carbs and 4 grams of protein. Thusly, they make my ratio with ease.

I have used Emer'gen-C powdered drink mix for years now, as an additive to my water. Emer'gen-C comes in small packets that weigh a piddly .29 oz. yet contain 1,000 mg of vitamin C, which is 1666% of your Daily Allowance as well as 500% of B6 and 416% of B12 plus it is high in potassium. This is something I strongly suggest you use.

I think one the best main staples to the wilderness bowhunter comes in the form of military rations called Meal-Ready-to-Eat, or MRE. These things are awesome and have a ton of calories, are convenient and are balanced in nutrients (carbohydrate, protein, fruit, etc.).

Eliminating the need for a stove is one of the best attributes of going with MREs. They come with a sleeve that you insert the main entrée into and then add a very small amount of water, which activates chemically a self-contained meal heating system. In minutes you have a hot meal. Some say that because these meals are already hydrated they are heavy, but, by packing MREs you will not need to haul a stove, cook set or utensils in your pack.

This is huge as every ounce is critical. MREs come in many different combinations of main meals, fruits, crackers, potatoes, rice, noodles, ham, meatloaf, etc. Plus the hydration quality of an MRE means that you can run your water reserves lower if need be knowing full well your MRE will give your body some of the fluid it needs to survive, which is the backcountry hunters #1 goal isn't it?

They also come with a number of things I do not want to pack, like instant coffee and Tabasco sauce among other things, but I simply take these out and discard, along with the heavy package the MREs come in, prior to my trip.

I have used MREs for years with great success, but my best piece of advice I can offer is get out in the field, eat some backpacking-type foods and find out what exactly you like best and would be most inclined to eat when fueling your machine is vital to the hunt.

From the Backcountry Kitchen of South Cox

BREAKFAST

I divide breakfast into two groups, cold and hot. As mentioned above, instant oatmeal is my usual first choice for a couple of reasons, mainly weight and size. I'm a pretty big eater in the morning, so I'll eat three packets of flavored oats. To add a little more interest I'll sometimes add some chopped dried fruit, like apples, apricots or banana chips. A hot chocolate helps keep me hydrated. To change up the monotony, instant cream of wheat or other hot cereals can be substituted for oatmeal. Mountain House also makes freeze-dried scrambled eggs for those of you who like protein right out of the sack.

Though heavier and bulkier, granola is a great breakfast option. I get a handful of sealable sandwich bags and pre-measure the granola and powdered milk. In the field you simply add water and eat it straight out of the bag. Some of the granolas out there are barely palatable, so I'd do a little preseason testing to make sure you aren't carrying "dead weight." Sometimes I'll add a little Frosted Flakes to make the cereal taste better, and again, dried fruit can also be added. On cold mornings you can add hot water. Breakfast bars make a good addition to the menu, but I've found they aren't substantial enough for me on their own.

LUNCH

To me, lunch has always been the biggest challenge. In the past it has usually just been continual snacking, but that always left me yearning for something more filling. A few years ago I bought a bag of bagels and brought them up to base camp with me. That has now become the foundation for one of the most looked forward to meal items. In base camp I'll spread peanut butter on my bagel, then in the field I'll add some jam from some pilfered restaurant packets. They are the perfect size for single use servings and keep your bagel from getting soggy. Another option is hard salami and cheese. Here again, raid the condiment rack on the way to the trailhead for some mayo and mustard. In the dairy section at Safeway I've found pepper jack cheese in individually wrapped packages like string cheese. Get the dried salami sticks and they'll stay preserved for a long time.

In addition to my bagel sandwich, I heavily supplement lunch with snacks. Jerky and trail mix are of course old standbys. Peanut butter crackers, corn nuts, cookies, fruit leather, dried fruit, bite size candy bars, pop tarts, cereal bars, and energy bars are great for eating on the go. In the past few years there has been an explosion of options for energy bars. On a recent trip to the health food store I purchased 20 or so different bars and gave each one a taste test (pre-season scouting). Out of the 20, I found a dozen or so that I liked, offering further diversity to my menu options. I also carry a small zip lock with some powdered Gatorade.

DINNER

Regardless of the length of my intended outing, I've always been a fan of freeze-dried meals for my dinner. After busting my butt all day, I'm looking forward to dinner and MREs don't do much to excite me. I feel like I'm getting a more substantial meal from a double serving of freeze-dried than an MRE, especially when you run into some of the less palatable sides. I don't mean to slight MREs; they are just not my first choice.

BAG O' BACKCOUNTRY FOOD

One of the things I've found very helpful is to separate out my daily meals into gallon-sized sealable bags. Breakfast, lunch, snacks and a freeze-dried all fit neatly into one bag making it easier to monitor your food supply. I do this all at home so that all I have to do when I return to base camp for refueling is grab a few bags and then head back out again.

Tents & Bivy Sacks

Finding Shelter in a Storm

As it has been chronicled in the pages of EBJ and through this book, solo bivouacking has been my ace in the hole in regard to backcountry hunting strategy and a good bivy sack like those offered by Cabela's or Outdoor Research makes it possible. A bivy sack takes the place of a tent, yet weighs only 31 oz. or slightly less than 2 lbs. This shell is 100% waterproof, which is key as even those late summer storms can hit pretty hard in the high country. And in reality, the only reason we pack a bivy sack or a tent in the backcountry is for protection from the elements or a "shelter in a storm" if you will.

My OR Bivy Sack is slightly larger than my sleeping bag. This allows me to keep my bag inside the bivy (protected from the weather even when lashed on my pack frame) stuff the whole kit-and-caboodle into the sleeping bag stuff sack. I call this "The System" and it has taken me years and many lessons learned the hard way to finally come up with something that works as well as this does.

According to my figures, if you're with one or maybe two guys, a shared tent is not particularly heavier (per person sheltered) than a solo bivy setup. For two guys sharing a tent like a Sierra Designs Clip Flashlight CD (2-person 3-season) that weighs in at 4.25 lbs. you are looking at about 2 lbs.

According to my figures, if you're with one or maybe two guys, a shared tent is not particularly heavier (per person sheltered) than a solo bivy setup.

per person sheltered. Now assume you're in a group of three. The Sierra Designs Clip-3 CD (3-season 3-person tent) weighs in at 5.5 lbs. and that equates to a very doable 1.83 lbs. per guy. This is assuming you can shuffle gear around adequately to balance the weight distribution out fairly.

If you are getting packed in with horses and hunting right out of base camp everyday, well then that is much different than the bivouac style of hunting off your back that I have been writing about. With the horses, weight is not nearly as much of a factor. Take what you want. See if they will have a big canvas elk hunter's tent to hunt out of, and throw in a big air mattress to sleep on. You know the ones. They are the mattresses that you take to the pool. Dang, those are comfortable. You can get away with these "perks" when a powerful horse has panniers emptied out just for you. Life is so sweet when we get an "in" on such a hunt. The problem, I don't and most of you guys don't get many "ins." So on your typical backcountry hunt, don't plan on spending much time on a floating air mattress from your last pool party.

Optics

Go Big or Go Home

I am not going to spend a lot of time on optics, because really this is one of the most over written topics in hunting. The bottom line is buy the best you can afford. Almost everyone knows what is the best and for those that don't, I will list it here just on principle. But again, there won't be much book space dedicated to optic selection.

With regard to binoculars, when I say, "Go Big or Go Home," I am not talking big, as in 15 power and definitely not in regard to size or weight. Having binos as heavy as the 15xs I've owned hanging off of your neck for a week would be miserable. Pretty soon you are tired of lifting those things to your eyes and resort to glassing only the most suspicious looking forms on the hill. This is not the way to work the high country with your optics.

At least as bad as too big or heavy of binos hanging off of your neck is cheap glass. I fully realize all of us are on some sort of budget, but honestly, this is not the area where you want to skimp. Keep in mind that you can't kill them if you can't find them. Without quality glass the huge expanse of the high country can seem void of life. When I say big in terms of binoculars, I mean 10x40 and nothing smaller. Those little 7x35s or 8 power glasses are simply not enough. But, perhaps more accurately, what I am really referring to is "Big" in terms of quality. I can promise you, once you own a pair of Leica or Swarovski binos nothing else will do, period. I have learned this the hard way. You will spend more time glassing, working hard to find a buck, if your binos are easy on the eyes.

With cheap binoculars, after a few hours, your head will be splitting. I have been there. It is pretty sad to be looking over miles of good deer country with a headache so bad you don't want to look through those optics even one more time—especially when there are suspicious, deerish-looking spots to confirm.

Here are my recommendations for binoculars

Top o' the heap: $1800+, Swarovski EL or Leica Ultravid, both 10x42s. Yes, this is having your cake and eating it too.

For kinda of a "tweener" I have one recommendation: The Zeiss Victory FL 10x42 for just under $1,700. Not quite tops in my opinion, but pretty darn close.

Next level, around $1,000, Leupold Gold Ring 10x42, Steiner Predator 10x42, Nikon Premiere LX. All of these are great glass. Not quite the quality of Swarovski, Leica or Zeiss, but hey I can sympathize with all those blue-collar bowhunters, which I am. For us, almost $2,000 is a lot to spend on one piece of equipment.

For bargain shoppers, the Cabela's Alaskan Guide 10x42, for under $600 is tough to beat.

Spotting Scopes

QUESTION & ANSWER WITH JEFF JANSSENS OF ADVENTURE OUTFITTERS

Jeff, it is no secret Swarovski makes great glass, but what I am looking for is a couple of other spotting scope options, that while not sacrificing quality may be a little lighter in weight and more compact. I hate how big and heavy those things are. Here I am shaving space and ounces, and then go throw on the 5 lbs of spotting scope, not to mention its tripod. Weight and space—always two keys for the backcountry hunter. A spotting scope

South Cox' Top 10 Wilderness Tips

From the pages of the book, "Bowhunting Trophy Blacktail"

1. *When glassing, get comfortable. I pack a small pad to sit on for extended stints as many times I sit in one place for hours.*

2. *When selecting binoculars, remember you get what you pay for. Sure, you can buy a pair of 7x35s for $40, but if you plan on doing any amount of glassing then you'd also better invest another five bucks in a bottle of Tylenol for the headaches that cheap glass is sure to cause.*

3. *I have become a firm believe in a product call Baer's Feet. There are other similar brands of these polar fleece booties that slip over your boots or stocking feet; the key is they all make your footfalls much quieter. A must have for close quarters hunting.*

4. *Use a pack, internal or external frame, that will allow you to pack boned-out meat. This will save a round trip back to camp to get a pack frame, which can be monumental in the wilderness setting.*

5. *In regard to packs, get one that is properly fitted and it will make your experience that much more enjoyable. Poorly fitted packs can create hot spots, blisters and really sore muscles.*

6. *Keep an eye out for and respect all bears, not just grizzlies. Those black bears can be feisty too. (Note: South was mauled by a California wilderness black bear back in 1992.)*

7. *A handy item I carry in my pack is a three-foot length of surgical tubing. I've used it to siphon water out of seeps or small springs. The dripping of melting snow can also be caught and "piped" into your drinking container.*

8. *Whenever possible, I like to approach a buck from above and to the side. This allows me to come down the ridge at an angle, making the footing a little easier as opposed to coming straight down the mountain.*

9. *When I get within about 200 yards of my quarry, I take off my pack and boots, leaving them in an easy spot to find. It helps to have a piece of surveyor's flagging to mark the spot as well, so you don't have to search the entire hillside later to relocate your gear.*

10. *Pack a good, lightweight spotting scope. If you are serious about finding and shooting big bucks, a spotting scope is a must.*

has always flown in the face of my ground rules.

Cameron, as far as top quality, compact, lightweight spotting scopes go you need to look at the Leica 62mm compact (16–48x) and the Nikon 60mm ED (20–45x or 20–60x). I would easily put them in the same class optically/visually as Swarovski and to answer your question, they're also smaller and lighter.

A Swarovski 80mm is 16½" long and weighs 59 oz. (3lb. 11oz.). The 65mm is 15¼" long and weighs right at 48 oz. even (3lb.). In comparison, the Leica 62mm (rubber-armored) is only 14½" long and weighs 46.5 oz. (2lb. 14½ oz.) and the non-rubber armoured is almost another 2½ oz. lighter at only 44 oz. (2lb. 12 oz.)! The Nikon 60mm ED (Extra Low Dispersion, High Definition) scope is only 12⅞" long and weighs 43 oz. (2lb. 11 oz.).

There is one other spotting scope that may be of interest to you, the Minox ("sister" company of Leica) MD62 ED spotting scope. It is an extra low dispersion, high definition (apochromatic, fluorite glass) 62mm scope of real good optical quality. The key with this unit is to get the ED model with the 21–42x L.E.R. (long eye relief) eyepiece instead of the standard one. This makes it an upper-end quality unit, superior to any Leupold, etc. or anything else under $900, and probably close to the Leica & Nikon I mentioned earlier, but of course, not quite "there." I mention it though because it is exceptionally good quality and it weighs only 39 oz., the lightest of all of them.

Just to give you an idea of how they come in cost-wise, the Leica 62mm straight rubber-armoured sells for $1,694 and non-armoured for $1,544 ($150.00 less). The Nikon 60 ED straight about $975, and the Minox 62 ED straight w/ L.E.R. eyepiece about $919.

For any optic related questions give Jeff or Kipp at Adventure Outfitters a call, toll-free # (1-888-935-HUNT / 4868).

The Bow & Arrow Rig

Choose Your Weapon Wisely

Successfully bowhunting the West for trophy elk and big bucks requires a complete understanding of your bow & arrow rig, its capabilities and a personal commitment to becoming proficient with this equipment.

I know full well that everyone shoots different combinations of equipment and all of us have our own preferences, but regardless of bow style or hunting style, I am convinced that for the western bowhunter the following topics play a huge part in whether you'll be lashing your tag to the antlers of a trophy bull or whether the lunch special at your house will be "Tag Soup."

Arrow and Broadhead Combo

This one is very subjective, but I would suggest simply focusing on the basics. I think arrows on the light side cause more problems than the speed gain can offset. Having a forgiving setup is key and a light arrow at high speeds might fly good if everything is perfect; release, no wrist torque, no canting, etc., but many times in the hunting woods things are not perfect. Going a touch on the conservative side will give you a little more margin for error. This could make THE difference.

Also, the selection of these two items simply has to make "sense." I see guys come into the local shop shooting 200s (very light carbon arrows) tipped with a 125-grain broadhead. This is like trying to push a bowling ball with a noodle. Today's bows are capable of great things, but don't make equipment choices that are going to handcuff performance.

A good calculation to run that will verify you're shooting a "balanced arrow" is called Front of Center, or FOC. When calculating FOC, find exactly the center of your arrow by measuring the full length of your arrow from the end of the point, be it a field point or broadhead, to the end of the nock. Then find the physical center of the arrow by balancing it on your finger, a pen or something similar. Finally, measure the distance between these two points. Divide by the length of arrow and multiply by 100 to express this number as a percentage. Experts say that 7 to 10% FOC (Forward of Center) is the proper amount for optimum stability and accuracy. You can tweak the FOC by changing the length of your arrow or the weight of your broadhead. There are a number of FOC calculators available on the Internet. I Googled "Front of Center + Archery" and had plenty of options. Check it out.

To ensure your broadhead and arrow selection is compatible you must "shoot through paper." This is a method many bowhunters use to tell if their arrow is coming out of the bow true. Most pro shops can instruct you on how to go about this process. Secondly, and this is huge for accurate broadhead flight, your vanes must have some helical. Controlling that broadhead is paramount and yes, helical does slow your arrow down a touch, but again, the speed gain is not worth the sacrifice. Building your arrows with straight fletch will be fine and dandy if all you do is shoot field points, but for hunting, you will be relying on your fletch to control a broadhead-led arrow.

Sharp Broadheads

This is another topic that everyone has probably heard hundreds or thousands of times, but I thought I should throw it out there anyway because I have recently seen guys practicing with hunting arrows right out of their quiver. I wouldn't shoot a broadhead even once that I was going to hunt with unless I changed the blades first. I am not saying don't practice with broadheads. You must do this, but do it by buying a couple extra broadheads to exclusively practice with (exact same head you'll be hunting with). This cost is not much of a sacrifice considering how much time, money and effort we put into bowhunting. You owe it to the animal and yourself.

I take the sharpness equation even a step further as I alternate which arrow I grab out of the quiver when closing in on animals. I can't help but think that sliding the same broadhead out of the foam in the hood of your quiver and putting it back in time after time won't dull it some, so I switch it around a little. Also, this past season in camp I touched up all my hunting broadheads every night with a sharpening stone matched precisely to the angle of my broadhead blades (dummy proof sharpening is exactly what I need). I know the every night sharpening thing might seem like overkill, but I have learned the hard way, bowhunting success is in the details. In my mind, leaving just that much more of an edge on the blade could lead to one more pin drop of blood on a pine needle, which could give me direction of travel on a tough tracking job. That's just something to consider.

So far as specific brands and types of broadheads go, I am sold on Rocky Mountain's Ironhead 100 or the G5 Montec. Both of these are as tough of a broadhead as there is and they both start cutting right on impact, which I think is huge. This allows for incredible penetrating ability. In addition, I have had great results with a few other brands of broadheads including Thunderheads and Steel Force. I don't think you could go wrong with any of the heads I've listed as they are razor sharp, good flying broadheads that most importantly are rugged enough to hold up on thickly muscled and heavy-boned bull elk.

Kinetic Energy

Exactly how much kinetic energy (KE) is enough is again a subjective topic because a few factors can make a big difference, like whether or not you're shooting a cutting tip broadhead, fixed-blade, or expandables.

As a general rule of thumb, I would suggest 40- to 50-foot-pounds of

KE for medium-sized game like deer, antelope, black bear, etc. and 50 to 60 foot-pounds for the big boys like elk, moose, grizzlies, etc. Don't go in under-gunned so to speak. It drives me crazy to hear stories about guys who say they hit a big bull perfectly and didn't get penetration. Again, you put too much effort into this deal to do everything right so far as finding the animal, closing to within bow range, estimating yardage and releasing an accurate arrow; then to have it hang up on a rib because your bow lacks energy is really a shame. You must ensure you're using the right tool for the job.

To figure how many foot-pounds of kinetic energy you're shooting, use this calculation: Arrow speed squared, divided by 450,250, times the weight of the arrow = the kinetic energy produced by your bow. I would suggest shooting as much KE as you can comfortably and accurately handle.

For example, my rig shoots a 420-grain arrow about 275 feet per second. The calculation would be 275^2 / 450,250 x 420 = 70 foot-pound of KE, which is more than adequate for anything I hunt out West, including trophy bull elk.

As I mention, in my opinion, too many guys put an overemphasis on the speed of their arrow. They think by shooting 300 fps they will have no problems so far as penetration goes. This type of thinking is simply too one-dimensional. Keep in mind that when you whittle away arrow weight (shooting a lighter arrow) without otherwise changing your bow, you are losing efficiency, i.e. kinetic energy or penetration power.

By running some sample numbers through our formula, we learn that to increase your bow's efficiency all you have to do is shoot a heavier arrow. This holds true up to approximately an 800-grain arrow. Beyond that, it is a case of diminishing returns.

Plus, when shooting a heavier arrow, your bow will be quieter. When a bull hears the loud unnatural sound of a bow shot at close range, they can drop, spin, rear-up or all of the above in an amazingly short fragment of time. The soft, muffled sound of a finely tuned bow releasing a properly weighted arrow is much less intrusive than the crack of a bow shooting too light of an arrow.

Practice

Yeah, I know this is not real cutting edge, but the bottom line is if you are going to bowhunt the backcountry of the West effectively it takes commitment. I shoot virtually everyday all year except the months of December and January.

This is show season, which means I am on the road and it is the heart of my off-season, so I take a little R&R in regard to shooting. But otherwise, you can count on me shooting everyday as sure as the sun comes up. This might sound overwhelming, but really it isn't when you consider that on many of those days I might shoot only a couple dozen arrows. This takes me about 15 minutes I would guess, and I shoot most of the time at 20 yards on these quickie sessions. Accurate bow and arrow shooting is all about consistency. You have to anchor, aim and release exactly the same to hit the spot at 20 yards as you do at 60 yards.

Shooting everyday gives me confidence in my ability and my equipment and really, 15 minutes is not that much time to set aside. I do supplement these short sessions with longer outings though, too. A couple times a week I will go down to the local pro shop and shoot against the fellas for dollar bills or shoot in one of the indoor leagues. One evening a week, I will shoot at my buddy's house where we stretch the distance out a bit, and then finally, I will partake in as many 3D shoots as I can during the summer, probably 10 of them most years.

One thing I would suggest avoiding is trying to get all of your weekly practice out of the way in one or two days. If you try to shoot for an hour or two at a time, most of that practice will be reinforcing bad habits or improper shooting form because of muscle fatigue. You've heard the old saying, "Perfect practice makes perfect?" Well, this couldn't be more true so far as shooting a bow and arrow rig goes. Short, high quality sessions, in which you are focusing on pinpoint accuracy, will pay huge dividends in the field.

Forgiving. If I can use just one word that is the one I want to describe my bow. I want a bow that will deliver an accurate arrow even with a less than perfect release. In my opinion, a bow around 36 or 37 inches long, with close to a 7" brace height is a good choice. Almost all of the big manufacturers offer bows that fall into this category. These include PSE, Mathews, Hoyt, BowTech and Alpine among others.

Beyond the bow, rugged accessories are mandatory when hunting the backcountry. My number one priority is hunting with gear that will help me on my quest to down a big bull. I have always found a way to use the best long before I had my first article published. You can bet that regardless of whether I was hunting for a living or just as a hobby, my bow would be outfitted with a Spot-Hogg sight, a Trophy Taker rest and a Winner's Choice Custom Bowstring released with a Scott release. These dependable

I commonly practice out to 80 yards. While I don't recommend shooting at animals at this distance, long range practice makes those 40-yarders when hunting seem like chip shots.

products will do what is expected, every time. Of course my bow has to be quiet and my rig reaches the "whisper quiet" level thanks to Sims Vibration Laboratories gear. These products make the extremely tough challenge of public land bowhunting just that much more attainable.

For those who are interested, here is the rest of my hunting gear. I have no problem recommending any of this stuff for serious public land hunting and in my opinion, I shoot the ultimate big game bowhunter's rig. How does yours compare?

- ***Bow:*** *Hoyt Trykon*
- ***Arrows:*** *Easton Axis 340*
- ***Broadheads:*** *Montec G5*
- ***Sight:*** *7 Deadly Pins by Spot-Hogg*
- ***Rest:*** *Shakey Hunter by Trophy Taker*
- ***String:*** *Winner's Choice Custom Bowstrings*
- ***Camo:*** *Mossy Oak Brush*
- ***First Layer Gear:*** *Under Armour*
- ***Optics:*** *Swarovski*
- ***Rangefinder:*** *Nikon*
- ***Other:*** *Sims Vibration Labs vibration dampening products*
- ***Release:*** *Scott Little Goose*
- ***Boots:*** *Lowa Tibets*
- ***Tent:*** *Bivy Sack by Outdoor Research*
- ***Sleeping bag:*** *Marmot Hydrogen +15*
- ***Sleeping pad:*** *Therm-a-Rest*
- ***Pack:*** *Adventure Outfitters & Badlands 4500*
- ***Watch:*** *Suunto Vector*

Shooting—Dead On Accuracy

Readers often ask, "What one piece of advice can you give that will help me to be more successful this bowhunting season?" That is tough to do, but if I had to give a single tip it would come in two simple words, "Bow familiarity."

It seems many bowhunters are looking for a quick fix or a shortcut to success. Bowhunting doesn't generally work that way. Whatever bow you decide to hunt with, outfitted with whatever rest, sight, arrows, etc., the bottom line is there needs to be a "connection" by the time season rolls around.

Dead on accuracy with a bow and arrow comes with repetition. Drawing, anchoring, picking a spot and a smooth release should all be part of the subconscious. In talking with Wayne Endicott from The Bow Rack, he tells me, "Cam, for me, shooting a bow is just about like standing here talking to you. Pounding the target butt with arrows is as natural an act as talking or breathing as far as I am concerned."

I guess this helps to explain his extraordinary success both in the woods and on the target range. Just this last season he arrowed a nice six-point bull and a bomber buck here in Oregon and for years he has routinely finished near the top of virtually any 3D shoot, marked yardage course or field archery tournament he enters.

Wayne shoots about 100 arrows a day, nearly everyday of the year. While this type of commitment is hard for many guys to match, incredible bow and arrow accuracy can be achieved with less. Personally, I only shoot about 25 to 50 arrows a day, which takes at most 30 minutes or as little as 15 minutes. If successful bowhunting is a priority for you, this shouldn't be too hard of an obligation to meet.

A natural transition will take place when finally, because of the daily practice and immersion in archery, your bow will become like an extension of your body. And, with this, will come confidence.

One of my bowhunting heroes, Chuck Adams, says in his book, *Life at Full Draw*, that he never doubts his ability to make a clutch shot. He says that because he practices so hard in the off-season and gets his gear so right that while he isn't cocky, he is very calm and confident when it comes to bowhunting. It is hard to question Chuck; he is the most accomplished bowhunter ever, right? And, while he references an "off-season" in that statement, he later clarifies, "For the great ones, there is no off-season."

Lastly, I recently talked with the king of "Dead On" accuracy in my opinion and one of the very best shooters bowhunting has ever known, Randy Ulmer. I would venture to guess that all serious bowhunters who have followed the sport have heard of Randy, who not long ago was elected into the prestigious Bowhunter Hall of Fame. Randy made his mark years ago by dominating the 3D circuit and quickly built a reputation as a great competitor with an uncanny ability for accuracy. When he talks bow and arrow shooting, I listen.

When asking him about his preseason shooting routine, Randy referenced the old adage, "Practice does not make perfect. Perfect practice makes perfect."

To try and achieve shooting perfection, he shoots the first five arrows and the last five arrows of the day from a distance of five feet with his eyes closed.

Randy continues, "During a normal shot, aiming and concern over where the arrow is going to hit completely occupies the conscious mind while the subconscious mind controls the shot process. In order to become more aware of what you are doing before, during and after the shot, you must remove the aiming process and the concern over where the arrow will hit from the conscious mind. Closing your eyes and standing a few feet away from the target will allow you to "feel" the shot. You will soon discover things you may have never known you were doing wrong and eventually you will discover what the "perfect" shot feels like. Once you've experience this "perfect" shot with your eyes closed, you can try to repeat it with your eyes open. If you can maintain this feeling, your shooting will rapidly improve. If you hit a slump, go back to shooting with your eyes closed until the feeling comes back."

Granted, for many of you, I have not revealed any new or groundbreaking information here. The fact is there is not too much cutting edge glamour involved with putting in practice time, but really nothing is more necessary. Bowhunting is a challenge and to be successful you will need to punch the ol' time clock when it comes to practice. Downing trophy big game with a bow is difficult to do consistently, and I realize that for the most part guys don't want to hear how "hard" it is, they just want to know, "How can I arrow a monster."

The answer comes in the form of a question. "About time for your daily practice session, isn't it?"

Sometimes the country is simply too steep or rough to ride the pack animals. By leading them, you can pick your way through some pretty nasty stuff.

Horse Packers

Best money you'll ever spend in the backcountry

One of the biggest questions a prospective backcountry hunter will face, especially when going after big bull elk is, "Should I walk in or get packed in?"

Obviously, this is up to the individual, but what I've come up with after having done both many times is the following guidelines: If you are hunting within five miles of the trailhead, you could probably hike in with your gear if you are in fairly good shape. If you will be hunting over five miles deep, I would hire a packer and get you and your gear hauled in and dropped.

There is a lot to be said for starting off "fresh." Take it from someone who knows and has learned this lesson the hard way. There is nothing worse than busting your tail just getting to your area, and then being too dang whipped to hunt like you're capable of. Burning a couple days off a week-long hunt to recover is not time well spent.

Where a horse packer pays off in spades is once your trophy hits the

Carrying your bow is the best bet when getting packed in. You can maneuver it around trees and brush. When it is lashed to the horse or mule, the risk of damage is great.

ground. This is especially true when it comes to elk. From weather (very warm Septembers) to fatigue and a multitude of circumstances in between that can potentially comprise your meat, the safe bet is to have a packer set up to come in and help you out.

Walt Ramage is all smiles.

I feel a great responsibility to the animal and believe that killing a bull elk deep in the wilderness on a solo hunt is not only irresponsible, but morally wrong as I don't know many bowhunters that can pack out an entire bull by themselves before the meat begins to spoil.

Bottom line: Honor the animal by having a meat extraction plan in place. I have never lost one ounce of meat because of spoilage since I've had the packer factor in place or even in all the years before this packing revelation for that matter. I have worked my tail off to ensure my harvest gets broken down and hauled out to the meat locker either by me or someone else. I will say though, having a packer on call by way of satellite phone just makes life much more enjoyable after a kill and has added years to the life of my back. Carrying an elk out miles and miles from the wilderness can be a brutal way to save a few bucks. Not worth it.

When using horses to get your bull out of the mountains, keeping the meat on the bone is the way to go. Quartering the bull as opposed to boning it makes it much easier to divvy up the load equally.

The Llama Option

First, I owe all my initial wilderness experiences to the fact that Roy and his dad, Ray, bought four llamas back in the early 90s. They were there for us to use, and use we did. We could have never hunted the backcountry if it weren't for these beasts of burden.

Second, I learned the hard way that you can indeed push llamas too hard. The backcountry wasn't an option for us before because we never had enough money at one time to pay for a drop camp or a packer that could haul our kills out of the wilderness. If nothing else, llamas are cheap—they don't eat much and require little maintenance so we could spread out the cost of owning them over the whole year. Llamas allowed us to hunt deep, period. That being said, if you can afford a packer, owning llamas does not pencil out as it does take time to train them and get them in shape, and as we know, time is money.

A few more thoughts on horses vs. llamas: I completely switched gears in regard to getting animals out of the backcountry. I used to be all about doing it all on my own. And, while there is still a great amount of pride in 100% Do-It-Yourself from A–Z hunts, I now almost always leave the packing to the professionals.

The first problem I had with llamas surfaced after I'd killed a great bull on opening day one year. Even though they were in great shape, the llamas were simply not fully recovered from packing all the gear up the hill the day before. They were exhausted and would never have made it down in the hole where I killed that bull, then back up the mountain and all the way out.

This meant that I had to bone out my bull, hang it and hike about 10 miles over to where my other three buddies were hunting and try to talk them into giving up some of their hunting time to help me get the bull out. Of course they did, but really it cost them their hunt as putting on that many miles in just a few days broke everyone down—way down. Lesson learned—If you can afford a packer, owning llamas does not pencil out.

Cameron, I have a quick question for you. You said that you typically pay about $300.00 to get your animals out on one of your wilderness hunts. Do you own horses or do you hire someone to come in and take the meat out for you, and if so how would I get in touch with someone like this? Oh, by the way I just received Eastmans' Season 6 TV Show DVD and watched your two backcountry hunts. Great animals, footage and great job at capturing what the whole backcountry hunting experience is all about. In my opinion it is truly the most rewarding and only way to hunt. Thanks for your time.—Glenn

Glenn, I pay the $300 or up to $400 at times to a packer and usually get ahold of him by climbing to the top of the mountain and hitting him on the cell phone. Of course this game plan is all set up well in advance.

At times, worst case, this means a 3,000 foot climb to get to a spot the cell phone will work, but it is worth it to get some help in

Now, this is a beautiful sight to the backcountry hunter. A great packer, Barry Cox, loaded down with a trophy bull and buck from my best wilderness adventure.

there to haul my downed animal out. Also, I don't think this type of arrangement is S.O.P. for most packers.

The packers I've used are men I have known and worked with for many years so they know when I kill something, the meat will be in good condition and I will have packed the quarters or boned out meat to a place their horses or mule can access. Notice I did not say easily access. My main go-to guy, Barry Cox, has an amazingly capable packstring and he is as good of a horseman as there is so, while the country I hunt always seems to be the most nasty there is, Barry has always been able to get his stock right up to where I've had the meat hung to cool.

Glad you like the backcountry hunts. Filming is very tough back there but it is so sweet when it works out like it did on the sheep and elk hunts you watched. Thanks for the positive comments.

Meat Care

Cameron, I have a question that has to do with field dressing your game. It is obvious you have this down pat. I am from south Texas and well, I never have to pack anything out. A truck is always there and quartering takes place on a single tree. Quartering is not a problem. The problem will

Heading out of the Wyoming backcountry with the 7x6 bull I arrowed on the eighth day of a great backcountry elk hunt.

be bagging and transport. How many game bags should I be carrying, should I plan on boning out the meat, and where can I purchase the correct game bags?—Dustin Ford

Dustin, for elk, I would pack at least three high quality game bags at all times. I know for a fact that three good sized and durable bags like those from Alaska Game Bags will hold and protect the meat from an entire boned out elk. My last sentence should answer the other part of your question. Yes, you should plan on boning out the meat if you will be the one doing the packing. You and or your buddies do not need to, and I would venture to guess probably don't want to, pack the leg bones and carcass out, just the meat. So, remove all of it from the quarters, rib cage, neck and etc.

Now, if you have access to pack animals, quartering the bull out will work.

With pack animals it is easier to divide the loads up evenly when there are two equally weighing fronts and hinds. Regardless of what animal you're relying on, horses or mules, balancing the weight of each side is paramount.

If you are using animals to pack, you'll probably need one more game bag at least for a total of four. One for each quarter and then you will have some miscellaneous meat to protect from the neck, etc., which I usually split up evenly and throw in with the front shoulders.

Keep in mind you will need to get that meat up off of the ground at least 8–10 feet when hanging if you have to leave. A bear or other scavengers can find it and get into it quickly if special precaution is not taken. This is why you will also need to make certain you have at least 50 feet of braided nylon rope.

And, even if it is freezing or in the 30s and just dark or after dark when I recover my bull or buck, I always at least gut my animal and prop open the cavity so it can cool properly. Elk are so thickly muscled and have such a tough insulating hide for those cold winters that they will hold a lot of heat if not opened up. A guy could lose some meat, even on a relatively cool September night if he doesn't at least yard those guts out. In such situations, I will then pull the hide off first thing in the morning and finish boning him out before hanging him. While this is a ton of work by yourself and believe me, I have done it many times on my own, it is the final gesture of respect we can and are obligated to show the animal.

Quick tips—remember to always have your knife ultra sharp and have a sharpener to touch it up. Even the best knife will need a little attention after cutting those hip sockets out (I never use a saw because I never want to pack the extra weight) and cutting the head off. Maneuvering the tip of your knife in, through and around those joints is guaranteed to bang it up a little.

In regard to knives, on the last two bulls I have killed in the wilderness all I've used was a little surgical style knife with a 2" or 3" blade that my taxidermist, Dan Smith, gave me. He uses one to do all his taxidermy work and guaranteed me that it was all the knife I needed. He was right. It is super sharp, holds an edge and is small enough to get in there and whittle those hip sockets out of the pelvis and do the precision cuts called upon when caping out the head.

Fellow backcountry bowhunter Kevin Law out of Nevada offered up a few additional tips on game and trophy care while in the field and some of the processes he follows:

Veteran horseman Barry Cox proved invaluable to me and father-in-law Larry Smith on a public land, D-I-Y bighorn sheep hunt.

Cameron, I like your tip about packing a small surgical type knife. That is one of the things that I do, too (and learned from an old taxidermist buddy, as well). I use a small scalpel type X-acto knife for caping in the field and at home. I have an actual "caping" knife, but prefer the small scalpel tool, especially when working around the sensitive areas like the eyes and mouth. I have a separate knife that I use for the cleaning and skinning of the animal.

When caping, I always make sure to leave as much extra on as possible around the eyes, mouth, nose, and ears. A quick talk with your taxidermist will help you to know exactly what he needs left on your cape and most times your taxidermist would probably be glad to let you watch him cape something out so that you'll better know how to do this and won't ruin your capes for him in the future, if you decide to do your own caping. There are also videos available on the subject for those interested in learning more.

At base camp, I always have about half a can to a can of table salt or an equal amount of Borax in a gallon Ziploc bag to use on the cape to help dry it out and better preserve it. This is especially a good idea if it's going to be a while before I get back to civilization while I'm helping my buddies on their backcountry hunt. I salt down the cape and lay it out in a nice shady

For me, there is a great sense of relief when my bull is off the ground, skinned, broken down, ready to be bagged and safely hung, cooling in the crisp mountain air.

spot to let it dry out and keep it covered with a piece of cheese cloth from a deer bag to keep the flies and bugs off of it. You'll also want to get it up in the air to avoid varmints getting to it.

I wrap up my boned meat chunks in cheese cloth deer bags and hang them in a shady tree to keep them cool. The less meat that you put per bag, the cooler it will stay, of course. Those fancy dancy deer and elk bags work great too and are actually much easier to hang, but they weigh more to carry and you have to bulk meat up in them more than with the good old cheesecloth deer and elk bags, unless you bring a ton of them.

Another thing that's worked great for me, especially on trips where it was a long way in and out, is to camp by a creek and put your meat chunks in those 13 gallon white plastic trash bags. After wrapped up in the waterproof plastic bags, I put them in the cold water of a dammed pool. This keeps them extremely cool and works great...assuming that you don't have a hungry grizzly or coyote close by. But even then, the cold water probably washes most of the smell away.

Though it can be super exhausting work (especially when alone), I usually won't stop until I get all of my animal skinned, boned, and hanging in a tree or in the creek cooling off.

Like you mentioned in your Q&A to Dustin Ford, even in cool weather, you can still lose some meat to spoilage around the neck and back region of the animal if the hide stays on overnight. I lost roughly 50 pounds of meat on an early January hunt a few years back due to me leaving my animal on a ridge top overnight in zero degree weather and having the heat from the animal trapped between his hide and the meat...even with him being gutted, propped open with sticks, and his opening facing into the biting cold wind. Learn from my mistake: Break that animal all the way down as soon as possible.

At base camp, I also keep a small bottle of formaldehyde, a hypodermic needle, and some disposable rubber gloves for taking care of the velvet on my deer. There are veins that go up through the velvet along the antlers that you can inject with formaldehyde and then rub formaldehyde all over the outside of the antlers (might want to do a couple coats). Then I make sure to keep those velvet-encased antlers in the cool shade, too. This is probably something that your taxidermist can talk to you about, too, and give recommendations on. Be careful when dragging or moving your deer because you can mess up those veins in the antlers and make them so the formaldehyde won't inject into them very well.

SECTION 4

Mule Deer

Backcountry Mule Deer

The Hardcore Bowhunter's Ultimate Test

"100% pure bowhunting" are the words that immediately come to mind when somebody mentions hunting the high country for trophy mule deer with a bow and arrow. It surely doesn't get any better than peeking into a remote mountain basin and having your eyes immediately drawn to a couple of suspicious looking spots on a not too distant ridge. Melting into the shadows while easing the binos up, your heart begins to race at a rate more suitable for a hummingbird. Fingering the focus knob, in a split second with 10x clarity, your optics are filled up with reddish-brown hide and the bobbing, velvet encased antlers of a monster buck leisurely feeding toward his morning bed. Time to strategize.

Matching wits with a big, high country buck is one of the greatest challenges a backcountry bowhunter can take on. Anyone who is successful in such an undertaking will have earned their trophy. When I see someone posed with a 170-class Pope & Young mule deer in a mountain setting, I take notice. This hunter automatically has my respect because there are no shortcuts to success on such a hunt. That is the greatest thing about mule deer hunting. There is basically only one way to tag one and that comes in the form of sweat equity. The bowhunter who pays his dues, puts in the time and can stay focused enough to place an arrow on the mark

when hunting the rugged country a mature mule deer calls home, in my opinion, is the real deal.

Mission Accomplished!
Boone & Crockett blacktail.

Interestingly enough, I first headed out on my own to the big country of Oregon after elk. Hunting mule deer bucks didn't seem to interest me in the least, as in the beginning of my bowhunting career, I'd always been enamored with the black-tailed deer in the valley. Honestly, my attitude was, "I don't want to go over there (eastern Oregon) in the early season and ruin my late-season, blacktail rut hunt by killing a mule deer. Well, as you may have surmised, things changed. I racked up a slew of pretty good Pope & Young blacktail and even achieved the ultimate for a bowhunter, arrowing an official Boone & Crockett buck with my bow back in 2000. So while not mastering blacktail by any means (I was humbled on a regular basis believe me) I had hunted them for years with above average success and itching to branch out a bit and try something new.

In the middle of this transformation, I got lucky in 1991 on my Steens Mountain monster, a true trophy mule deer. For a few more years after that, I went back to my roots and hunted Roosevelt elk and blacktail with good success and wrote my first book, "Bowhunting Trophy Blacktail."

My hunting focus stayed with these species until I arrowed that big B&C blacktail in 2000, and that was enough for me. It was almost like I said, "Mission Accomplished on the Trophy Blacktail Pursuit." From that point on, I have been concentrating solely on trophy mule deer throughout the West and have never looked back. I love the ultimate challenge of those big-antlered bucks in the mountains. Personally, I didn't know anyone who had arrowed more than a couple of decent bucks, so this seemed like the exact kind of hearty challenge I love. Could I find long-term success where no one else I knew could?

Mule Deer the Species

The majestic mule deer may symbolize the wild West better than any single big-game animal. And, although this magnificent creature is regal in appearance and almost mystical in legend, he is also the most fragile to Mother Nature's effects of any of the deer species. The lion's share of the mule deer population calls the Rocky Mountains or similar high elevation climes home. Living life amongst the high country, for as long as the weather allows, requires migratory travel when the "big weather" hits. This can be a time of high stress to even the hearty mule deer.

When extremely harsh weather wreaks havoc on their wintertime range, severe winterkill can result, as was the case across much of the West during the winter of 1992. In a number of states, like my home, Oregon, mule deer populations are just now starting to show strong, tangible signs of recovery.

More Challenges

The mule deer is also subjected to other formidable challenges. Loss of winter-range habitat from booming human population and drought-like conditions during the summer months, not to mention predation can adversely affect the "fragile" mule deer. Drought not only reduces availability of the highly nutritious forage mule deer depend on to brace themselves for the winter and rutting trials, but also, the parched land is less able to sustain life in the form of rodents and other food sources for the predators that share habitat with the mulie. This limited menu results in an increased number of mule deer deaths at the claws and fangs of cougar and coyotes.

The range of the highly adaptable mule deer stretches from Mexico through the western United States and into Canada.

The overwhelming most popular method for tagging a big mule deer buck is by using the spot and stalk approach. Closing to within bow range of a mature buck can be a tough proposition. One had better be capable of extending their shooting range out to at least 40 yards before traveling out West in pursuit of the great mule deer. In fact, the average shot for recorded Pope & Young mule deer is from 30 to 39 yards, which indicates that while some trophy bucks are killed under that range, an equal amount are killed beyond.

Oregon isn't known as a top producer of trophy mule deer. Regardless, I have had some great hunts in its backcountry.

Where to tag a trophy

Historic mule deer hotbeds such as Arizona's Kaibab or Utah's Paunsaugunt continue to produce monster bucks, but in my opinion, the Colorado and Nevada backcountry offer the best trophy buck opportunity for the hardcore D-I-Y bowhunter. Although most states up and down the Rockies generate bucks that will surpass the 145-point Pope & Young minimum, like Idaho, which offers tags over-the-counter to bowhunters, it is simply a matter of quality deer density.

Where I grew up hunting in Oregon, seeing one or two true trophy bucks a day is something to write home about, whereas in the prime areas of the Nevada high country you could expect to see five times that amount. The difference? Excellent winter range and little competition from elk for prime food sources have created a big buck hot bed in Nevada.

I had heard many stories about the excellent opportunities to arrow a record book buck in the state more known for casinos and bright lights than backcountry bowhunting. Finally, I got a chance of finding out for myself about Nevada's trophy producing potential in 2005. I can tell you now it was worth the wait, but we'll get to that story later.

To me, and most D-I-Y public land bowhunters, a buck that stretches the tape to 160 Pope & Young is a trophy.

I have had above average success by sticking to an area and really learning it.

I've had above average success in good, average, and the best mule deer producing states. What is important to understand is I didn't do anything different when preparing or hunting Oregon as opposed to Montana, Wyoming or Nevada.

In Oregon, it took me years but after time I found pockets that always have and likely always will produce at least one or two good deer a year. The reason this never changes is because since I hunt designated wilderness, the area will never be affected or drastically altered by man. No new roads punched through, no logging clear cuts, etc. The deer and elk, for that matter, have been doing the same things for years. Even without scouting, I can go back there and get into animals right out of the gate. My goal on any hunt is each evening I want to find something to hunt in the morning. After the morning hunt, if it didn't work out, I want to be able to glass up a buck to hunt that evening. No matter where I have hunted, again from the best to worst, I've pretty much always been able to do this. I've always had a plan…

something to go after. And believe me, if I can do it, you can too.

Mule deer in the mountains all act and react pretty much the same. If they smell you they are gone. If they see you or if they hear you, you wait them out. The biggest difference has been in deer numbers, which hasn't been a deal breaker for me. I don't need to see 50 or 75 deer a day. I just want to have enough deer in the country to hunt. In country where the deer are more sparse this can be tougher, but I have done it by sticking to an area and really learning it. In states teeming with mature bucks, learning the terrain and the deer's habits or tendencies is not nearly as important.

Bucks in the Backcountry: Go Big or Go Home

Hunting the high country for trophy mule deer on your own is not for the faint of heart. To successfully find and arrow a buck in the backcountry, you'll need to head to BIG, remote and rugged country, use *big*, high quality optics and be ready, willing and able to put forth *big* time effort.

Think of these three *big* factors as the legs of a stool. With only one of the three legs, obviously the stool will topple, with two out of the three legs the stool again will fail. It takes all three to give yourself a better than average chance of filling your tag on the caliber of buck I consider a "trophy", which in my world and in this book is anything that exceeds 160 Pope & Young.

Keep in mind I cut my teeth on trophy mule deer in Oregon. Not exactly a state known as a mule deer Mecca. Some seasons I would only see a handful of bucks over a 10-day hunt, but realistically, this is all you need. All I wanted was something to hunt every day and no matter where you are, I doubt if you'll be getting more than two quality stalks a day on trophy animals if you do it right. Seeing more deer sure is nice, but not necessary.

In fact, the big herds of bucks like I've had to battle with in Nevada make it really tough. I would much rather have a buck on his own, battling just his eyes, ears and nose than the 23 bucks I had to beat in Nevada in 2005.

Memoirs from the Rimrock

By Cameron R. Hanes

Originally appeared in Eastmans' Hunting Journal *issue 39*

Not a part of any range, Steens Mountain stands alone in the desert of southeastern Oregon. The gigantic mountain is made up of almost perpendicular lava that looks as though it has been thrust skyward through the earth's surface. When approaching, its spectacular appearance is accentuated by the lack of any real foothills. At 9,740 feet this majestic mountain seems to materialize out of nowhere, standing solitary guard over the vast desert.

The immense glacier-created gorges that cut deeply into Steens Mountain are named as if they were beings, or entities...Kiger, Blitzen, Big Indian and Little Indian to name a few. Ageless and mighty, each has fended off many would-be hunters. These gorges are rugged and unforgiving, but it's the size that can be deceptive, easily betraying the unwary.

To quote E.R. Jackman, "One who decides to climb a nearby hill before breakfast may be late for lunch."

The arid mountain air and near-zero humidity combine to suck the moisture from exposed skin, causing hands and lips to dry and split. Climbing feels like a type of self-inflicted punishment and is done in short exhausting bursts as the thin mountain air starves lungs. Leg muscle recovery time is extended, making those short, catch-your-breath breaks longer and longer as the hunt progresses.

This mountain offers splendor, beauty and history as well as pain and agony; not to mention some of the best mule deer hunting to be found in the state of Oregon. These far reaching gorges will never be overhunted as good judgment will not allow it.

Bucks can be found above 7,000 feet where it is cooler, the feed is greener, the wind is fresher and the distractions are fewer. As the sun unveils this mountain each morning, the bucks will be in transit heading for their sanctum we refer to as rimrocks. A big buck will almost always be found backed up against the base of a vertical rock wall protecting his backside. While facing downhill he will monitor the rising thermals of midday, keeping himself well-informed of any likely danger approaching from below. This defense is basically unyielding except in the rarest of cases.

Joining me on this quest for trophy mule deer would be longtime hunting partner, Roy Roth, Wayne "Mr. Steens" Endicott, Jeff Brooks and Dwayne Leavitt. Wayne practically grew up in this country, hunting it since he was old enough to carry a weapon, hence the nickname. Jeff and Dwayne have spent many years amongst the rimrocks chasing big bucks, learning some important lessons and developing time-tested tactics that repeatedly put them in on mature animals. Although each of these guys has had multiple opportunities throughout the years, "Murphy's Law" time and again dictated the outcome of any potentially successful stalks. All they had to show for their years of hunting on Steens Mountain were numerous unforgettable experiences and tales that unfortunately began with the words, "If only…" Such is bowhunting.

Hunting the rimrocks in this country will test you mentally and physically. My confidants and I felt we were up to this test of wills though we were seemingly reduced to the size of ants as we descended into one of the mountain's most impressive gorges.

The first stage of the five-mile pack into this country is the most difficult because the trail is hard to follow through the rocks and the occasional spattering of snow, not to mention you are losing elevation at a very uncomfortable rate making for some interesting and unplanned alterations in your descent. Once reaching the creek the traveling is "easy money" as the domestic cattle have cut a wide swath paralleling the creek through the bottom of the gorge.

Wayne's four pack animals proved to be worth their weight in gold and our creekside camp reflected this. We were blessed with good food, water and the serenity of a complete, well-stocked camp. All this and deep into prime mule deer hunting country I had to wonder, "Does it get any better?"

Opening morning found us about ¼-mile up the west side of "our gorge," glassing east and picking through the rimrocks for signs of life. Almost immediately bucks were spotted. In time, two were singled out that we felt deserved extra attention. Each of these bucks was a mature, big-racked bruiser, but more importantly they were in locations that left them susceptible to a close quarters approach. They were also bedded which meant their position would not change dramatically. After a quick conference, Jeff agreed to stay and monitor the bucks while the

rest of us traversed the east wall in an attempt to get above them. Dwayne and I planned to concentrate on one buck as Roy and Wayne tag-teamed the other. Both groups would rely on hand signals from Jeff as the stalk entered the critical stage.

As expected, our journey to the rimrocks proved taxing. We began by weaving through the quaking aspens that nestled in the bottom of the gorge exhibiting their riotous colors of fall. Our 2,500-foot vertical climb then began in earnest. Progressing through the scattered juniper and sagebrush we scanned ahead for our next footstep on the unstable, ancient lava slides that make up much of this mountain. As we neared the end of our climb, our hands grasped for the mountain mahogany in an attempt to contribute to the ascent. All told the climb took over three hours which was as planned since the sun had by then made its impact felt in the gorge causing the thermals to begin their upward rush. These conditions leave a buck vulnerable to a strike from above.

Making frequent communications with Jeff through hand signals, we each closed in on our buck's location. Wayne and Roy blew out their buck almost before their stalk began so they traveled back to our predetermined meeting place.

With Jeff guiding us in, we snaked down through the rimrock until he indicated we were directly above the buck. Knowing we were close but unsure of the precise location of the buck, Dwayne and I split up. Dwayne traveled about 100 yards and peeked over the edge of the rock shelf searching for the buck. I eased up to the edge, side-stepping along a narrow ribbon of rock to attain a better vantage point. With an arrow nocked, I crested the shelf and fixed my eyes on a sight that made my heart skip a beat. The buck was up and feeding as he was likely in the midst of changing his bed. His body size and rack were amazing...he had the total package!

In one fluid motion I rocked back and drew my bow, then leaned forward bending at the waist. Immediately, I realized how difficult it is to shoot straight down over the edge of a cliff. Envisioning my broadhead slicing between his shoulder blades and into his chest, I was horrified when on release I felt a tremendous tug on my neck and watched my arrow fly harmlessly over his back. Apparently as I leaned forward to shoot, my binoculars got caught up in the bowstring causing the described nightmare. For some unknown reason, the buck stopped after running only 50 yards. Blessed with a second chance I quickly nocked another arrow, drew and released. My arrow disappeared into his shoulder and he lumbered off.

The sound of falling rocks marked his retreat long after he was out of sight; then it became eerily quiet. Feeling as though I was having an out-of-body experience, I had to ask myself, "Did that really happen?" Using extreme caution, I crept in the direction the buck had traveled hoping to glass his escape route in the event he made it farther than I expected. Catching movement, I watched him take his final bed.

That moment brought closure to a memorable adventure and a hunt that made history as my buck is currently ranked the fourth largest mule deer in the Pope & Young record book from the state of Oregon. His final official score was 179⁰⁄₈ and he grosses nearly 185.

This experience was one of revelation. I felt grateful for the company on this hunt as I never would have had the opportunity to harvest a buck of this caliber without the shared advice and knowledge of my hunting partners.

The circumstances under which I harvested this once-in-a-lifetime buck are truly remarkable. By circumstances I am referring to claiming him on opening day, first stalk of the year, missing him once and then getting a reprieve. At times I feel undeserving of such an extraordinary trophy, but I am convinced the harder you work, the luckier you are. However, I think after this hunt I may be a little overdrawn in my bank account of luck!

Hunt Report Card – Hindsight is always 20/20

What I learned on this hunt: *Gratefulness.* If not for Wayne Endicott's invite to join him on this trip into the Oregon backcountry, who knows when I would have had another chance?

I was not at a stage in my life where pack-in trips were a real possibility. This buck, while not my first record book animal, was my first real quality kill. I owe it all to Wayne as do many others whom he has introduced to the lifestyle we know as bowhunting. He is as good of an ambassador to the sport as there is. Oh, and also I learned what a great invention the bino-system is. As opposed to what I had during this hunt, they make those straight down shots possible by keeping your binoculars out of the string.

What I did wrong: Where do I start? From not being in good enough shape, to wearing all the wrong clothes (material-wise), including...cotton socks, there was very little I did right. I got realy lucky in killing my buck on opening day because my lack of conditioning guaranteed that I would have hit the wall physically on day three or sooner. While I wasn't overweight, I was by no means ready to hunt for days on end at 9,000–10,000 feet. The country was so rough and it was so arid that the bottom of my buddy Jeff Brooks' feet split down the middle on the third day, I think it was. That pretty much ended his hunt. From that hunt forward I became a student of the conditioning game, as it is so vital to the backcountry hunter. Also, learning from Jeff's plight, I started beating up my feet in the summer months prior to season with long runs, hikes, etc. My goal then and now is to toughen them up because as we know, you can be in the best shape of your life, but without healthy feet, it won't matter in the least. The hunt is over.

Learning from Jeff's plight, I started beating up my feet before season.

Of course, this was before there were magazines out there like EBJ or books like this one designed to educate the backcountry hunter, which meant lessons back then were learned the hard way.

I literally had blisters on my feet for years until learning the wonder of synthetic socks, but blisters were nothing compared to the night after I killed my buck. I was out with the other guys helping to find deer for them to try and hunt when we made some serious rookie errors. One thing led to another and we got farther and farther from base camp. Keep in mind, this was long before we had even heard the word bivouac.

Finally at dark it was time to head back, but we were many miles and many big ridges from camp. It took so long getting back that in our weakened state we made some huge errors. For one, Wayne drank straight from the creek and got "Beaver Fever," which didn't kick in for a couple days but lingered in his body for years. Also, Roy had walked and sweated so much during the day that he got "Diaper Rash" for lack of a better description.

At about midnight, he was unable to walk any farther so while the others kept going, Roy and I lay down to sleep. It mattered little that we had not near enough clothes and of course no gear to sleep out, but to magnify our screw up, we tried to bed down in the very bottom of a canyon by the creek, where it was at least 15 degree colder than anywhere else. Dumb. After a couple hours of misery we forged on and got to camp just as the sun was rising. That was one long night.

At 184 Pope & Young, this big high country buck was my first "signature" bow kill. Truth is I probably didn't deserve to kill such a great trophy in only my third year of bowhunting. I am still grateful for my good fortune.

The one and only thing I didn't screw up was my shooting. I used to shoot for hours and hours a day and despite the other notable deficiencies, I could pinwheel anything out to about 60 yards and judge yardage about as good as anyone. Such is the life of a bachelor right? I had plenty of time to dedicate to these disciplines.

Grade: Regardless of why or how I was in position to shoot that buck or if I even deserved the opportunity at such a trophy I did come through in the clutch and made what many would consider a very tough shot while in a harried state. But truthfully, the fact of the matter is I was more lucky than good on this hunt. **C**

Glassing

Picking apart the shadows

Wary old bucks love to bed tucked up against rock ledges with their backs protected, monitoring the wind and where they can stay as cool as possible. It is here that they feel all but hidden to the rest of the world. It seems like they also like to bed in the shadows of a small patch of trees up high on the hill where they will easily see, hear or smell anything coming up their way. The key is to glass the dark spots.

Without really picking apart shadows, nooks and crannies, you simply will never find those big bucks unless they are feeding, which is typically for a very small period during daylight hours.

I believe a big buck, when bedded, tries to become invisible to four-legged predators and humans alike And, really they are unless you truly scrutinize the likely bedding spots of a mature buck. It takes time to learn where bucks are likely to bed, but spend some time in the hills and before long, if you treat mule deer hunting like a science, you will start making educated guesses on bedding areas that become increasingly accurate each day and

Get comfortable and prepare to spend hours at times behind the glass.

each season.

The bigger bucks seem to like flat spots (benches or just a small flat next to a tree) high on the ridge, but not at the top and definitely not in direct sunlight. You can count on there being feed available as often times, even during the middle of the day, they might get up to stretch, move their bed or get a midday snack. But, water? Not necessarily. The times I have seen big bucks at "real" water have been few and far between. A mule deer is night and day different than elk, which need water at least twice a day, so don't waste too much time glassing creeks or ponds for mule deer. They get much of what they need in regard to water from the feed and from dew.

When glassing, always stay hidden and let your optics do the walking. My buddy South packs a small pad to sit on (a kneeling pad he bought in the garden section of the local Home Depot) so he is more comfortable and less inclined to move around. He will sit for hours when in prime mule deer country, working the hill in grid-like fashion over and over. Patience is key and it takes time to pick apart the hillside. South sticks with it until he is thoroughly convinced there is not a shooter buck in the basin.

My 1991 Steens buck here is bedded in a classic mule deer bed. Rest assured though, if I hadn't arrowed him, he would have moved once the sun lit on him.

I usually focus on the dark shadows under rock ledges and watch for the flick of an ear or tail or the twist of an antler. Other than my first pass over the hill, I seldom look for the entire body of the deer. I will scan the open areas first, especially at first light as the deer may still be out feeding. If I don't see anything obvious, I start from the top of the hill and work my way down, slowly left to right, drop down a section, and then back right to left. First off, I hit the base of cliffs or strips of timber up high if there are any, and then work slowly down letting the optics do their thing.

In regard to timber, deer seem to love working the "edges" so to speak. They will feed in the open at night, then head for timber where they might bed, but if it is still early, they will buy feeding time by working the timber edge always just one or two steps from the security of cover. I slowly and repeatedly work these edges with my glass and have found many bucks by doing exactly what I've described.

Stay tucked back in the shadows whenever possible in mule deer country. Low impact is the key when hunting big bucks.

Above all else, when glassing or hunting, never, ever skyline yourself. If I need to cross over a ridge, I always do it through brush or rocks that will break up my silhouette or drop to the ground and slowly ease over the ridge. This is the biggest mistake a mule deer hunter can make as those wary old bucks can pick up a human form standing on top of a ridge from miles away. I know I have irritated many new hunting partners with my psychosis when it comes to this. Yarding them back by the top of their pack frame before they stroll over the top of a ridge is never a popular move, but adhering to the "No Skyline" rule is a must for the serious mule deer hunter.

Spotting Scope – To pack or not to pack

Two schools of thought here. I've hardly ever packed a spotting scope; South always packs one. To me, the five pounds was simply too much weight to be carrying every step of the way during a long backcountry hunt. I reasoned that five pounds could really enhance my lunch and dinner options back there.

And, besides, I know what a 160 or 170 buck looks like, 4x4 with eyeguards, 26" outside spread, 21" inside spread, 22" main beams, 15" G-2s, 10" G-3s and 8" G-4s. I've never thought I needed a spotting scope to scrutinize such a buck. If I saw one about that size, he was a shooter, period. If he scored 159 or 164 or 170, I would be happy. I've never had to get down to the inch on a buck, wondering, "Is he 190 or 189?" Maybe someday, but not now.

Saying all that, after our 2005 hunt in Nevada, South and I spent some time hunting together and I now can definitely see the advantages of hauling

Wary old bucks love to bed tucked up against rock ledges with their backs protected, monitoring the wind and where they can stay as cool as possible. Precise optics work is required to find a buck tucked away in a spot like this.

a scope around.

In fact, I started packing that thing myself, because it was me who was dominating its use. I think the big difference there was there were so many bucks in that country similar in size that if we were headed way down or over to one, we wanted to make sure it was the biggest of the group. Just glassing with the binos, the big four-points all looked about the same. But with closer scrutiny, there would be up to 10 to 15 inches of difference in some cases, which is substantial, especially to South. His goal was to kill a 180-plus. To make sure we picked the right buck for him, the Swarovski spotting scope was key.

Like I said, in Oregon where I cut my teeth on trophy mule deer hunting, I would often times see one or two bucks at a time. I could tell with the binos whether or not I wanted to go after them. If there was more than one, once I closed in, I could again use my binoculars to gauge which one was the largest and shoot him.

This got me wanting to learn more about spotting scope options. Maybe there were some high quality lighter and smaller options for guys like me. Backcountry guys who wanted the increased magnification at the lightest weight possible. Check out the results of this search in Section 3, Chapter 6.

Inching on my butt down the hill toward this Montana 4x4 I was able to get 10 yards away. Now that is slam dunk range for about anyone.

Stalking

Mission ~~Im~~possible: 13 Wicked Tips for Stalking Trophy Bucks

During my long bowhunting career, I have been lucky enough to hunt some of the West's best backcountry for trophy mule deer. And, in doing so, I have killed a fair number of 4x4 or better Pope & Young mule deer. Regardless of where I was hunting these tough to arrow animals I have learned to rely on 13 tips that have largely contributed to my success. By keeping the following tips in mind on your next mule deer hunt, you too might very well be lashing your tag to the antler of a monster.

- **Stay in the shadows.** Sunlight is always the enemy. You can get away with much more in the way of movement when you are in the shadows. A glint of the sun off of your binocular lens, your broadhead or the flash of the back of your hand can draw the attention of a wary buck and sabotage your stalk.

- **Be patient and never force a stalk.** Getting aggressive on elk is one thing; getting aggressive on mule deer simply will not work. When in close, taking it slow and staying in control is key. Mule deer hunting can test your patience like nothing else can. I have lain for hours in the blazing sun, 20 yards from a big buck, praying for him to stand and expose his vitals. Over this time it was like I'd formed a silent, one-way bond with the buck. With an arrow nocked, waiting, I studied every inch of his rack, every point, knob and burr, and watched him roll his head around, shake off flies and flap his ears. I would tense up with his every move, as I just knew, "He is getting up. This is my chance." And then, with one gust of fickle wind, my heart and our bond was broken. Nothing hurts as bad as being so close for so long and then having it fall apart. But, this intimacy is what makes bowhunting so unique and that hard-earned success so special.

- **Close in only when the wind is steady**—wait out those switching thermals. The air currents are the worst in mid-morning when the sun warms the mountains. What was once a steady breeze going down becomes first unstable, and then begins rising up as the heat of the day builds. I always wait until the air warms and rises as this complements another must, as in you must come in on your buck from above. This should only be done with the wind blowing steadily in your face.

- **Come in on your buck from above.** Big bucks will nearly always bed with their back protected while watching for danger from below. Popping in from above is the #1 way bowhunters can kill a trophy mule deer.

- **Use the contour of the land.** On almost all my successful stalks, I executed an approach to get me in the Red Zone under the shield of cover or land contour as opposed to moving through the open. Once in range I then popped over a bench, rock ledge, from behind boulders or whatever the land contour was I used, and deftly placed my arrow in the buck's vitals.

- **Pick out landmarks.** You must pick out landmarks to guide you in on your buck. When you move from where you first spotted the buck, everything changes so far as perspective goes. Many guys have located a buck, started their stalk and then when getting to the other side of the canyon lost track of where exactly the buck was bedded. This can be the ultimate in frustration. I've learned the hard way to always take the time to select distinct landmarks before heading out.

- **During the stalk, be certain to check the wind often.** Terrain contour can alter prevailing wind direction. A non-scented powder works well for this. If it gets whacky on you, back out until it stabilizes. You have no room for error on this one.

- **Always assume the buck is still where you last saw him.** Just as soon as you think, "He's gone. I blew him out already," and jump up on a rock to have a better look around, there he is, still bedded. But, guess what? Game's over because now he is gone for real. The size of the country mule deer live in can be very deceiving. You might think you should be right on top of the buck but in reality he is a little farther than anticipated. Be patient and always assume the buck is still there until you know without a shadow of a doubt. And, oh yeah, pick those landmarks.

- **Choose your battles wisely.** The Nevada buck my buddy South Cox killed in August 2005 is the perfect example of this tip. We had a big buck, slightly larger than the one he ended up killing, we named the "G-4 buck" that was bedded, but it was not in position for a high percentage stalk. While many probably would have gone after G-4, given where the buck was bedded and the proximity of the surrounding deer made success all but impossible. South went after his second choice, "5x4" which was in a much better location. South got in tight and well, the results speak for themselves. Make a good decision in this regard—big bucks usually only give you one chance.

- **Wait for the buck to bed.** Others might have differing views on this, but in my experience all my big mule deer bucks except one were bedded when I shot them. Knowing their exact location is such a huge advantage to the spot and stalk bowhunter, I think you're making a big mistake taking off after a buck before he beds.

- **Don't get lazy.** Hey, I want success as much and as quickly as the next guy, but taking shortcuts or not going the extra mile sabotages many mule deer stalks. It is such hard work even getting into prime mule deer country not to mention finally finding a trophy to go after; you owe it to yourself to make the most of it. Keep working hard and the odds of closing the deal increase exponentially. Sometimes it is just a matter of gaining a little more elevation to get the wind right or dropping down to skirt other deer. While the shortest distance from point A to point B is a

With Mike Eastman filming, I snuck in to 21 yards on this big buck in his bed. Using the contour of the land, I came in on him from above sending an arrow through his vitals without him ever knowing I was within 100 miles.

straight line, the path you take when closing in on a big buck will often times be ripe with detours. Deal with it.

- **Bowhunters are a slave to their psyche.** It is no secret that bowhunters can be superstitious among other things. A bowhunter's psyche many times runs the full gamut of emotions from being overconfident, lacking confidence, or as my wife Tracey claims, to include a touch of obsessive compulsiveness. With the mind in mind, above all else the #1 key to successful bowhunting is you have to believe with all certainty you will make the shot. Many bowhunters, especially new ones, shoot at animals and hope their arrow hits where it is supposed to. Whereas when the most successful bowhunters loose an arrow they know without a doubt that they will hit spot on and truthfully are shocked if for some reason it doesn't.

  South displayed this level of brimming confidence on our recent Nevada hunt as well as exhibited a little physiological quirkiness. Get this: Just before beginning the stalk on his big buck, South took a practice shot. He hit so perfectly on the 80-yard practice poke that he was

Quick Hitters

- Relish the challenge that is bowhunting.
- Respect the animal.
- Be patient, and...be aggressive. Timing is everything.
- Respect Mother Nature.
- Watch the wind. As they say, you can fool their eyes and you can fool their ears, but you'll never fool their nose.
- Respect your fellow hunter.
- Stay in the shadows. Nothing stands out like a human form in the sunlight.
- You will fail and dreams will collapse. The question is, "Will you bounce back?"
- Get out of your comfort zone and push the envelope.
- It is never too late...because it only takes one arrow and one opportunity to turn the worst hunt ever into the best.
- Focus on desired results. Pure and simple: Winners dwell on the rewards of success. Losers focus on mistakes and failure.
- Don't skyline yourself, ever.
- Make sure you have your tags and licenses in your pack.
- Believe in yourself.

compelled to put a new broadhead on that #6 practice arrow and use it to kill his buck. South was so calm and confident in his ability and his equipment that changing out arrows and broadheads minutes before killing one of his best mule deer on film was no big thing. In such a situation, most guys would be battling surging adrenaline and a churning stomach. The last thing on their mind would be messing with their equipment, but South was as cool as the other side of the pillow and it showed in crunch time.

• **The little things make the difference.** We've all heard this before and most of us have probably said it a time or two, but do we live by it? When hunting mule deer we should. The little things that come to mind for me are: Felt on your riser, so if by chance the arrow gets knocked off the rest it doesn't "tink" on the metal riser. Take off your shoes and finish the stalk in stocking feet when you get into the Red Zone. Dab on a little face paint to avoid "moon face" which is about like a spotlight shining on a bedded buck if you poke your head up in the sun and he is looking your way. And lastly, above all else, don't ever try to save a little money like my buddy Wayne Endicott did a number of years back (20) and buy Easton Gamegetters in Autumn Orange and then try to make them camo with spray paint.

This seemed like a great idea until he was eight or ten yards directly on top of a smoker buck on Steens Mountain. From there he decided that the buck was in perfect position, so he rocked back and started to draw. Much to his horror with every inch he drew his arrow over the springy rest, a blood-curdling screech rocketed off of the contact point. A big mule deer might stand for a wayward pebble rolling down the hill but fingernails across a chalkboard x 10 will not fly. The buck boiled out of there and Wayne was left with nothing but a valuable lesson learned and a great story.

More on Stalking Bucks—Random Thoughts and Theories:

Treat every stalk like it is your last. *I have found myself at the end of a hunt or the end of the season, praying for the chance I had at the beginning of the hunt. At the beginning of the hunt it is easy to take opportunities for granted but realize for high country mule deer, the hunting almost always gets tougher. It is not like they are moving toward the peak of the rut or anything. Your repeated presence will educate a big buck and get him on edge or blow him out of the high country. Plus, once that velvet is gone, those older bucks head for the timber. When bowhunting a high country buck, time is of the essence.*

When in tight on a big buck, never stare him directly in the eye. *If they lock on you, especially if you're within 50 yards, look down at the ground in front of them and try to shield your eyes with the brim of your hat. Animals are all about body language as this is largely how they communicate with each other. If you stare them down, so to speak, I believe this aggressive, predator energy is felt and it will result in a blown stalk.*

When in tight on your target buck, *which is sure to be a deer of trophy proportions, you need to take controlled movement to the next level. It is always a tough call as to what to do with your bow when closing in from 40 to 20 yards or closer. There is simply no room for error when packing your bow and arrows in this game. If you're too nonchalant with what you are doing with your bow during the stalk and accidentally raise a bow limb above the brush line or in a manner that the buck spots it, that is obviously not good. My point is there should be no extra movement whatsoever.*

One stalking tactic *that can work to restrict bow movement is when crawling* *in a four point stance, easing in on your target animal, put your bow up on your back, laying it flat and ease on forward staying as low as possible (obviously, this can only be done when you're not wearing your pack). Despite what you might be thinking, it is really not that hard to keep it up there and out of the way for short stints of time. In doing this, you are able to use all four appendages for balance as opposed to using one arm to lift and place your bow further ahead on the path you're taking in on the buck (I do use this tactic quite often as well by the way). Plus, with the bow out of the way and on your back, it is easier to stay even lower all in all as you can move forward crouched with arms bent the entire time, like a lion. With the bow in one hand the other arm has to be pretty much straight, which puts your head and torso up at least 6" higher. And, with that bow in hand I guarantee you inadvertently wave it around a bit when leapfrogging it along with you and you have to find a place to set it every time. A buck can pick up the flash of your bow in a millisecond when in the Red Zone.*

A good way to pack your bow *when easing in tight on a tough-to-approach buck, is on your lap as you slide downhill toward the buck on your butt. It is easiest to go slowly and movement is extremely minimal when on your butt inching forward. If you get semi-busted by getting caught in a bad spot, in this position it is easy to drop down on an elbow or completely flat until the buck settles down. The bow has no problem staying balanced in the lap. I have used this tactic many times over the years. With this example in mind, maybe you will butt slide in on your next buck.*

Last but not least, remember, failure is a prerequisite. *You will not be successful every time out. In fact, the most successful bowhunters are not those who have never failed; the most successful bowhunters are those who have learned from failure and moved on. I have used failure as a motivating tool. I don't like the feeling of failing in the form of a busted stalk because of my impatience or a clean miss, so I take measures to correct my mistakes and you should too. This is all part of the process. Bowhunting is tough and will be ripe with failure. The key is how you respond.*

A hunt in Nevada's high country illustrates many of these points perfectly. Follow along with the action of this backcountry adventure, which could have easily been entitled, "Blueprint for Trophy Mule Deer" or "Backcountry Bowhunting in Mule Deer Heaven." Instead, with much less flair, I called it, *Nevada 2005 Big Buck Diary.*

NEVADA 2005

Big Buck Diary

Day One—Friday 8-5

Season opens tomorrow on the 6th. Horse packer hauled me, Shon Simpson and South Cox deep into the rugged mountains of some great looking Nevada high country. This is my first time hunting Nevada and it looks just like the kind of terrain I love—big, rugged and remote. We dropped base camp and quickly threw together our packs, bivouac gear and five days worth of food. We made our way a couple miles over to a big ridge at the head of a killer-looking basin to do some evening optic work and ended up glassing about 15 bucks. One sure shooter, a 170 P&Y, was in the mix. Having "a plan" is such a good feeling and with all these buck sightings, we definitely had a plan for the opener.

Food item of the day: *Two Peanut Butter and Bacon sandwiches.*

In regard to the daily special of "peanut butter and bacon sandwiches" these are one of my very favorite backcountry staples. They might sound weird, but they are ideal for this type of hunting. My wife, Tracey, usually whips up about eight of them before I take off on a hunt. I live on these for the first few days of the hunt, which really helps to break up the MRE monotony.

To make: fry up a bunch of bacon, an entire pack usually. Toast some wheat bread, spread a generous portion of peanut butter and put on three or four pieces of bacon per sandwich.

These will last for many days, as cooked bacon of course is fine for a while, toasted bread is the same and peanut butter, I don't know, but I have never seen it go bad. I figure these sandwiches have about 900 calories each, are chock-full of protein and carbs, plus they taste good—1,800 calories total. Good solid backcountry food.

Day One Food: 2 Peanut Butter and Bacon sandwiches, 1,800 calories; 1 Nature Valley Granola bar, 180 calories; 1 Quaker Granola bar, 240 calories = 2,220 calories

Day Two—Saturday 8-6

Opening day of season. Rolling out of my bivy at first light I immediately glassed up two good bucks. They vanished but soon after Shon and I located a herd of 23 bucks including a great 170-ish 4x4. We watched the deer for a good 30 minutes, picking landmarks and planning the best route to get in tight on all those eyes, ears and noses. This would not be easy, but it sure did seem possible. Glassing from a few hundred yards above the bucks, we had a number of benches in between us. As we closed in there was little doubt the country would look a little different and it would be tough nailing exactly which bench the bucks were bedded on. This is where a lot of stalks get blown. The key with our stalk was that we had a dead tree just below the deer that would serve as the perfect reference point. The tall cedar stood out from all the others because it was dead and red in color.

Staying locked on the "Red Tree" we circled around to get the wind right and get into position to come down on top of the bucks. At about 100 yards, we were perfectly concealed by the break of the bench directly above the deer. I could glass through the trees and see bucks shaking their heads and flicking their ears. Taking a deep breath and getting mentally ready, it was showtime as we entered Slo-Mo mode. Taking it nice and slow was not that difficult, as Shon and I had slipped our boots off and dropped our packs about a half-mile back. We miscalculated how far we had to go and then didn't want to go back to get our stuff after realizing our gaffe. Suffice to say, by the end of the day, our feet were hamburger. The Nevada high country is not a place to be running around for hours in your socks. Was it worth it? You be the judge...

Easing off the lip of the bench just up the ridge from the deer, we were careful to stay in the shadows. Shon, with camera in hand, and I inched ever so slowly on our butts through the black shadows of a dark stand of cedars. We had closed in to this point very quickly, relatively speaking, by using the contour of the land for cover but now it was a much different story. To get in bow range, I had to move painstakingly slow given all those eyes. As it was playing out, given the cover and the big buck's location, it looked like my only shot was going to be straight down on the big buck. This is not the easiest shot to make in the world with a bow, but is one I have practiced thousands of times. If your goal is to arrow a trophy mule deer this is a shot you are going to have to master.

The Straight Down Shot: *If your goal is to arrow a trophy mule deer this is a shot you are going to have to master.*

The big 4x4 was bedded unaware of my presence as I inched to 53 yards. The problem was there were four other bucks facing me, boring holes through me every time I even twitched too quickly. I had to be very patient while trying to get my bow drawn back without blowing all the bucks off the side of the hill. Finally, after taking probably 10 full minutes to get my knees under me and my bow up, I slowly got those cams rolled over. With adrenaline buzzing in my ears, I anchored in hard against the wall, leveled the sight bubble and settled the red 40-yard pin tight behind the buck's shoulder while gently fingering the trigger of my release. In a flash the arrow was streaking toward the animal.

The angle of the shot was so steep that despite taking off 13 yards, I still hit higher than I wanted and a touch farther back than I would have liked. This is where razor sharp broadheads are worth their weight in gold. While the hit wasn't in the 12 ring so to speak, it really wasn't that far off. One positive in regard to the shot angle was that the arrow came out the very bottom of the buck's chest cavity, which meant there would be a heavy blood trail. Thanks to some handy trailing help by South and Shon, we recovered my Nevada trophy near a small creek up and over a finger ridge from where I hit him.

I'd been blessed with "Opening Day Magic" once again. For whatever reason, either because I put so much into preparation and am on top of my game or the animals are kind of caught off guard by the opener, I have killed some of my most memorable trophies on opening day. This trend goes way back to 1991 when I arrowed my best ever mule deer in the Steens Mountains, my best Eagle Cap bull in 1996, a beautiful cinnamon colored black bear in 1997, Saskatchewan whitetail and Montana antelope in 2003 and so on. I expect success every day I hunt and prepare for it obsessively, but on opening day luck has been on my side.

After shooting some photos and video we quickly skinned and boned the buck out to cool. We were in the bottom of a nice basin and by a creek as I mentioned which meant it would cool down pretty good during the night. We needed it to. It was HOT during the day. After breaking the buck down and hanging the meat, we all yarded out our bivy gear and some food. Spirits were as high as could be expected. One day hunting, one bomber mule deer down.

Day Two Food: 2 Peanut Butter and Bacon sandwiches, 1,800 calories; 2 Nature Valley Granola bars, 360 calories; Jerky, 80 calories; Peanut Butter and Crackers, 210 calories; Chewy Granola Bar, 110 calories = 2,560 calories.

Day Three—Sunday 8-7

We all woke at first light, ate a few bites, took a few more photos and made plans to get my buck to the trail. We had used the satellite phone to call our packer, telling him of our success. Getting the meat taken care of was our paramount concern given the weather and of course the packer understood this. He planned on leaving the trailhead at first light and meeting us near our base camp at 2:00 p.m.

Shon and I emptied our packs of gear and replaced it with meat. We left our gear at the spike camp, as did South. While we humped the meat and antlers up to the trail some three

In my opinion, a trophy public land mule deer arrowed in the high country is one of bowhunting's greatest achievements.

miles, South scurried around the mountains looking for something to sneak an arrow into.

Getting the meat to the trail and meeting the packer went perfectly. I felt relieved watching my harvest heading down the trail on the backs of the packstring as I knew in just a few hours it would be in a walk-in-cooler back in town. I had closure. With empty packs and an overall good feeling of relief and accomplishment, Shon and I bombed back in to spike camp to see what South had been up to all day. While we packed meat, South had found a few bucks in a neighboring basin, but nothing too crazy big. It was easy for him to hold off on going after them, as our goal was to get his kill on film. We still had a few hours before dark so we all loaded up our packs and worked back up to the top of the ridge to put ourselves in good position for the morning's hunt. After a steep and grueling two-mile climb, we peaked out with a few minutes to glass. Bucks were popping up everywhere and we found at least two shooters for South to pursue the next morning.

That night, under the bright stars, we made plans for the morning while snacking on food and pouring over topo maps by the light of our headlamps. Another good day in the mountains—sleep came easy.

Day Three Food: 1 Peanut Butter and Bacon sandwich, 900 calories; ½ Mountain House Spaghetti, 400 calories; 1 Nature Valley Granola bar, 180 calories; Chewy Granola bar, 110 calories; Peanuts, 290 calories; mixed fruit, 200 calories; Doritos Crackers, 240 calories = 2,320 calories.

A sweet sight. Headed out of the high country tagged out.

Day Four—Monday 8-8

Let me make it clear here and now, South is a great hunting buddy. Need proof? On this fourth morning on the hill, Shon and I woke up to a hot oatmeal breakfast thanks to South. Enough said as that is a great way to start your day in the backcountry.

Just after daybreak we all slowly angled up from our spike camp toward the peak of the ridge, staying just off the spine so as not to be skylighted. South and I glassed both sides as Shon took photos and videoed. It was a great morning. Through the Swarovski big glass, I found a real nice 5x4 with crazy long eyeguards bedded on small bench with a younger buck bedded nearby. We videoed him and planned a stalk for a closer look. After about an hour and after losing about 1,000 feet in elevation we popped over the ridge just 64 yards from where he'd been and...he was gone. Such is spot & stalk mule deer hunting! We glassed for quite some time but could never relocate him or his smaller buddy. Sometimes it seems they vanish in midair, but in actuality, I am sure those bucks moved out of the sun to spend the bulk of the day in some secluded and cool hideout. We hoofed it back up to the top of the ridge and continued on.

We made our way to a decent-sized but short drainage that looked to be prime mule deer country. Our first impression was right on as we glassed up two beautiful bucks. I should note now that on our first optic sweep of this canyon we found only a handful of bucks. It wasn't until I suggested we drop down about 500 feet and glass off a little bench, which I felt would open up some more country, that we saw what we were after. It is this type of extra effort that oftentimes makes the difference in a hunt. No one wants to drop down and lose elevation but well, you know. Gotta do what you gotta do.

Don't be lazy—extra effort is rewarded

It wasn't until we dropped down about 500 feet in elevation to peak over a little bench that the canyon opened up. We were rewarded for this effort by immediately spotting two big bucks.

The two biggest bucks of the drainage were shooters by South's standards, which is saying something. He wanted something comfortably over 170 Pope & Young. I know this because I had glassed up a good 165–170 buck earlier, showed it to him in the spotting scope and he shrugged it off saying, "That is not really what I came here for." Impressive.

Watching South Cox sneak to within 36 yards of this brute then send a perfectly placed arrow through the buck's lungs was amazing.

What we'd found in this basin was a buck we called "The 5x4" for obvious reasons and a great 190-class buck we'd given the moniker, "The G-4 Buck." He had a monster frame with huge splits; his only knock was a short G-4 on his left side.

The 5x4 was in ideal stalking position and as we have learned, you have to pick your battles, so South decided to put something together on him. Incidentally, he looked to be about a 180-class trophy almost anyone would be proud of. Shon and South peeled off after the buck while I stayed to film with a backup video camera from my hideout about 200 yards from the bedded 5x4. He was surrounded by five other bedded bucks and a doe, which would make things interesting for sure.

South closed to about 80 quickly, then things slowed way down as he was forced to cover a wide-open expanse to get within bow range. While the country was open, what should also be shared is that there was just enough contour in the hill to effectively shield South's approach from above the bedded deer. As the ever savvy bowhunter, South also got serious by covering his face with camo, taking off his boots and slipping on a pair of thick wool socks. Remember, it is the little things that make the difference. Shon set up on a huge rock outcropping where he could film over South's shoulder. Shon was about 100 yards from the deer and if the stalk worked out would get a great bird's eye view of all the action.

When South got within about 35 yards of the bedded buck, he crested the slight swell of the hill he'd been using as cover and things began to go haywire. One of the deer must have seen him and spooked, taking two of the smaller bucks with him. They didn't really know what was up, but knew something wasn't right. The big boy was up, not yet fully spooked, but definitely on edge. In my experience, what I think happens is unless the biggest buck, or another of similar age, is actually the one that sees, smells or hears the threat (you), they are not real excited to bound off just because a squirrelly little forked-horn or doe gets wound up. In the case of the big 5x4, he was in a perfect spot to bed for the day, it was hotter than hell on the side of that mountain and he hadn't a clue as to what all the fuss was about and as I alluded above, he probably didn't 100% "respect" the judgment of the deer that spooked. He seemingly had to be convinced the threat was valid or he wasn't going to budge. This didn't change the fact that South had to act and act quickly.

South stayed calm, cool, collected and most importantly, in control in the face of all this excitement. As all the deer except for the big buck intermittently scurried off, South in "cool as the other side of the pillow" mode, took a reading on 5X4 with his rangefinder, eased his bow back, settled his 30-yard pin, and then sent a razor sharp broadhead through the buck's lungs. The big deer bounded down the mountain a short 56 yards before faltering. Shon's video work caught all this action which made the experience just that much more special. We have relived this great bowhunting moment in the mountains hundreds of times with our families from the comfort of our living rooms. Good times.

After quickly taking some photos and capturing a little more video, we got busy breaking the deer down. My Suunto wrist computer's thermometer read 111 degrees.

We were on a boulder-strewn sidehill as the baking sun ricocheted off all that white rock making the deer-processing chore all that much more fun. Hey, but it is all part of the experience right?

South boned out the meat, caped the head and loaded up his pack. Shon and I split South's gear between us as we busted our humps up and out of the top of the basin. The plan was to get to the top of the ridge, swing by our spike camp, load up all the rest of our bivouac gear and line out three miles to a patch of snow where we would bury the meat. I know it seems odd that there was still snow given the baking heat, but being at 10,000 feet helps, plus there were a number of snowdrifts that sat on the backside of a couple of ridges which virtually never see the sun.

After a few long hours, we made it to our mountain meat locker and set up our bivys for the last night. A call on the satellite phone to our packer telling him we had "Tagged Out" was a good feeling. He made plans to start the five-hour ride in the next morning at first light, which would be perfect for us as we had about a four-mile hike back to base camp.

Day Four Food: Oatmeal, 200 calories; 1 Nature Valley Granola bar, 180 calories; Chewy Granola bar, 110 calories; MRE Pineapple, 200 calories; mixed fruit, 200 calories; Doritos Crackers, 240 calories; MRE Wild Rice Pilaf, 240 calories; MRE Turkey Breast, 450 calories; Bagel & Summer Sausage, 500 calories = 2,320 calories.

In Summary

Once it was all said and done, our 10-day backcountry mule deer hunt was cut in half to five days. I killed my buck opening day, South killed his on the third day and we were heading home early. This is rare indeed and is surely something my wife should not get used to. What a perfect hunt. We both stalked and killed great bucks, made good shots and compiled an amazing backcountry bowhunting video.

Section 5

Elk

Backcountry Elk

Heart pounding, hair raising, spine tingling...

Many of us have used such references when trying to describe the adrenaline-fueled emotions that race through our bodies when a big, rutting bull elk is in bow range. A backcountry bowhunter who can stay calm, cool and collected when in close proximity to one of the West's most regal animals deserves a lot of credit. This bowhunter is also in the minority.

Most of us simply attempt to manage our emotions rather than control them, which is an uphill battle if ever there was one. If the truth was known, the solid thud of those heavy hooves striking rock and hardened earth as the bull comes in redlines most of our heart rates. If the mud-caked, urine-soaked bull lays his heavy antlers back and lets loose a thunderous, spine tingling bugle through the crisp mountain air while just a stone's throw away from your hunkered bowhunting form—staying focused has never been tougher.

This situation is the exact reason we bowhunt for elk, is it not? We all long to be set up in the perfect spot, arrow nocked, broadhead shaking ever so slightly as we fight an all out battle for composure while we wait. With a mouth as dry as the desert, we wait, aching for the chance to bend that bow back and pick a spot behind the beast's thickly-muscled shoulder. This is the exact situation we've waited, practiced and dreamt for all year. This is "Crunch Time" and it all comes down to mastering the moment.

I think mastering the moment is tougher yet for the guy hunting deep in the backcountry. The reason is we put so much into it. To get in posi-

You don't know if you don't go. Having only one day to hunt, I killed this bull on a "Banzai" trip deep into the wilderness.

tion to kill a wilderness bull, we have been working for months—planning, strategizing and shooting. If you've done it like I do, basically your life has revolved around getting ready for that one chance at a big country bull. To say this is a moment ripe with emotion, it would be an understatement.

Adrenaline has never screamed through your veins faster than when a big bull comes at the tail end of a long backcountry hunt. Is this a different type of emotion than a guy who hunts from his rig feels? You bet it is. This is backcountry elk hunting and this is as raw and as real as it gets!

New elk hunters take note. Simply put, there may be no better time than the present to be bowhunting for trophy bulls. For new-to-the-sport archers or long-time bowhunters who will be pursing elk for the first time, in this, the age of many elk, locating a Pope & Young bull is simply not all that difficult if you do a little homework. All of the western states that hold elk will produce bulls that score over the P&Y minimum of 260 points or inches. When you consider the vocal nature of rutting bulls, the herd's affinity for yellow grassed meadows at and above timberline early and late in the day and the highly visual characteristics of these buff-colored, horse-sized

Almost ready to throw in the towel after nearly a week of nothing, I arrowed a Pope & Young buck and then this bull on consecutive days in the Oregon wilderness.

animals, locating elk may very well be the least of your problems.

As I mentioned, for an elk hunter these are the "good ol' days," to be sure; good ol' days in a couple of different ways. First, elk numbers are peaking like never before and secondly, some absolute monster bulls are being killed. For proof of this look no further than the pages of nearly every single issue of *Eastmans' Bowhunting Journal*.

However, for the new elk hunter, setting goals such as tagging a Boone & Crockett class animal or arrowing a Pope & Young bull may be a sure recipe for disaster. For the beginner, I feel like what is most important is garnering overall elk hunting experience. One gets this by simply hunting and perhaps more importantly, successfully hunting.

When I first started chasing these buff-colored beasts in the late '80s, I trophy hunted for all of one morning, and then it was anything goes for a couple years anyway. I surely wasn't born a trophy hunter, but from that first day in the field I started a natural transition from an elk hunter who would be happy simply getting something on the ground, to presently, a hunter who has the patience to be a little more selective.

The transition I reference should be gradual. In my opinion a good goal

Setting up a public land hunt like the one in which I arrowed this 7x6 Wyoming trophy is realistic for the hardcore D-I-Y guy.

for a rookie bowhunter is a spike bull. Of course a bigger bull would be great, but arrowing any bull the first year out is surely something to be proud of. I know I was. Walking up on that spike bull as a greenhorn was something I'll never forget. From there, any branch bull, then a mature bull like a big five-point, and then set your sights on any 6x6.

The next stage of a trophy elk hunter gets tougher for most blue collar guys like us. In my opinion, after about five years worth of serious elk hunting experience with a bow, you'll be in the right frame of mind and should have accumulated enough backcountry savvy to move up to this next level. By this time, if you do your homework and hunt hard (yes, I am simplifying things), I'd think it would be realistic to hold out for a 300-inch Pope & Young bull. I am a regular guy and to me and almost everyone I know a 300+ bull is the trophy of a lifetime.

Now for the baddest of big bull hunters there is another level. Letting up to 320-class bulls walk would seem ludicrous to many guys, but the upper echelon bowhunters out there do it regularly. These guys don't even consider a bull unless it is 330 Pope & Young, but there are a few extenuating

While always wanting to tag a bull like this 350 Pope & Young monster out of Colorado, it took me nearly 20 years of bowhunting to make it happen. I wouldn't want it any other way.

circumstances here.

First, don't kid yourself, as just like you and me, they have come up through the ranks. Second, they hunt areas where the bulls routinely grow up to 330-class, which requires a few key components: Genetics, age (over five years old) and good winter range to name a few.

In heavily hunted areas, the bulls are oftentimes killed before they can get old enough to reach their full potential. In areas like the Eagle Cap Wilderness in Oregon, the lack of a quality winter range makes surviving so tough they have little "juice" left to fuel mega antler growth. Of course almost all elk country produces big bulls, but in the Eagle Cap where some big bulls have been killed over the years, it can be like finding a needle in a haystack. Whereas in certain areas of say, Wyoming, a 300–320 class bull might be considered a satellite bull. The lesson here is to make sure your goals match the country you are hunting and its trophy producing potential.

During my first couple elk seasons I would go through waves of frustration, but because I would attempt to take any legal bull, I mixed in just the right amount of success to keep me focused and hungry to learn. Elk hunting is very difficult; there is no other way to say it. And as a new elk hunter, if you take something that is already incredibly tough and make it exponentially tougher by setting lofty goals such as holding out for a 6x6, or a big 5x5, you can be making a big mistake. Days, weeks or years marked by frustration will create desperation and take the fun right out of chasing your dream. Elk hunting is hard, but it can also be one of the most rewarding and enjoyable experiences in your life.

In Summary

When the majestic elk is your chosen quarry, start at ground zero by setting realistic goals for success and rely on basic common elk sense when hunting, scouting or studying maps. If nothing else, the beginning of this chapter illustrates two important points. One, as I mentioned earlier, I wasn't born a trophy hunter or a wilderness expert. To become both takes time, years in fact, and if you're like me this process will include many valuable and sometimes painful lessons. I wouldn't have wanted it any other way.

Committed to the Wilderness

By Cameron R. Hanes

Originally appeared in Eastmans' Hunting Journal *Issue 46*

The Wallowa Mountains of northeastern Oregon are awe-inspiring in their appearance. Out of respect for this grandeur, they are sometimes called the Oregon Alps in obvious comparison to the legendary mountains of Switzerland. The imposing snow-covered summits, high alpine meadows, bare granite peaks, ridges and u-shaped glaciated valleys will always be protected in their unsullied state by the boundaries of the Eagle Cap Wilderness. This is Oregon's largest designated wilderness area, stretching 30 by 60 miles. Inside this protected sanctuary, the wilderness is home to a bevy of big game animals, including bighorn sheep, mountain goats, mule deer, bear, cougar and Rocky Mountain elk, to list a few.

Smack dab in the middle of country with as much wild character as any Oregon has to offer, this classic elk habitat is home to its fair share of trophy class bulls, which brings me to what kindles my interest in this wilderness. I will sum it up in four simple words—big, remote, trophy bulls. Don't assume that I mean there are bulls lurking behind every tree or bush. This wilderness is huge, and if you're looking in the wrong place, you can wear out a pair of boots without so much as seeing an elk. For those who are up to the supreme challenge of hunting big country elk, I will share the tactics and strategies that have made my hunts successful.

I believe the ability to successfully hunt elk in Oregon's most remote, expansive and rugged backcountry starts in one's heart. If you plan on venturing miles into some of the harshest country in Oregon or anywhere for that matter with the hope of harvesting a trophy class bull, the "need to succeed" should have been burning in your soul long before you pull up to the trailhead. The mental challenge of wilderness hunting is easily as formidable as the physical challenge. I have hunted this wilderness for a number of years, and each fall for days on end I face many trials and tribulations in my quest for a trophy. In no special order I deal with fatigue, sleep deprivation, unforgiving country, the ever-present threat of merciless weather, seemingly eternal solitude, sore feet and the frustration of pursuing extremely high-strung animals. If one heads into a challenge like this half-hearted, the chance of success is as remote as if you had stayed at home.

Some will say that you don't have to endure this much to harvest a bull in Oregon, as elk populations are extremely healthy throughout our state. I agree there are areas with higher concentrations of elk, but with that comes a higher concentration of hunters. To me, wilderness elk hunting offers the right mix of trophy bulls and hunting pressure.

Once you have all of your mental ducks in a row, it is time to concentrate on strategy. I believe the key strategic element to successful wilderness hunting can be summed up in one word: Efficiency. I achieve this by having my camp on my back at all times.

Traveling to and from camp each and every day is not only a waste of time but is also an unneeded depletion of that ever-precious commodity...energy. In the not-so-distant past I would leave base camp two hours before light in the morning and return two or three hours after dark. This was a tremendous squandering of energy. When I decided to bivouac out, and never concern myself about where I was as long as I was in elk, potential harvest opportunities increased dramatically.

I bought a piece of equipment called a Bivy Sack made by Outdoor Research. This was a key ingredient in my master plan of mobility and efficiency. The Bivy Sack is a compact, waterproof shelter with room for a sleeping bag to fit snugly inside. The sack is constructed of Gore-Tex fabric and each seam is waterproofed with Gore-Tex seam tape. Couple a Bivy Sack with a top quality sleeping bag and pad, and you can survive virtually any hand Mother Nature may deal you. This is a tremendous asset in obtaining the peace of mind necessary to be completely focused on your mission.

The day before season I was perched on a rock outcropping 14 miles into the heart of the Eagle Cap Wilderness glassing for elk. Darkness was fast approaching when the high-pitched shrill of a bugle wafted its way up the ridge to my hidden post. About 600 yards away, 10 cows came single file out of the adjacent drainage up onto the marshy flat I had been glassing. They were followed by a spike bull and a nice five-point. Bringing up the rear was a beautiful 6x6 that I judged would go about 300 P&Y. I had a hard time prying the binoculars from my eyes as the bull was putting on quite a display, alternating between chasing cows, bugling and running off the younger bulls. I would have stayed there longer if not for the cool night air that would soon carry my scent directly to the elk. Having the bivouac camp allowed me the option of skirting through a saddle to the backside of the main ridge, and sleeping within half a mile of the herd.

Living with the elk can have its pros and cons. In the case of this herd, I became startlingly aware of a big con when the herd bull bugled not 100 yards from my camp at about 5:00 a.m. Obviously, I had not backed off far enough as I was forced to look for another bull rather than hunting spooked elk.

The search for more elk was a short one. I decided to go back through the saddle and sidehill it over to the head of the big drainage where the elk had appeared the night before. This particular drainage was not only miles into the wilderness, but also five miles off any pack trail.

I immediately glassed up a second, 300-point 6x6 in the company of four cows and a spike approximately half a mile away and directly across the drainage from me. After glassing for a short time, it became apparent the small herd was headed down to the cool timber near the creek to bed for the day. I would have to close in on the bull from the top, so I decided to grab a bite to eat and bide my time until the sun's warmth sent the mid-morning thermals rushing upward. The bull never bugled as he wasn't yet feeling the full effects of the rut. He did, however, stop and tear up a tree or two as he picked his way down the rocky slope.

Not long after I downed one last Power Bar and swallowed the last of my iodine-purified water, the bull disappeared into a thick clump of timber. I crossed my fingers that he would bed there because it was not in the bottom of the canyon but more up on the sidewall where the sparse timber was broken up by intermittent meadows and rock outcroppings.

I glassed the timber patch intently for upwards of an hour until I was satisfied the bull had not slipped away. By that time, the sun had finally come up and warmed the bottom of the drainage enough to send the thermals on their daily trek up the canyon.

Prior to beginning my stalk, I picked landmarks and plotted a path of travel that would take me into bow range of the big bull. Having distinguishing landmarks is of the utmost importance on any stalk, but in this big, open country where size and distance can be very deceiving, it is even more critical.

I felt confident of my planned approach as I made my way to a landmark that was directly across a small meadow from the bull's selected bedding area. The wind remained steady as I slowly eased my way down off the canyon rim and into the bull's sanctum. Within about 45 minutes I was straining to see into the shroud of darkened timber where the bull had disappeared. Bringing my binoculars up, I was about to begin picking apart the shadows for a tine or flicker of movement, when I heard an elk rise to its feet. I could see the shape of the motionless bull on my edge of the timber patch, but he was still almost completely obscured by the low hanging limbs of his timbered fortress. As my mind raced, trying to calculate both his and my next move, the bull stepped clear and offered me a 43-yard quartering away shot. I slowly bent my bow back, anchored in with my 40-yard pin locked on high lung and released.

After the shot, I hit the cow call a few times, trying to relax both the bull and his small herd.

The rest of the elk never really knew what had transpired as they ambled off in a state of confusion. With an arrow nocked out of habit I suppose, I sat down and replayed the shot and the bull's reaction in my head a thousand times, while staring blankly at the tip of my broadhead. As I settled in to wait the obligatory 30 minutes before tracking my bull, I become acutely aware of my surroundings. It seemed although everything had come to a screeching halt, the deafening sound of silence was so all-encompassing that it was almost unsettling. Minutes passed at a time-warp-like slowness that allowed me to slip into a state of deep contemplation. My thoughts were of how strange it was that I felt so insignificant in the hundreds of thousands

of acres of wilderness and yet I could come in here and commit an act of absolute significance by entering this bull's domain and potentially wrench him from his majestic prime of life.

The blood trail told the story of a mortally wounded bull hit by a razor sharp broadhead that entered the quartering away elk mid-body, dissecting through the liver and one lung, finally coming to rest on the far shoulder. I knew it would be a short tracking job long before I saw my bull lying in his last bed a short 100 yards from when he was hit.

Perhaps I was being overly cerebral, but it was hard for me to not be caught up in the moment as I sat there next to my bull in the middle of this impressive expanse of untamed country. I suppose it was because I took the life of an animal I respect like no other, for the country he inhabits, and for the unequaled manner in which he displays his dominance. Although I harvested this bull on opening day of the 1997 season, I had truly been hunting him since I first stepped into the woods with a bow some nine years ago. Finally, my hunter's rationale returned and I was able to fully appreciate the feeling of accomplishment and fulfillment that comes with the harvest of a long sought-after trophy.

Some 36 hours later, my partners Greg, Tim, Joel and I were sitting in a pizza parlor in the little

Harvesting a bull of this caliber in the backcountry of Oregon seemed impossible to me for many years. I don't think I've ever been more proud than when I walked up to this 6x6 that lonely day deep in the backcountry.

town of Enterprise, Oregon, after successfully packing out the hundreds of pounds of boned meat. We were filthy and exhausted, but that special time with close friends brought closure to a personal dream and made memories that I wouldn't trade for anything. Wilderness hunting offers new challenges and experiences that are there for the taking; all you have to do is want it!

Hunt Report Card – Hindsight is always 20/20

What I learned on this hunt: All of us set goals. Some bowhunters' goals are different or loftier in comparison to others, but they are a standard to shoot for nonetheless. Shortly after getting my feet wet in the obsession we call bowhunting, my goal had always been to shoot a good 6x6 bull. I considered a 300-point bull to be a good one, especially for Oregon and especially on a D-I-Y, public land hunt. Secondly, my first ever wilderness hunt resulted in the arrowing of a spike bull shot too far from the trailhead. It took a lot of work for me and Roy Roth to get that thing out, but since that hunt another one of my goals was to kill a wilderness bull on my own miles from anyone with my bivy camp on my back. I achieved both these long sought after goals when I arrowed this bull.

The most important lesson I learned is that whether your goal is to kill a 400-inch bull, a 300-inch bull or any bull, stick with it, stay committed to achieving your dreams, keep working hard and it will happen. I set, achieve and then set new goals annually and suggest you do the same. Having something to work toward makes all the difference.

What I did wrong: My first screw up was that I lost a custom knife my father-in-law, Larry Smith, had just spent a decent amount of money on and given me as a gift prior to the trip. Secondly, I know now that you can push llamas too hard. I can't bag on the llamas too much though. It was only when Roy and his dad, Ray, bought four llamas back in the early 90s that the backcountry was really opened up to us. It wasn't an option before because we never had enough money at one time to pay for a drop camp or a packer that could haul our kills out of the wilderness. If nothing else, llamas are cheap – they don't eat much and require little maintenance so we could spread out the cost of owning them over the whole year. Llamas allowed us to hunt deep, period.

The problem on this hunt was I killed my bull on opening day and even though they were in great shape, the llamas were simply not fully recovered from packing all the gear up the hill the day before. They were exhausted and would never have made it down in the hole where I killed that bull then back up the mountain and all the way out. This meant that I had to bone out my bull, hang it and hike about 10 miles over to where my other three buddies were hunting and try to talk them into giving up some of their hunting time to help me get the bull out. Of course they did, but really it cost them their hunt as putting on that many miles in just a few days broke everyone down—way down.

Another mistake I made and looking back maybe it was for the best was that as I was packing the head and tenderloins up out of the drainage I had killed the bull in, my bow kept hitting on stuff, getting caught in brush, etc., so I stashed and kept on truckin'. This was all fine and good until I popped around a bend in the trail and came face to face with a big P&Y 3x3 buck that was bedded only 20 yards away. The good thing, I had a valid deer tag in my pack. The bad thing, I now had no way to kill the sucker. I did get some pretty good photos though as he stood there, let me wrestle the pack off of my back, dig my camera out and snapped about six or seven shots. Two lessons learned from this encounter: One – in the wilderness anything can happen. Two – never, ever go anywhere without your bow.

Grade: Even though the stalk had more of a mule deer flavor than elk, it was textbook. My logistics in regard to getting the bull out needed work. Lucky for me we didn't kill more, as we'd have been in a bad situation. I have done a better job of planning since this hunt. **A-**

Learning the Ropes

Decoding the ways of the wapiti

When I hunt, I learn something every time out. Essentially this serves as a highly effective form of scouting. When hunting, I am more in tune and cognizant of my surroundings than when trips are scouting-specific. I have averaged approximately 10 days in the field for each of the bulls I have killed. It should be noted that as archery hunters we are generally privy to a much longer season than a rifle hunter would be. This elongated time in the woods allowed me to learn a great deal about elk in just a handful of seasons. To expound, here in my home state of Oregon, rifle season lasts for about seven days or in some cases as little as five days. When one can only spending a handful of days chasing elk each year, wapiti savvy accumulates slowly.

Another key attribute to my ongoing elk hunting education happens when I am lucky enough to tag out, early or otherwise. When faced with such a 'dilemma', I never pass on a chance to spend time in the elk woods during elk season. I often find myself tagging along with one of my elk hunting buddies in an effort to learn more. I have been with friends and family on at least as many successful elk hunts as animals I have personally tagged. Also, when accompanying others I've been able to not only hone my blood trailing skills, but also become more adept at dealing with that demon known simply as 'elk fever,' which can single-handedly sabotage the most ideal situation. More time spent with and around elk has allowed me to get better at holding my composure in crunch time.

Make no mistake, hunting is a great time to scout, but I still spend many hours afield scouting. Elk may be one of the easiest big game animals to scout due to their large size and the not so subtle behavior of rutting bulls. When I scout, I couldn't care less whether or not I see an elk. The sign they leave gives me ample information on elk numbers in the area I am focused on. A herd of elk tears up an amazing amount of ground, creates trails quickly and browses heavily, which are all calling cards that can be interpreted quickly by even a novice.

When scouting during the summer prior to elk season, again I am not concerned as to any actual elk sightings, as they may very well summer in an altogether different area from where they will be during the breeding (bow) season. This holds true for summer areas as they relate to fall (rifle season) haunts as well. Above all else, never lose sight of the fact that the cows dictate everything this time of year. When scouting prior to season a lot of guys get wound up by finding bulls. Don't fall into this trap. When I scout, I look for signs of rutting behavior because as a bowhunter this is when I will be pursuing the beasts. This is not too difficult, as a bull will tear up many a tree in a display of dominance or in an effort to burn some of his spare testosterone.

I have found most rubs will be around bedding areas, which typically will be located in the cool big timber of north facing slopes. I believe the reason for this is that bulls are on edge during the rut (breeding season) and often pace around the perimeter, amongst or through his bedded herd. The rutting bull spends very little time bedded, so while his harem rests, he wanders and with peaking aggression, tears up trees. When I find these bedding areas that are littered with rubs I know I am on to something. The next step is to determine likely travel routes that link feeding to bedding areas.

Yet another easily distinguishable sign of bull elk is a wallow. A wallow is basically a mud bog in which the bull will flop, roll, rake, urinate, splash and generally have a good time making quite a mess. You see, elk are big animals. During bow season, which most often runs during very warm periods of late summer, they will need a good water supply. As such, you can count on them frequenting water daily at least once and more likely twice, and when near water you can rest assured the bulls will create a wallow in an effort to cool off, or perhaps simply display classic rutting bull behavior he has seen displayed by previous herd masters.

How to make that hard work pay off.

When in the field, bow in hand and all the hard scouting work has paid off meaning you've found elk, you might be asking, "Now what do I do?"

Good question. First, don't barrel into the middle of the herd at half draw scanning frantically for a bull like I probably did during my first elk hunt. It would be nice if I could remember exactly what I did, but unfortunately I had an "Elk Fever Blackout." I finally came to about five minutes after the herd had left, which left me choking on their cloud of dust, wondering what just happened. It didn't matter back then; all I wanted to be able to say was, "Got into some."

Somehow, some way, by the grace of God, I was able to arrow a spike bull elk that very first year of bowhunting. I had to pretty much drop out of school to do it. I remember to this day that I killed the bull on September 13, which had been my 18th straight day of elk hunting. My college professors were none to pleased with that move, but hell, they just didn't understand. I remember one of them asking me what I thought my odds were of actually killing something with my bow if I hadn't been able to do it in the two plus weeks I'd already missed of his class.

Walking me halfway to my truck to say all of this, he finished up with something like, "Cam, aren't you ever going to learn when to say enough is enough?"

I replied with remnants of camo left on my face from the morning hunt, "Don't know, but I gotta get going now if I am going to have any chance at all of killing something today and besides Professor, I am in love with the struggle."

"The what?" he fired back with a tone of irritation.

"The struggle, you know, the challenge...I love it. Sitting in class and getting good grades is something anyone can do. On the other hand, not everyone can go kill a bull elk with a bow and that is why I like it. I'll see you when I finally kill my bull," I called over my shoulder on the way out to my truck. Thinking back on it now, some things never change. I am still in love with the struggle.

The next year I again found myself in pretty good position with some elk in my sights, only this time I chilled out and glassed for at least 30 minutes to get a good gauge on what they were going to do. See, I was learning.

By their actions, I could tell they were looking to bed down. They had been slowly browsing their way up an old logging skid road and were now starting to mill as they neared the edge of some second growth. There was a good 5x5 bull in the mix that I would be ecstatic to run an arrow through if he'd let me. I eased along behind, just far enough to where they didn't know I was around. Hanging up as they just worked into the big timber, it looked to me like they were setting up shop for the morning. I watched and waited. The bull looked to be checking all his cows as they bedded. Once I was certain they were settled in for the morning, I started my sneak up the grown-over road.

The elk were bedded on either side of the road, with five cows on one side and three on the other. The bull was pacing back and forth between them. He wasn't bugling full fledge, but he was glunking. It would have been tough to hear the glunking had I not been so intimate with this herd. In his distracted state, I was able to sneak in when the cows would allow it. Finally and painstakingly, I had closed in to bow range but the bull was on the wrong side of the road. With an arrow nocked and kneeling along the side of the old skid road like a cagey veteran I waited, watching under the bill of my hat as the big 5x5 slowly ambled from one set of cows to the next, passing by at only 25 yards. I didn't try to draw until he had worked past me a little as I didn't want him to catch movement.

Being close to elk like this in their natural environment is the greatest thing about bowhunting and is where I've learned the most about elk behavior. Some rifle hunters never in their life have an experience like the one I was lucky enough to have on this special morning. As the bull worked over to check on a cow, I readied myself for the shot. He got to her and when he bent his head down to nuzzle her, I rose up and eased my bow back. At full draw, I picked a tuft of hair just off the last rib of the quartering away bull, put my 30-yard pin a touch high above the tuft as the bull was at what I guessed to be 35 yards, and gently squeezed my release. The arrow hit hard, quartering up through the bull's vitals with full penetration. He wouldn't go far.

He didn't bleed much as I expected because there was no exit wound and the arrow stayed in the entrance, blocking it a bit from letting too much blood spill. The lack of blood wasn't a big issue as the big bull was hurt and I was easily able to follow the tracks his heavy hooves tore up. After following blood for about 40 yards, I could see him. He was down. I had taken my first ever Pope & Young bull during my second season of elk hunting, and it

Backcountry Bowhunting Collector's Edition

Note from the Author

Cameron R. Hanes

Make no mistake, I always dreamed of being a hunting writer. Not just a hunting writer per se, but a hunting adventure writer. How-to articles on tying in your peep sight bore me to tears, to read as well as write. My goal was to paint an *edge-of-your-seat, raw, real, blood-and-guts* picture with words. Yes, much easier said than done.

After penning my first article back in the early '90s, seeing my name in print and my story given life in the pages of a magazine, I became obsessed. I wrote a few articles each year and sent each carefully packaged manuscript/photo bundled (long before the days of the Internet) to each editor of the "big" bowhunting magazines. I longed to make it! Like clockwork I had each submission sent back, most often with a hastily scratched out, "Thanks but no thanks".

Undaunted, I pushed on. Finally, after getting some freebies published, in 1994 I sold an article for $25 to *Oregon Hunter* magazine. I made a copy of the check, which I still have today. I'd finally earned compensation as a writer! It was a start but I wanted more . . . it was all I thought about.

Biding my time, I hunted like a man possessed, scouted all off-season, took hundreds of photos of everything I did. I just about went broke paying for 1-hour photo developing so I could see them as soon as possible. I shot my bow incessantly, hung out at the bow shop talking about the sport I loved so much, and bought every hunting magazine I could find. After reading each article, invariably I thought to myself, "I can write as well as these guys, and, I probably hunt harder. Why do I keep getting shot down?" I told myself it was just because I didn't have connections and that was why I wasn't being given a chance. A victim of the good ol' boy system, I reasoned. I was young, impatient and, yeah, a touch delusional. *Blissful ignorance* are a couple words that come to mind.

In 1999 I decided I was going to take this big time writer deal into my own hands. I was going to write a book on the animal I grew up hunting, the Columbian blacktail. I couldn't find a publisher interested in my concept, which was a problem I easily solved. I'd just publish the dang thing myself. What did I know about self-publishing a book? Nothing. I'd learn on the fly. That was a huge mistake, one of many to come.

To self-publish *Bowhunting Trophy Blacktail* I had to borrow all the money for the project. Married, with a house payment and at the

***Overleaf:* I would trade packing my kid's animal for my arrowing the trophy of a lifetime any day. Here I'm packing out a nice forky my son Tanner anchored early in his hunting career. Over the years, he's proven to be a great shot.**

As a young hunter, Truett has shown to have ice in his veins. Every one of his kills has been filmed for TV. He got it done a couple times on bear in Alaska and in Hell's Canyon country of eastern Oregon. Also, in 2010 he made a great shot on this dandy Oregon Coast Range 4-point blacktail. My sore back has never felt so good.

time, two small kids, everything I made went to bills. To make matters worse, I decided this book was going to be first class all the way. I bought photos instead of using all my own, paid contributing authors and editors, went hardback with thick glossy paper and full color throughout. I wrote from the heart and the book swelled to more than 300 pages. I printed 5,000 copies which, with all expenses added, cost me $56,000. I had to borrow $21,000 from my wife's parents, Larry and Judy Smith. As a concrete contractor and secretary closing in on retirement, they did not have a bunch of extra cash to loan out for some poorly-thought-out-pipe dream. Believing in me, they did it anyway, as did my mom and stepdad and a couple of grandmas. I hit them all up, confidently telling them my book would sell, and I'd get them paid back in no time. Apparently, in *Camspeak*, "no time at all" meant *a number of years down the road.* After that bumpy start, I can happily say I've paid back everyone now and, incidentally, Larry and Judy were the first to be reimbursed as the books sold, with interest I might add. In the end, I never made a dime on the book, and with just a handful of that print run left it doesn't look like it is going to be the cash cow I was hoping for.

Big bank accounts and Teddy Roosevelt writing fame notwithstanding, I will always be very proud of *Bowhunting Trophy Blacktail.* I had some of the most accomplished and knowledgeable blacktail hunt-

I have been on a lot of tough bow hunts over the years and while many have been in much more rugged country, spot and stalk antelope hunting on film ranks right up near the top of the most difficult and frustrating challenges a bowhunter can take on.

ers in the world play a role in compiling my first book, and I will always be grateful for their generosity.

Since we are all friends here I can tell you there were times when I honestly wondered if I might have to file for bankruptcy on the heels of publishing my blacktail book. I am just grateful Tracey stayed true to the "in good or bad times, for rich or poor" just as she vowed (I had to remind her of that a few times). The positive fallout from taking the reins on the book project ultimately earned me opportunity in the writing world, which gave me a chance to earn free exposure for my book. Exposure promoted sales, which was exactly what I needed. Things were turning around.

Not long after finishing my *Bowhunting Trophy Blacktail* book Eastmans' hired me to moonlight as editor of their bowhunting magazine, which exploded in popularity and was a great vehicle for me to get my blue-collar-bowhunting, family-man, come-up-from-nothing-but-live-your-hunting-dreams story out there to other public-land hunters just like me. And, this persona wasn't an act, it was real, so I connected with what the industry called the "Average Joe" hunter because I was one.

In the midst of a decade-long run of being the editor of Eastmans' *Bowhunting Journal* magazine, I decided to try my hand at another book. The result of that decision is what you hold in your hands. Only this time I wasn't going to have to come up with all the capital on my own. I would write, Eastmans' would publish. That took the fundraising pressure off me so I could just focus on my vision for the book.

Now, here we are, on the 6th printing of *Backcountry Bowhunting*, five years after its initial release. The success of *Backcountry Bowhunting, A Guide to the Wild Side* has been hard for me to grasp. I still feel like that young bowhunter fighting for a chance, winning support and overcoming doubters. The amazing success of my second book has been humbling, and more than anything I am extremely grateful there are so many mountain loving bowhunters out there. I poured everything I had into this book, just as I do on a hunt in the mountains, but as a writer, you never really know if your words will hit home with the reader. I just hoped we'd sell a few thousand and what I wrote might help a few guys find success in the backcountry. No visions of grandeur here.

I can't tell you how many emails I've received about this book from readers who have been inspired to "dream bigger and achieve more." Guys who had never hunted the mountains before, but because my book armed them with knowledge, they had the confidence to get out of their comfort zone and after doing so found success on the backcountry bull or buck they long desired. As a writer I couldn't hope for any more.

I've made another observation in corresponding with many who have bought my book over these past few years. There are a lot of guys who've read the book and realistically, because of physical limitations, mental reservations, distance from the mountains or simply put, money, might never hunt the backcountry and that's ok. *Backcountry Bowhunting* is not just a how-to-hunt-remote-country book; it represents a dream. A goal to work toward for like-minded bowhunters who, after being immersed in my memoirs from the mountains, find themselves filled with the desire, realistic or not, to roam the lonely, rugged mountains of the West, bow in hand, wind in their face. To test themselves in a grand arena. Whether or not they ever make it so far as the trailhead, this calling has motivated many to make positive changes in their lives regarding fitness, diet, commitment and perspective. This type of influence is special and hard-earned. I know that, which is why I appreciate it so much. I never could have dreamed of such acceptance. To all of you who have shared your stories of self-improvement with me, thank you so much. Hearing from all of you means more than you know. You all motivate me to be the very best I can be every single day because I don't want to let you down.

What's amazing is even after having 20,000 copies of *Backcountry Bowhunting* on the streets, which makes it one of the best-selling

I traded in what many might call a "dream job" for something far more valuable—time. During Tanner's senior basketball season I was able to watch nearly every single one of his games, 27 in all, home and away. And, I was able to do this without packing my laptop to the games, as I had in years past, since working during the game was the only way I could stay caught up on emails and editing.

In the five years since *Backcountry Bowhunting* was originally released, much has changed. Namely, my kids. Taryn is turning into a young lady and Truett a handsome young man. My passion for bowhunting? That remains as strong as ever.

bowhunting books of all-time, my book is still in high demand. Who knows, at this rate maybe we can usurp Chuck Adams' *Life at Full Draw*? (Great book by the way—for a bowhunting junkie like me, it is a classic.) As it is, there isn't a day that goes by I don't receive numerous emails from guys wanting to know where they can get a copy of *Backcountry Bowhunting*. I recently have seen hunting forums with postings from guys talking about the difficulty of finding my book, lamenting that the only place they can find a copy of *Backcountry Bowhunting* is on eBay for $200.

If the book has sold and is still selling, why would there not be any available? A couple years ago I decided to quit working for Eastmans' in order to spend more time with my family. I've heard a lot of other theories regarding my decision to leave, but that was the true reason. I've been holding down a regular 9–5 at the local water and power utility here in town for the last 15 years, which meant serving as editor of Eastmans' *Bowhunting Journal* (EBJ) took up much of my "free" time. If EBJ left me a little time, I had family obligations to do my best with and after that, training as an endurance athlete for Under Armour. Part of my compensation package when leaving Eastmans' was that after 18 months I would get the full publishing rights to *Backcountry Bowhunting*. That brings us to today.

Welcome to the Collector's Edition of *Backcountry Bowhunting, A Guide to the Wild Side*. I decided to print this special edition of *Backcountry Bowhunting* because, as the publisher, I can do what I want, but mostly I did it to commemorate passing 20,000 copies printed, which is an impressive number for a specialty hunting book. For me, selling this many books is the realization of a dream I have literally chased for a lifetime.

For this limited edition I wanted to come out with something unique, and I feel my new "looking over sheep country" cover perfectly captures the spirit of the passionate backcountry bowhunter. Along with the striking cover I've added this 24-page bonus section, sharing a few powerful memories of hunts and accomplishments in my life since *Backcountry Bowhunting*'s release in 2006. This section is punctuated by the ultimate backcountry bowhunt, Dall sheep in the rugged mountains of Alaska, with my long-time hunting partner Roy Roth.

Most of all, I want to say thank you. Keep hunting hard and remember, *the greater the sacrifice the greater the reward.* –Cam

Cameron R. Hanes

www.cameronhanes.com

I grew up hunting Roosevelt elk. In fact a spike Roosevelt bull was my first ever bow kill back in 1989. I can't tell you how many times I envisioned arrowing a bull like this. Finally, in 2010 my dream became reality as I was able to arrow this Boone & Crockett monster Oregon 6 × 6. I had some help on this one. Thanks to the general elk hunting knowledge of Jody Cyr and the calling of Kevin Akers, who both stayed true to our mission of targeting this particular bull, we got it done. Thanks fellas.

It's been a good run. This big blacktail, which I killed in the rain back in 1988, was one of my last rifle kills. He is loaded up in the back of my beat up Toyota 2WD standard cab pickup, aka "The Blue Bomber." As a side note, this was the only vehicle Tracey and I owned when we first were married. After Tanner was born we would wedge a baby seat in between us, which made shifting that 5-speed four cylinder a challenge. Then thankfully Tracey's sister, instead of hauling it to the wrecking yard, gave us a gutless free-of-charge Ford Escort station wagon with simulated wood paneling that actually ran fairly well. You've heard of high-rollers? That was not us. The only animals I hunted back then were deer because elk tags, at almost $30, were too expensive.

I have hunted blacktail with Chad Montgomery for over 15 years. He has filmed me killing some of my best bucks. In 2010 the tables were turned as I filmed him arrowing this giant blacktail buck, one of the largest ever killed on video. You can see all the action on my DVD, *Bowhunting Trophy Blacktail.*

When I think of Roy Roth a few things come to mind . . . honest, tough, caring, optimistic and a natural leader. Roy has been one of my best friends since back in our high school days. There is no doubt Roy is a good hunter, but more than that he is a great man.

I have killed eight straight 6-point or better bulls. I pray that this run of luck continues. Hunting big bull elk has become quite a passion of mine, especially since I began working for the greatest conservation group in the world, the Rocky Mountain Elk Foundation.

Back in 2007 this photo was the Hanes family Christmas card. I can't think of a better one as I was able to have my family help me commemorate arrowing another good blacktail buck, which is the species I have hunted more than any other. Counting my young rifle hunting days and the last 23 years with the bow, I have been hunting Oregon blacktail for nearly 30 years.

I took this Wyoming backcountry bull on an amazing hunt I shared with good friend Nate Simmons. I enjoy hunting the mountains with Nate as much as anyone. He is a tough guy, good elk caller and does a great job on the camera. All that added up to our making a killer TV show on this hunt for Eastmans'.

This photo was taken during the Western States Endurance Run in 2010. I ran 100 miles in the mountains of California in 22 hours and 41 minutes. Why? To help toughen my mind and body for the challenge that is bowhunting mountains of the West.

I had the opportunity to run with the legendary Lance Armstrong in the 2008 Boston Marathon. This was quite a special trip as I travelled to Boston with one of my bowhunting heroes, Dwight Schuh, who ran Boston as well. I was able to run stride for stride with "the-greatest-endurance-athlete-of-all-time" for 13 miles before sneaking over the finish line 12 seconds ahead of him. Surreal experience and one I will never, ever forget.

Under Armour put me in contact with Wounded Warrior Kelly Gravitt from Washington. Then with the help of my good friend Wayne Endicott, we invited Kelly down to the annual bowhunting get together we have every July at The Bow Rack in Springfield, Oregon. In front of over 600 passionate bowhunters, we awarded Kelly a bowhunt for black bear in Alaska with Roy Roth and me. It was an honor to meet Kelly and show our gratitude for the sacrifices he's made serving our country.

Meeting others who love bowhunting as much as I do is one of the reasons I love putting on seminars throughout the West. I am so grateful for every person who takes time out to attend one of my shows, or buys one of my books or videos. Bowhunting has changed my life in so many ways, I can only hope that it will impact others in the positive manner it has me. Building the sport of bowhunting is something I am tirelessly motivated to do.

Alaska Dall Sheep Less Than Zero

By Cameron Hanes

Roy asked before the hunt, "So Cam, what makes you so different than everyone else who drew this tag?

The Setting

Towering, rugged Pioneer Peak, a 6,398-foot mountain in the Chugach Mountains, sits over the Knik River just nine miles south of Palmer, Alaska. Pioneer Peak is a prominent landmark in the Matanuska-Susitna Valley and the mountain I tackled looking for a Dall sheep to arrow. The climb to sheep country is brutal and one I won't soon forget. The starting elevation is basically at sea level, which is a lot (5-6,000-feet) lower than sheep country. And, since my hunt, the DS 140 West late season archery hunt, ran from Oct. 1-10th, I knew chances were we'd be dealing with hardcore mountain weather.

Sheep country and any "weather" is a bad combination, making the use of crampons and an ice ax mandatory at times. It also helps to have a savvy, woods-wise, tough and reliable partner. In pretty much a dream circumstance, my high school friend and long-time hunting partner, Roy Roth, had been working as an Alaska assistant guide. As most know, when hunting sheep in Alaska as a nonresident a guide is required. Being that Roy was working under the supervision of an Alaska contracting registered guide-outfitter meant he could personally guide me on my sheep hunt. This was my 15th hunting trip to wild Alaska over the years, but my very first for sheep and my very first with a guide.

All my other trips—Sitka blacktail, black bear, caribou and moose were do-it-yourself trips Roy and I set up together. Hunting the backcountry on our own is the kind of adventures we long for. Being able to share my first ever Dall hunt with Big Roy meant the world to me. We learned the backcountry bowhunting ropes together 22 years ago and have shared many campfires since. As I've heard Roy say, we are different in so many ways, yet exactly the same. Goal oriented to the max - a common attribute we share is being able to keep our eyes on the prize even when all hope seems lost. What I am certain of, there is no one I respect more in the mountains than Roy Roth. Our bowhunting passion has burned deep since we were young men, and this passion has offered us so many life-enriching moments and experiences it was only right that he be on the mountain with me for this monumental occasion.

While this ram surely isn't the largest Dall ever arrowed, he is a mature, 4½ year-old, Pope & Young animal (he green scores 133 6/8 . . . P&Y minimum is 120), loaded with great genetics, but most importantly, he is mine! I couldn't be more proud of my first bow ram and the mountain lessons I learned on this tough hunt.

I was nervous about this hunt from the get-go. Being a blue-collar bowhunter, raising a family and holding down your run-of-the-mill, 40-hour-a-week job, I knew full well that this could very well be the only sheep hunt I go on in my entire life. I was putting a lot of pressure on myself to make the most of it. Many have read of the intense mental and physical preparations I put myself through leading up to the hunt. I remember vividly writing a web-account titled, “Sheep & Suffering”, which can still be read in the archives on my website, www.cameronhanes.com. In that piece, in part I wrote . . .

Sheep & Suffering

Why run ultramarathons? Truthfully, I run out of my comfort zone (and, yes, an ultramarathon in the mountains will definitely get you out of your CZ) to not only build confidence but also to increase my ability to suffer. I want to hurt. I want to hurt in training because I know I will hurt during tough hunts. In almost every ultra I want to quit at some point and likewise on most of my hunts I have thought to myself something like, “This is stupid. I am never going to kill anything. I am wasting my time.”

Bowhunting is a test and so is endurance running in the mountains. How much pain and suffering will you go through for success? On most my hunts this is what has probably made the biggest difference. The ability to suffer more. This is not to say that I don’t enjoy my hunts. I do. I love that challenge that is bowhunting. But, I have yet to be on an easy bowhunt, so I train for epics. The polar opposite of an “easy” bowhunt is no doubt my upcoming Dall sheep hunt in Alaska. Sheep hunting is tough no matter what the time of year, but mine gets

even more daunting as this hunt takes place in the rugged mountains of Alaska in October. I am ramping up my training this year more than ever to combat what I know might very well be the most difficult bowhunting challenge I've ever faced. This is my first ever sheep tag and I am going to do absolutely everything in my power to head out of the mountains loaded down with meat and horns.

I love this journey. Seemingly every day I learn more and more what the human body is capable of if you work hard and believe!

The Numbers Don't Look Good

This hunt has been circled on my calendar for many months. While I've been focused and committed to success on all my previous hunts, I knew that for this one to end like I'd envisioned I was going to have to be at the very top of my game.

If my motivation to work hard ever waned, all I needed to do was look up the success rates for this hunt from seasons past. The hunt allowed the harvest of any sheep, but I was focused solely on a mature ram. For the five-year span I researched on the Alaska Fish & Game website (1997-2002) the most rams killed by bowhunters in one year was four. In 2000, there was one ram killed out of 100 tag holders. I've been around hunting long enough to know that 1% success is not high. Part of the reason is because the hunt is so late. Weather can make effective hunting nearly impossible and because the hunt is the last sheep hunt of the year, they have some history with us human hunters. In other words, they've been pressured. We learned first hand that it doesn't take much of a bump to push them into the cliffs, or "goat rocks" as Roy calls

As I scrambled over ice and snow toward my trophy, the only thought in my mind was, "I have to grab my ram before he goes over the cliff." I grabbed his horns just as the fatally hit ram started to go over the edge of a 400-foot drop off. Had he gone over the edge, I don't know if I would have ever recovered him.

them, which are completely inaccessible to man. So, best case, out of the 100 tags issued less than a handful of bowhunters would end the hunt holding sheep horns in their hands.

To Roy's question before the hunt, "So Cam, what makes you so different than everyone else who drew this tag? Why are you going to be one of two or three guys who tags out?" Hmmm . . . good question? All I came up with was, "Because Big Man, it's no surprise to you that I pretty much suck at most things, but you know, in the mountains with my bow, for whatever reason I can get it done. Maybe this is what I was born to do? Scratch that last part. That sounds pretty stupid actually. What I do know, on this hunt, success is my only option. I am not even putting any energy or thought into not getting it done. I will tag a ram!"

The Hunt is On

I will save the boring details of the four-hour quad-burning, calf-busting, devil's-club-thrashing, slow, step-after-painful-step hike to a bench where we set up camp halfway up the mountain the day before the opener. Just after shrugging off my 50-plus-pound pack I spotted sheep. I put the spotting scope on the big group of ewes and lambs excited to see them!!! They were miles away still, but then I noticed a couple other sheep closer to me, and one of them was a ram. He was only a half curl but man I was pumped. I couldn't wait for daybreak and the opening of sheep season.

Looking off the other side of the mountain, we could see town. I will say it is weird how it seemed we were on top of the world looking down on the valley below, so close to civilization but at the same time we may as well have been a million miles away. It can almost give you a false sense of security as you can see the lights of the city and headlights moving along the highway. But make no mistake, if you got in trouble on the mountain, there is nothing anyone in the valley could do for you. Alaska sheep country is as unforgiving a place as there is, regardless of the view.

Morning broke and it was beautiful. Sun in sheep country is a godsend. After another four-hour leg of packing camp to the top of the mountain the next day and after putting on many miles hunting some of the roughest country I've ever roamed, I spotted another ram, bedded in perfect position for stalk and by himself!!! We were filming the hunt, but I was real nervous about two guys (me and the cameraman) trying to sneak into bow range on my "once-in-a-lifetime hunt". Opting to play it safe, I had the cameraman, Phil Quick, stay to film from our vantage point, which, while not over-the-shoulder would still give him a great view of the stalk and all the action. And, little did I know at the time, but the stalk was going to be sketchy.

I tried to drop in on the ram from a number of different routes, but couldn't find one that was humanly possible. Finally, though, I took a chance and after lowering my gear with a rope, I was able to latch on to a cliff enough to lower myself to a height I could jump from. From there I was good to go and actually couldn't believe how easy of shot I had earned. As I closed in, I had little doubt I'd arrow my ram. Just as predicted, I indeed arrowed my ram. Yes, it was a kill shot, but I knew full well there would be some blood-trailing involved to recover my trophy. Gut-wrenchingly, I topped off my "perfect stalk" with a very much less than perfect shot.

At the chip shot range of 23 yards, directly above the ram, I tried to sneak my arrow over a rock into the ram's vitals. Just after release I heard an almost inaudible "tick" as my arrow arced towards the ram. A blade had caught stone, and deflected into the ram, low. I made a bad hit! I had confidence I could thread the needle. Maybe too much confidence it seems.

I pride myself in my dedication to the sport of bowhunting and my shooting (Yup, I was the same guy who wrote an article titled,

Sheep country and hardcore weather is a bad combination making the use of crampons and an ice ax mandatory at times. We lucked out on this hunt and were able to set up our tarps and bivy sacks right off the top of the mountain. I arrowed my ram very near the peak of Pioneer. It was an awesome setting. I owe Mother Nature big time for giving me a break.

"Striving for Perfection" in regard to bow shooting) and in spite of this, I made a bad hit on my dream animal. My goal in the discipline of bowhunting is perfection and I work toward it every day of the year. I had failed miserably and I was sick about it. I thought about one of my favorite Mike Tyson quotes—"Everyone has a plan until they get punched in the mouth."

Blowing a 23-yard shot on a record book Dall ram was definitely not in the "plan" I had envisioned thousands of times and, yes, it felt like I'd been punched in the mouth and gut for that matter. I sat on that lonely ridge and reflected on my failure after watching a puff of long, white, winter-coat sheep hair float off in the wind after being cut loose by my razor sharp broadhead on impact.

Did I Not Sacrifice Enough?

Walking over and picking up the hair, I inspected it and wondered, "is this the closest I'll ever get to my ram?" My heart ached as I watched the ram intently through my binos as he slowly navigated his way through the rocks. I questioned, could I have sacrificed more? Was I ill-prepared for crunch time? Did my focus wane because I felt the shot was a gimme? My goal is to be on autopilot, but I didn't remember "picking a spot," which is of course a step of the aiming process I obsess over. I thought of all the effort it took to get 23 yards from my ram. The hours of shooting, miles of running, logistics, travel, the time away from my wife and kids, the money, humping it up the mountain, trudging through the snow, living in a Spartan camp in extreme conditions, etc.

I knew in my heart that I would NEVER, EVER have a better chance at a Dall. It simply doesn't get any easier than a 23-yard, broadside, all-the-time-in-the-world shot on a ram looking downhill away from me. How could I screw that up? Such is the exact situation where I expect myself to be infallible. I don't remember ever feeling lower. Emotionally I was less than zero.

However, I have learned over the years that successful bowhunting is more about overcoming obstacles than anything else. Yes, my lip had been bloodied. I was depressed, and I let myself down big time, but I had no other choice but to suck it up and get to work on what was sure to be a tough blood-trailing job. Without saying a word about it, Roy and I were on the exact same page. We were prepared to give all we had to make it right. More than anything, I owed it to the animal. I think respecting the life of the animals we hunt is THE most important part of the hunter's creed.

Time to Get to Work

We got on blood, just as we had so many times over the past two decades of bowhunting. "Blood, blood, got blood, good blood here . . ." Every once in a while a guy catches a break, and I did this time. I was so thankful there was an ample amount of crimson colored blood staining the powdery snow and splashed over rocks marking the ram's path. In the steep, rugged country we kept working, unraveled it and eventually I was able to sneak in and finish off my trophy of a lifetime. He died at the edge of a sheer drop off we estimated to be 400–500 feet. I made the final shot at 25 yards and hustled down to him over snow-covered ice. I grabbed his horns as he began to slump and slide over. Struggling, I held him as he kicked violently in his final death throes. I thought for certain he was going over the edge and potentially I would join him in a freefall to the snow covered rocks far below.

Looking back, it was a highly questionable decision to try to hold him inches, and one false move from certain death, but this was MY sheep. I had waited a lifetime for this moment. I held a dream in my hands and I wasn't going to let it go for anything. And yes, for those wondering, we caught this entire sequence on film.

Finally, after about a minute of struggle, he died. I was out there with my sheep, by myself, fighting to hold him as most of his body hung over the rock edge. I knew I wasn't going to be able to hold him long. As the cold mountain breeze swept over the mountain, I wedged his ground-side horn into a crack in the rock, using my body weight to anchor him while I fought to get my pack off. After slipping it off, with one hand I unzipped a pocket and fished out a length of nylon cord. Throwing the cord with my left hand, while holding my trophy with everything I had, crampons digging in, I pseudo-lassoed one of his back legs and pulled it toward me. Letting go of the cord I quickly snatched his leg. By using every ounce of strength I had, I was able to somehow yard his body up on the small rock ledge. I don't know how I did it, but I did. So, yeah, the shot and recovery weren't textbook, but I got it done.

In the treacherous conditions, Roy and Phil methodically made their way down to me where we then snapped a few cherished photos, shot some video and broke my ram down. As you can probably guess, it was a VERY long, tough, slow hike up and over the top of that mountain loaded down with my sheep and gear, but such is sheep hunting I suppose. Roy had to hack footholds with his ice axe virtually every step back up the mountain. Each step took intense focus, as there was simply no room for error. No such thing as an easy sheep hunt and I am thankful for that. Because of the sheer difficulty in arrowing a Dall ram in the unforgiving country he lives, the accomplishment is as sacred as it gets for bowhunters.

As luck would have it, we got off the hill just in time it seems. We had a few days of incredible Alaska weather to sheep hunt. The day I killed, the weather began to turn and on the way down the mountain the next day, loaded with my ram, camp and hunting gear, it was snowing and so foggy we couldn't see 50 feet. Roy said that rain, snow and fog are what you can expect typically in sheep country and that during normal October conditions we never would have been able to camp where we did. We set up our tarps and bivy sacks right off the top of the mountain and I hunted very near the peak of Pioneer. It was an awesome setting . . . I owe Mother Nature big time for giving me a break.

Trophy of My Lifetime

And while he surely isn't the largest Dall ram ever arrowed, he is a mature, 4½ year old, Pope & Young animal (he green scores 133 6/8...P&Y minimum is 120), loaded with great genetics, but most importantly . . . he is mine! I couldn't be more proud of my first bow ram and the mountain lessons I learned on this tough hunt. From less than zero to one of my hunting life's sweetest rewards. This is an achievement I thought I'd never, ever realize. Dreams can come true and one did that special day on Pioneer Peak . . . October 2nd, my Birthday Ram!!!

Note—I would like to give a special thanks to Irene Kemp and Ian Thomas of the Chugach State Park for helping me navigate through the filming permit process to film in the park. The Chugach State Park is an amazing setting that deserves to be protected. I am thankful I was given permission to share photos and video from my once-in-a-lifetime trip. Commercial Activities Permit #08-128.

Lastly, I want to give a special shout out to my friend Phil Quick, Lower 48 sheep fanatic, who tagged along to experience his first-ever Dall sheep adventure. He was a great camp mate, tough dude and really helped me capture some powerful photos and memorable video—especially, those clips of me wrestling my ram on that snowy ledge.

felt so good. I had been blessed to be sure. I remember thinking now I could have my very own elk horn belt buckle. Hey, I was 20 years old—life and dreams were simple back then.

As this story alludes, I started off hunting areas that because of logging roads, even if they restricted motorized vehicle use, were more easily accessible than where I hunt now. It didn't take me too long to figure out that

Just like with this bull, I have killed many animals at the tail end of long wilderness hunts.

if it was easy for me to get into the elk country I was hunting, it was easy for everyone else as well. Getting away from the crowds was the biggest reason I started heading as deep as I could into the most vast wilderness area I could find. That being said, I learned a lot about elk while hunting off of logging roads and about how they respond to pressure. Besides, this was the only elk hunting I had access to. I didn't have enough money or time to head to the backcountry. I did the best I could at the time, and became a better hunter because of it.

Blood, Sweat and Bulls

By Cameron R. Hanes

Originally appeared in Eastmans' Bowhunting Journal's *premier issue.*

It had all the makings of the classic Shakespearean tragedy. The *it* I am referring to is the '99 elk season here in Oregon, which from my perspective, definitely was rank with the impending stench of heartbreak some five days into an "all or nothing" wilderness sojourn. For many, my alleging to such emotions tied to a sport that is supposed to be enjoyable might seem a touch melodramatic, but to the cynics I reply, "You just don't understand." Tragedy defined: trag·e·dy a. A drama or literary work in which the main character is brought to ruin or suffers extreme sorrow, especially as a consequence of a tragic flaw, a moral weakness, or an inability to cope with unfavorable circumstances.

As the main character in this literary work, believe me when I tell you I was indeed suffering extreme sorrow while trying to cope with an unfavorable circumstance. To expound, this hunt is my season. If I am not successful in arrowing a bull on this annual Do-It-Yourself trek into Oregon's largest wilderness area, The Eagle Cap, I am in for a very long off-season. You see, my fall calendar does not include multiple out-of-state hunts, essentially allowing me to jet set around the West in search of an aspirant bull on which to tie my tag. I have 10 days to down a bull elk—period.

Inexplicably, during the first five days of this hunt I had yet to see an elk. Not a bull mind you, but an elk, any elk. As this real life tragedy is now probably becoming clearer to the outsider, my quandary becomes painfully obvious when one considers that on hunts prior to this, which encompassed six separate trips into this beautifully remote high-alpine elk Mecca, I had never went a full day without seeing an elk.

On most days I was in bow range of elk, some days intimate with bulls, all the while biding my time for a slam-dunk opportunity at the "big boy." As it was, it seemed my theory of hunting fewer elk (there are a number of areas in the state that harbor more elk) with very little or no two-legged competition (I have yet to see another hunter off the trail during my years of hunting this wilderness) some 14 miles into an extremely rugged wilderness area had finally gotten the best of me. People have told me that I work too hard while hunting too few elk, and to this my standard reply is somewhere along the lines of, "I would rather hunt a fewer number of animals, if I am assured that I won't see another person." This is simply the right mix for me. Furthermore, if I had to have a vice, hunting too hard is one I can live with.

However, with the effort and planning involved in making this hunt happen, if it goes sour, it's "too bad, so sad!" Pulling stakes and heading off to another area is not an option as that would waste what precious little time I had to down a bull.

Back to the present: What really had me miffed was the fact that I had visited and/or glassed all of my old haunts during these first five days of trudging around this unforgiving wilderness. Places that before this season I would have wagered my youngest son on the odds of whether or not I'd see elk. Not only was I covering a minimum of 10 miles a day, but also I had glassed thousands of acres of prime elk habitat at elevations between 4,000 and 8,000 feet. The results were in a word—ludicrous!

During the many minutes upon minutes, hours upon hours and days upon days that I spent talking, coaching, arguing, belittling, brainstorming and second-guessing myself, I wondered if my partners on this hunt, Tim Thompson and South Cox, had fared any better. I had not seen them since wilderness wrangler, Barry Cox, dropped us and our gear off five long days ago. Tim was an old veteran of The Eagle Cap, having been back here with me before, but he'd yet to lash his tag on the heavy antler of an elusive bull. South had never hunted elk before, but had mucho wilderness experience and lived what many would call more that his share of successful bowhunts sprinkled throughout the last third of his 30 years of life.

While walking the top of a huge ridge that ranged for miles at elevations between 7,000 and 8,000 feet, I had an unrivaled vantage point from which to spot game. I could look into the hole where only two years prior I had arrowed my best Rocky Mountain bull elk, a sweeping 6x6. I could glass the natural funnel where just last season I positioned myself for an opening day lunch break and was rewarded with the "Ambling Bear Special."

I set down my trail mix and arrowed the beautiful chocolate/blond black bear as he picked his way through the boulder-strewn saddle where I had chosen to take my midday sojourn. These lasting memories carried me through yet another "elkless" morning, and although I did get an opportunity on a very nice 4x4 mulie with matching eyeguards, this stalk ended along with my cover some 100 yards from the velvet buck. As I lay in the dirt and rock, sun beating down on my weary body, and watched the buck slowly meander directly away from me, I found myself wondering if I might go home with all of my tags (elk, deer, bear and cougar) intact. An unsettling thought to be sure.

Gathering my gear, I slowly made my way back up over the top of the ridge and began picking my way toward where, a couple days prior, I had found the freshest elk sign on the mountain. I would lunch and perhaps nap in a spot where I could glass a few basins, knowing that sooner or later I would end this elk spotting famine. Just then my forlorn gaze caught movement a couple hundred yards up the barely distinguishable trail.

Bringing my Leupolds up and steadying them on top of my upper bow limb I focused on five mulie bucks feeding downhill across the trail. The group consisted of a good hard-horned 4x4, a small 4x4, a good 3x3 and two forked-horns. The fear of getting shutout coupled with the fact I had never arrowed a mulie buck on a wilderness hunt solidified my decision at the time to arrow any of the deer.

The stalk was cake and before I knew it I was 43 yards from an unidentified buck as he racked his horns on a bushy sapling. My arrow flew true and as the buck lifted his head, wild-eyed out of the vegetation and began his death sprint, I quickly counted four points total. Although momentarily surprised, I was not disappointed. I would have loved to down one of the bigger bucks, but I will never downplay the significance of taking the life of an animal just because of the size of his headgear. I was happy and have great memories when this episode is recalled. After the photo shoot I quickly boned the buck and hauled the meat back a couple miles to a patch of snow where I would stash it overnight while I searched for elk.

That evening and the following morning were uneventful in terms of elk sightings, so as day six sped by, I loaded up my 70 pounds of meat and headed back the six miles to base camp for the first time. The closer I got to camp, the more anxious and hopeful I was that either Tim or South was there. I wanted an update and the chance to exchange stories and field notes. A couple hundred yards from camp I could catch fleeting glimpses of the tent and could have sworn I saw movement, yes, someone is there, it is...South.

He heard my footfalls and looked up as I called out, "...and the killing has begun..." while swiveling around allowing him to view my buck's rack. His unsure response followed, "Uh, alright,"

likely wondering why in the heck I shot that little buck. It was then I spied the rack of a good 5x5 bull leaning against the tent. To my surprise, the killing had already begun prior to the arrowing of my young buck. South had downed a bull the day before my harvest. A P&Y class bull elk on his first wilderness elk hunt. That *dog!*

We spent the early afternoon eating real food (I had taken about three days worth of pseudo food and had been gone six—you do the math.) and drinking quart after quart of water while exchanging hunting tales. It seemed South had been in on elk since day one. He missed a big 6x6 our first day in and passed up a number of lesser bulls in between that initial miss and the downing of his bull.

South had seen 70 some elk thus far and 12 bulls. I was a tinge on the jealous side understandably, considering this was my elk area and he was supposed to be an elk hunting rookie. However, I will say after hearing of his travels, South is "The Man" when it comes to wilderness hunting. This country has broken many a good men and South came in blind, hunted hard, covered miles upon miles of ground, lived with the elk and ultimately arrowed his bull from 35 yards in the 2:00 p.m. heat after spotting it at noon.

Many would-be wilderness hunters would have been back at camp licking the wounds from the harsh environment, lamenting about the sweltering and incredibly dry conditions. Granted the rutting activity was slow and we didn't know it at the time, but the tagging of a bull is a battle many of archers across the West would lose this archery season, as the bulls simply were not responding to the call. Apparently, the heat had the rut stymied. Nonetheless, South made it happen, which in my opinion is what bowhunting is all about, defying the odds!

I filled South in on my hunt thus far and my plan for the remainder of the hunt, which included much of the same for me as I was still very confident in the areas I had been concentrating on. I felt the odds were increasingly swinging my way. Sooner or later I would find the elk on my side of this huge wilderness. I had seen a number of bucks besides the group I arrowed mine out of and the 170" buck I stalked before that.

This information caught South's attention considering he still was packing a valid deer tag.

I offered an invitation and after refueling we loaded up our packs and headed out together. Normally, I hunt alone, which is how I like it, as I am not there on a camping trip with my friends, I am there exclusively to bring home a bull. But, from what I surmised, South wouldn't be slowing me up at all (an understatement) and his extra set of glass would give me added spotting power, which might parlay itself into opportunity.

That evening we glassed up mountain goats, bighorn sheep, bucks and just before dark elk! What an awesome day. The 356,000-acre Eagle Cap Wilderness is as wild as wild gets and one of the most picturesque places in Oregon. What a setting for a late summer bowhunt.

South and I bivouacked out on a small rock shelf, which overlooked an extremely large expanse of rugged, elk friendly country. From our vantage, we spied three herds of elk and fell asleep that night 256 yards (via laser rangefinder) from eight bighorns, with bugles wafting through the crisp clear mountain air.

At first light the next morning I set up my spotting scope to gauge the size of the respective herd bulls and make a plan for the day. We selected the most stalk friendly mature bull and planned a tentative approach route. This route would cover 10 miles and 10 hours from 6:00 a.m. to 4:00 p.m.

Many would have parlayed this stalk over into two days if even attempting it, but it is my experience when wilderness hunting that you have got to jump on an opportunity when you can. Consider, I had not even been within bow range of one elk yet and I was now into my seventh day. I had to make something happen. The stalk would be tortuous physically as we were at 8,000 feet, had to drop to 4,000 and then climb back to the herd's elevation which was at 6,300. The 4,000-foot drop was considerably worse than the climb, as my 60-pound pack helped disintegrate further my already fatigued quads and advance the sorry state of my feet.

Despite the rudimentary challenges of simply closing the distance, by 4:00 p.m. we had successfully skirted over and past a lonely spike bull and a raghorn four-point, which now put us close to my target bull.

Taking off our boots and donning Baers feet we gingerly moved toward a large stand of mature timber that the elk fed into and thusly we surmised should serve as the herd's daytime bedding area. With me in the lead, South shadowed my travel while packing our boots. I followed the herd's fresh tracks on an ancient elk trail which sidehilled into their cool, north-facing sanctuary.

Fresh scat and rubs marked their path as we inched forward, wary not to get picked off by one of those meddling cows or calves. I spotted the bull at the exact same moment South jabbed me with his bow. He saw the bull, which was bedded and looking downhill, and wanted to alert me before the beast caught our movement. Instantly, we collapsed to the ground and surveyed the situation.

The bull was bedded straight downhill from us at an extremely steep angle. This can pose judgment problems for an archer, which was compounded by the fact that my rangefinder was picking up some small tentacles of brush about ¾ of the way to the bull. I couldn't get an accurate reading and my whispers to South for an estimate went unanswered, as he, telling me later, didn't want to be held accountable for any errors in yardage judging.

I felt like the bull was a touch over 50 yards away, well within range of my equipment and ability, but given his downward position, I drew, anchored and held my 40-yard pin just off his spine. This is where I wanted the arrow to enter given the angle, as the broadhead would travel through the lungs and heart and exit the bottom of the bull's chest. My whole hunt and season came down to this one defining moment.

My release was fluid and the arrow hit exactly where I wanted—money! I could not have walked down there and stuck it in any better. South was lying beside me watching the whole show through his binoculars and the hit of my arrow was immediately followed by his exclaiming, "Oh-my-God, Dude! What an arrow!" With emotions peaking I gave a quick hug to my partner on this hunt and collapsed to the earth like a wet rag staring into the treetops. What an ordeal. What an awesome ordeal. I was emotionally and physically drained.

We excitedly exchanged guesses of the bull's size. I knew he was a pretty good one for this country, which was of little consequence now. The woods were silent and given our certainty of the shot placement we did not wait too long before inching down to inspect the bull's last bed and commence on the short blood trail. The big, P&Y class 5x5 went about 100 yards before piling up in a tangle of brush. South and I took a ton of pictures and began the boning out process, which wasn't finished until after 9:00 p.m.

Unfortunately, the day wasn't over yet as we had to get up to the top of the huge basin we were in to call the packer on South's cell phone. We felt obligated to alert Barry of our bountiful harvest to ensure he brought enough stock to haul us, and our take-out. My bull was 21 miles from our trailhead and South's was 16. This fact alone added another day onto our trip as the packing out process had to be a two-day affair. This, The Longest Day On Earth, finally ended at around midnight. It took all of about four tenths of a second for me to fall asleep and/or pass out from exhaustion.

I don't know whether Barry was impressed or irritated, but he and his stock did an incredible job. I don't think he expected us dorky looking drop-camp bowhunters to down this much game. Surprise! Not to mention, South's boned out bull was in some of the steepest country I have ever seen elk in and Barry's Spanish Mustangs hauled that thing out with nary a hitch. The day spent getting to the bulls and getting them back to base camp was quite an endeavor in itself, but nothing in comparison to hauling the beasts out on our backs or by way of llamas, as has been the case in years prior.

This hunt encompassed all of the intangible qualities I want in a bowhunt. Indescribable emotional experiences like loneliness, fatigue, exultation, despair, passion and triumph are what it is all about for me. This hunt had all that and more as it also included my first "Wilderness Double," which was accomplished by releasing just two well-placed arrows. A hunt that started out sharing similarities to a Shakespearian tragedy ended up as my "feel good story of the year" which was a pleasant and welcome transformation. Sharing all this with good friends who second as good hunting partners made it even better. The only thing that would have rounded out the trip would have been if Tim somehow could have downed an animal. He was close and had some good opportunities but just could not close the deal. That too is an integral part of backcountry bowhunting!

Hunt Report Card – Hindsight is always 20/20

What I learned on this hunt: This hunt more than any other taught me the importance of staying strong mentally. I remember it being very hard to not throw in the towel as I thought to myself, "Hell, I can get shut out and not see any elk much closer to home."

South Cox made good on his first backcountry elk hunt. I on the other hand struggled.

What I did right: Obviously sticking it out was a good decision. I was feeling more pressure than normal on this trip because we were just getting ready to launch the very first issue of EBJ. I knew that everyone was counting on me to kill something on this D-I-Y trip and write a good feature for the magazine. This was the first of many pressure packed hunts I've been on over the years. I have since come to use the increased expectations as motivation.

What I did wrong: Looking back on it now some years down the road I realize there are a few mistakes I made. Firstly, I probably should have been more steadfast in my commitment to shooting only a record class buck. I let the tough hunt get to me and shot a smaller animal than I should have. I was and am still proud of the clean one shot kill and of the great eating meat, but I simply should have been more patient. I am certain I could have killed one of the bigger bucks in the herd in that situation—it was perfect as they were unaware of my presence and slowly feeding toward me.

Secondly, I was looking for elk where they had been and not where they were. As I mentioned in the story it was a very dry year, the hottest and driest in years. That meant the meadows and feed up high on the ridgetops were burnt up. Normally, the elk bedded in the timber and fed up in the evenings, staying on top all night rutting then work their way back down to the timber in the mornings. During this hunt they stayed low in the chutes where the water and the lush feed was and did not come up at all. I wasted a week walking and glassing the tops wondering where the elk were. Finally, I found them lower on the mountain and killed a decent bull, but if I would have been smarter about the weather situation and how it affected elk movement, I could have had more opportunities and perhaps killed a bigger bull. And, likely I wouldn't have killed the "Frustration Buck" just because it stepped out first.

Grade: While dedicated to success and showing some drive I severely lacked in the intelligence department. **B–**

This Pope & Young Roosevelt bull was my first 'trophy." Notice the bear claws glued to my quiver hood. I am proof positive that bowhunters can be quirky and superstitious. I am convinced the bear claws made the difference on this hunt.

Defining a Trophy

The evolving big bull hunter

The first rung in regard to a trophy bull for the public land hunter is a big 5x5 or likely a 6x6 in the 260–280-inch range P&Y. This will typically be a 3- to 4-year-old bull and if he is at the lower end of the scale, toward 260 inches, he will probably not be a herd bull. A five-point in this class will have a large looking frame and decent length tines. A six-point will have tines that appear shorter, but if they're all there and fairly uniform in length you will make "The Book."

The second-level trophy bull is an animal in the 290- to 310-inch range. This will be a 4- to 5-year-old bull and because he hasn't fully matured, a bull of this size is only 75 percent of his max potential for body weight. This size of bull will almost always be an average-sized 6x6.

The third trophy bull category is 310 to 330, which is when the animal really starts to fill out body-wise. He will be five to six years old now and will have developed 85 to 90 percent of his maximum body weight. This size of bull is really starting to look like the classic, "Big Bull." His fourth points or sword points, at around 14", are longer than the other tines and the main beams stretch the tape to about 45".

For the D-I-Y public land bowhunter a bull like this 6x5 Pope & Young qualifier is a nice goal for many years.

The top o' the heap in my opinion for the blue-collar bowhunter is a bull that exceeds 330 Pope & Young. This will be a bull that is usually at least seven years old and looks like a monster in body size and antler configuration with 16" to 18" fourths and main beams that will be approaching 50". For most of us, deciding whether to shoot this bull is a no-brainer if there ever was one. If you have a chance at a bull you think might be around 330, quit field judging and figure out a way to get within bow range of that beast.

There is Trophy Hunting and Then There is *Trophy Hunting*

For most bowhunters, a Pope & Young record book bull is the goal and a worthy one at that. For some though, a 260-inch bull isn't quite enough. The second level of trophy hunting is usually a 300-class bull. I don't know too many guys who would pass on a 300–320 P&Y bull, but believe me, there are a handful out there who would and do regularly. Some even pass on bulls that exceed the 350 P&Y range if you can believe that!

I only know a handful of these upper echelon guys: Randy Ulmer, bowhunter extraordinaire, and Dan Evans, of Trophy Taker fame come to mind. Another bowhunter who has let a number of BIG bulls walk while waiting for a monster is Jeremy Houston out of Utah. He is a hardcore

In my opinion, the evolving trophy bowhunter should start with trying to kill any bull, then a mature 5-point, then a 6x6 Pope & Young bull. The next step is a bull like this one, which is a trophy near the 300-inch mark.

bowhunter if there ever was one and spends an amazing amount of time out in the woods learning the ways of not only the elk, but deer as well. Here are some thoughts he recently shared with me in regard to hunting Jurassic-sized bull elk.

I asked Jeremy if my take was accurate in that calling in these ultra bulls is not the easiest way to kill them with a bow. His reply was, "You nailed it Cameron. No calls for the big boys. My experience is you are better off simply trying to ease in there, spot and stalk style, and whack 'em," which is exactly what he did last year in Arizona.

After packing into a remote area, some four miles, he snuck to within 38 yards of a 7x7 hog. A short time after releasing a perfectly placed arrow he was holding antler in his hands and lots of it. Jeremy's 2005 bull grosses just over 383, and with an estimated 20 to 23 inches that had been broken off of a few tines, his bull would have grossed 403 to 406 Pope & Young. Wow.

"On my hunt last year in Utah (2004), we called in a lot of 300–350 class Pope & Young bulls, but no ultra big ones," remembers Houston. "I made

Truthfully, I think a 330 Pope & Young bull is the top of the heap for the blue collar bowhunter. In my home state of Oregon, a 350 bull like this one is about like finding a needle in a haystack. Of course anything is possible, but my advice is set realistic goals and work your way up to the top of the trophy hunting ladder.

a big mistake and played my game too tentatively on a 390-plus bull that I think if I would have just ran in on him, I would have got a chance at him. As it was, I was too timid and he eventually got away." Jeremy did make good on his Utah tag last year by arrowing a 375 bull. That'll do.

"I have never had a problem sneaking up on elk with the wind in my favor. In my experience," Jeremy continues, "it seems that most 370-plus P&Y bulls are old and pretty call shy. This is not saying they won't answer a call; they just won't come in."

Jeremy has killed three good bulls the last three years (the two mentioned above and a 340 P&Y 6x5 – Idaho 2003) and not one of them was called in. In his opinion, really big bulls need to be ambushed or like I refer, "Go old school on 'em."

Jeremy adds, "I also think a lot of it has to do with the hunting pressure on the herd as well. I am sure there are a number of 370 plus P&Y bulls called in every year and killed in low hunting pressure areas as well, just not in country that I hunt."

Brush Country Bulls

By Cameron R. Hanes

Editor, Eastmans' Bowhunting Journal • *Colorado 2005*

The brush country of southern Colorado that Guy Eastman and I hunted the fall of 2005 is elk hunting heaven if there ever was one. Guy hunted the week before I arrived for my hunt on September 13th and while looking for a big bull to hunt at the same time scouted for me, which was pretty sweet. Calling his cell phone from my home each evening the days prior to my departure, I would get a play-by-play of the day's action and if I wasn't excited enough already, this definitely put me over the top.

Our hunt took place on the famed Hill property owned by Bobby and Dottie Hill. I personally have never hunted in such incredible elk country especially in the company of such great elk hunters. And, granted, I am a D-I-Y guy at heart that loves the challenge of bowhunting public land, however, when the opportunity came up to hunt and live a Primos video-like experience firsthand, I was more than happy to give it a shot. I might be dumb but I am not stupid. No one in their right mind would pass up a chance to hunt this country, and honestly, I felt more pressure on this hunt than any of my solo D-I-Y adventures because of the expectations. I knew everyone expected me to come through in the clutch and arrow a monster. As we all know, this is easier said than done. Fair chase bowhunting anything, anywhere is tough.

In 2005 Guy Eastman and I experienced a surreal week of elk hunting in Colorado. Knowing I must have been dreaming, I had to pinch myself to make certain it was real life.

From missed shots to boiling over emotions to swirling winds, there is much than can stand in the way of success. I knew full well that this hunt would be the cornerstone for Eastmans' new bowhunting DVD and that a chance to hunt here might never be thrown my way again. The pressure was on and I loved it. Proving myself to, most importantly, myself is what drives me.

As a Do-It-Yourselfer, anytime I have been required to hunt with a guide, I have always had kind of mixed feelings. It definitely changes things in my opinion as I have found that what I am willing to do and the extreme measures I am willing to take for even a sliver of a chance at success is not exactly on the same page as everyone else. Bottom line, hunting with a guide is definitely different and not ever my first choice. I feel handcuffed in many respects.

However, when it is required as it is in Canada or in the case of the Hill Ranch, being accompanied by a guide is all part of the deal. I will say though, on this Colorado elk hunt, I got lucky big time in the guide department. Our guides on this trip were brothers, Pat and Mike Lancaster, who are hands down two of the best in the elk hunting business. Words couldn't do justice to what these two know about elk. In addition, Mike Eastman was on hand to provide guidance and film Guy's hunt. With all of this elk hunting experience was there any way the hunt could go wrong? Of course there was. As we know, it is called hunting for a reason. As I alluded to before, it is common knowledge how tough it is to kill a big bull with an arrow, especially when the goal is to capture the entire hunt in vivid Technicolor made possible by our brand new Canon XL-2 video camera.

With all of bowhunting's many variables there are a plethora of "little things" that can doom success. Throwing a camera and another human in the mix to run said camera is a little like trying to put out a fire with gasoline. But, like I always say, if it were easy everyone would do it right? I like my hunts hard, serious and meaningful. It is the tough ones that make us who we are.

A place like this has all the elements of a successful hunt, which means little unless Guy and I do our part. We were committed to hunting only the most mature and biggest bulls of this area. Passing up mature animals waiting for "The One" can be a surefire way to head back to camp with an empty pack frame and home with a tag intact. But, as trophy hunters, this is the challenge that Guy and I are drawn to and seek out. Guy, who was hunting with his custom Weatherby .30-378 has had the pleasure of hunting the Hill property before and this trip proved his previous success here in years past was no aberration.

Imagine if you will Guy passing on a number of 320- to 340-class bulls before finding the one he wanted, a 360-class monster. Then, patterning the big bull with the patience of a polar bear sitting over a seal hole in the ice, Guy waited. For four days he waited before the shy bull finally exposed himself. The big 6x7 had holed up in a secluded pocket and was only found because Mike, Pat and Guy spent hours behind their Swarovskis waiting and watching. Finally, though, the reward was worth the effort and the big bull, with sweeping antlers and a massive top end, stepped out from the brush about 250 yards away from Guy's position on a parallel ridge. While Mike filmed, Guy did his job and the rest is history.

Then it was my turn. The first morning out, we called in a smallish six-point to about 10 yards, but decided to let him walk. That was easy and it made great film. Later that day, a pretty good 320 P&Y 6x7 crashed in and stopped 15 yards from me. He stared down my tiny statue-like form sitting in the middle of the forest for a few long minutes before apparently deciding that he did not like me? I say this because then he tried to bugle the face off of my skull with a bugle-scream that began sounding like a jet engine ramping up then dropped down a few octaves, but kept all its force to a sound that resembled a 500-pound African lion roaring his dominance to other jungle dwellers. That was intense. When watching on TV you'll probably have to turn the volume down a few clicks. The bull then turned and stopped again at 15 yards quartering to me. I ended up passing on all these less than perfect chances, as it was the first day and he was not quite to my goal of a 330 bull.

So, the hunt continued and I came no closer to realizing my goal. I began to wonder if I'd made a big mistake. I had passed up a number of bulls in slam-dunk bow range that had been bigger than any bull I'd killed previously. However, I believed in this area and I believed in myself. I knew that if the bull I wanted put himself in a compromising position, he was mine. This finally happened on day five of my hunt.

We spotted a bomber bull Guy had named "Mud Buddy," prior to my arrival due to his fondness for an isolated mud wallow. Mud Buddy was working up the bottom of a creek drainage about a half mile away, so Mike Lancaster, Guy and I made like a bunch of coyotes running down empty creek beds in an attempt to get in front of the fast moving herd.

We had made our move and now we eased along ever so slowly through the thick oak brush. Suddenly, there on the top of the ridge was Mud Buddy bugling his head off. Mike stayed back in the creek, while Guy and I headed up. We got in close, to about 40 some yards and while I eased forward, Guy stayed back filming. Guy felt that he could do a pretty good job from where he was and thought that two guys trying to get in on a big herd bull's harem probably wasn't real likely.

As I eased closer I could not believe my fortune. The big bull was facing straight away from me on a small ridge, bugling at another smaller bull across the way. I came to full draw at 30 yards but kept inching closer, closer and closer, all the while at full draw. After about a minute of this, I began to get fatigued a bit but the adrenaline screaming through my veins provided plenty of strength to hold that bow back hard against the wall. I needed him to make a move and, finally he did. As he turned to walk quartering away from me, I swung my bow arm until the 20-yard sight pin locked on the middle of his ribs. Once the pin was there, I quickly leveled the bow, and evenly squeezed the trigger sending my green-fletched arrow screaming toward Mud Buddy, who later taped out at just under 350 Pope & Young.

Guy Eastman and I have been through some tough times trying our darnedest to get trophy bow kills on film out West. Finally, after many years, we have started to get pretty good and have become great friends along the way.

I had just arrowed my biggest bull elk on film, spot and stalk and it was awesome. If I wasn't the one who did it, I guarantee I would still be dying to see it. It is pretty unique and powerful footage. That is, if you like bugling, glunking, slobbering and screaming monster bull elk up close and personal. Check out *Eastmans' Bowhunting Volume 3* to experience this hunt with me.

Note: The Hill Ranch offers trophy elk hunting in southwestern Colorado and has been featured in the *Eastmans' Hunting Journal*, *Eastmans' Hunting TV*, and Eastmans' video, "Hunting Trophy Elk." Guy adds, "Bobby's ranch has some of the best elk country in the West. Nestled in the San Juan Mountains bordering New Mexico and the famous Vermejo Park Ranch, this place offers some of the best free running elk hunting in the West today."

Calling Them In

Pulling those big bulls in tight

While I have killed a number of bulls from Oregon to Wyoming, including quite a few herd bulls, the biggest of which being the 350-inch Pope & Young monster I arrowed during the 2005 bow season in Colorado, what might be surprising to learn is that I have never bugled in and killed any of these bulls. In fact most of them I killed by way of spot and stalk. Granted, a couple of my bulls were lured into bow range with a sweet sounding cow call, including my 7x6 Wyoming wilderness bull of 2004, but not a one died because of the bugle.

My philosophy in regard to elk hunting or any bowhunting, really, is a simple one. If I can get into bow range without the animal even knowing I am in the same state, I will. My preference is low impact all the way. I know in this day and age of awesome elk calls, killer videos and the excite-

Elk Calling Champion Walt Ramage's Big Six

SIX TIPS THAT'LL HELP YOU GET THAT BIG BULL IN CLOSE

1 ***Always keep in mind*** *what the wind is doing. You can make the sweetest elk sounds, but if you don't do your best to stay downwind from the bull/elk your calling will be for nothing. I know, easier said than done, which is why I suggest using your wind checker to help keep track of the wind.*

2 ***When setting up,*** *make sure you have some shooting lanes open. Don't set up behind brush so that it hinders you from being able to take the shot when one presents itself. Get used to being able to use a diaphragm mouth call, that way your hands are free so you can take the shot when the bull moves through a shooting lane. When using a team calling technique I usually set up anywhere from 50–100 yards behind the shooter (depending on the terrain).*

3 ***I typically set up*** *for about 45 minutes or so on each calling sequence. I start out cow/calf calling softly for about the first 30–45 seconds and then get a little louder for about another 30–45 seconds. About five minutes later I will do the same thing. Every 5–10 minutes I will go through a calling sequence. After about 15–25 minutes I start throwing in some estrus cow calls and some short bull squeals. I will get louder and more aggressive the further I get into my calling sequence.*

4 ***In the morning,*** *before light, I will usually start off with a loud estrus cow call into a canyon and if I get no response follow it up with a bugle. Once I locate a bull I will usually try to get the wind in my favor and move into his comfort zone (100–300 yards). I won't call again until I don't think I can get any closer. I will then set up and try to call him into me. I try to get a feel for a bull's mood. If he is really hot I will throw everything at him. Don't be afraid to create some excitement. If he calls every so often but keeps moving away, run in on him. Again, get in his comfort zone then give him that call.*

5 ***The more versatile*** *you can be with your calls the better. Elk will sometimes respond to one call or sound and not another. It just puts the odds in your favor if you can effectively make a wide range of elk sounds.*

6 ***Some of my favorite*** *Primos calls are the Terminator, Bull Horn, Hoochie Mama, sound plate diaphragms, Hot Lips (estrus cow call) and Wind Checker. A great learning tool would be our new Mastering the Art DVDs. They explain all of our different calls and how to use them. Also on the DVD is some footage from hunts that we used some of our different calls on.*

Walt Ramage is a member of the Primos Hunting Calls Pro-Staff and 2005 Rocky Mountain Elk Foundation World Record Elk Calling Champion ment that calling in a bull brings, my approach might seem old school as I mentioned to Jeremy above I think it likely goes back to the fact that I am used to hunting public land where elk are bugled at and cow called to for months and months every year. In regard to hunter calling tendencies, big bulls get educated very quickly. I have seen even the most call susceptible satellite bull turn tail and head out with just one unfamiliar sounding cow call.

I should give a quick disclaimer; I am no elk calling guru, so take my personal advice on this topic with a grain of salt. However, before disregarding all my thoughts, consider that I have hunted with some of the best in the business and what I have found is that in all but the most perfect of situations those big, older bulls simply will not leave their cows. Why would they? They have the girls. Leaving their herd to fight or chase off a rival I think involves too much risk and not enough reward.

This past season in Colorado I was hunting during the peak of the rut, in some incredible elk country, with many bulls running around and I was in the company of elk call masters, Pat and Mike Lancaster. You'd think that if there was ever a situation to get a big bull in, this was it. Over the course of the week we were successful in enticing many bulls into bow range but none of them would have broke the 330 mark. We had around a dozen bulls in the 300 to 320 class come screaming into 20 yards or less, but those big bulls would not budge. We saw two or three bulls near the 340 mark and with every bugling sequence, while they would fire back a fire breathing response, they wouldn't take more than a step or two our way. As I mentioned above, in the end I was able to arrow a huge 6x6 (in my book) after you guessed it, spotting him and stalking to within 15 yards then slipping in a perfect arrow on the quartering away bull.

I know, most reading this will say, "Hey, what about all those 320 bulls?" I am with you. On any of my normal hunts, like my typical Oregon wilderness hunt, which usually results in me arrowing a mature, Pope & Young class five-point, I would have been ecstatic with any of the 300 plus bulls I passed on in Colorado, especially the 320 6x7 that came into 15 yards on the first morning of the hunt. That was tough. The lesson here is, "When in Rome do as the Romans do." In other words, I adjusted my game given the conditions. On this hunt I wasn't hunting Oregon or Oregon bulls. The situation was similar to those who draw out in Arizona or New Mexico. Most seasoned bowhunters don't wait for years to draw a tag, then go down there and shoot the first six-point they see. They are disciplined and let the 300–320 satellite bulls walk, hoping to get a crack at the bull of a lifetime.

Another question my recent Colorado hunt might elicit is how did you guys get all those bulls in? Like I mentioned, I was with some of the best callers in the West. Mike and Pat have called in more bulls than anyone I know other than Mike Eastman maybe? Above all, the one thing I noticed they did was create excitement. Creating excitement when elk calling is not a revolutionary approach, but the way they did it was. Mike Lancaster likely sets the standard in this regard. He bugles, squeals, glunks and growls with just his mouth, rakes trees with branches in both hands, rolls around, throws rocks and believe it or not, pees to more realistically mimic the sound of a urine spewing *hot* bull when it bugles. So, now you know – to get bulls fired up beyond belief, take your calling to the next level, the Lancaster Level. I have never seen as many slobbering, heaving, rage-blinded bull elk in all of my years of bowhunting combined as I did in Colorado.

So, unless you are going after those magnum caliber bulls, 350 or better, where going in silent might be the most deadly approach, you might want to give the Lancaster approach a try, or in regard to calling advice where better to get it than from a world elk calling champion. I am lucky enough to know fellow Oregonian Walt Ramage and he has graciously agreed to let me include some of his best advice for getting big bulls into bow range (see sidebar p. 210).

Dr. Phil's Guide to Relationships

All right, this advice was not contributed by Dr. Phil. I hate Dr. Phil. But, this is a guide to relationships. How to start one and the importance of creating a relationship with your target bull as told to me by Wayne Endicott.

For a little history, Wayne has been there from the very beginning of my bowhunting career. He has owned the pro shop here in my hometown since I began bowhunting going on 20 years now. And, it was in Wayne's area and only after his personal invitation that I traveled with him to some of Oregon's most famed trophy mule deer country and arrowed my first noteworthy trophy, a 180+ buck on opening day back in 1991. For that I will always be grateful. Of Wayne's many talents, calling in bull elk has to rank right up there near the top. He has called in countless elk and killed a staggering number of trophy bulls over the years. Along the way, he has developed a calling strategy that many could learn from.

As Wayne tells me, there are such good calls out on the market nowadays that sounding like a bull isn't all that difficult. The hard part is sounding authentic. Those older public land bulls, he says, have been through the

routine more than once.

What he likes to do first is hunt relatively unpressured wilderness bulls if possible or if not wilderness, big country elk that other hunters won't do what it takes to get in to. Once elk are located in this setting he tries to work to within 300–500 yards from the herd, at which time he creates an association or a relationship with the bull(s) by entering into their communication without being overly aggressive. The aggressiveness deal is key. He calls sparingly, just enough to where the bulls hear his bugle and become familiar with the sound. When you transform from the "relationship" mode to the calling in and killing mode, Wayne feels that if you've been able to spend two to three hours in this "zone" the likelihood of coaxing the bull to within bow range is near 100%.

Deep in the wilderness of Montana this past fall, Wayne and one of his hunting partners, Bryan Richardson, were hunting unpressured elk if there ever was such a thing. They worked into the same drainage of seven to eight bulls, which were taking turns sounding off to each other. The biggest bull in the canyon would start the discussion, then the bull across the canyon would light off, and so on.

After getting set up, Wayne worked his way into the rotation, so as to familiarize his calling tendencies and the sound of his "voice." After a few

Here Wayne Endicott displays the double-fisted Hoochie Mama calling technique. Wayne is a master at sounding like an entire herd of elk all by himself.

hours of calling just once about every 30 minutes, Wayne and Bryan had figured out where the hottest bulls were and slowly worked in between them. Then they set up and called with dynamic results. The bulls had become accustomed to Wayne's bugling and were convinced he was a rival bull, so they came storming in. Bryan passed on the smaller bull, which was a decent 5x5, could have forced a shot on a 325 P&Y bull in close that just didn't give him the right angle, and then finally had a monster 360 bull hang up at about 60 yards—fast and furious action to be sure.

Another thing Wayne tries to do is to create curiosity. It is common knowledge that curiosity killed the cat, but what might not be well known is that curiosity has also done quite a number on bull elk. To do this, patience is the key. You must make the bull believe you're an elk, which means sounding authentic is paramount. A real antler to rub with pushes the authenticity factor over the edge. Bulls can tell what is real antler tearing up a tree and what isn't. Convincing them will make all the difference.

You know how you don't like when you're telling a story or reading someone the riot act and they cut you off? Same thing goes for elk. Cutting the bull's bugle off can make them boiling mad. Wayne had good luck doing this in Idaho recently.

While Wayne Endicott has killed many big bulls, he gets just as much satisfaction helping new bowhunters. He called in this Oregon state record non-typical Roosevelt for Chris Phillips. The "Scorpion King" was Chris' first bowhunting bull.

After exchanging bugles for about 45 minutes, Wayne thought he would try to push the bull a little bit. As soon as the bull would start a bugle, Wayne would bugle over the top of him and then grunt for longer than he had been. Wayne believes that bull elk almost get into an arranged agreement or understanding that, "You listen to me and then I'll listen to you." If you'll notice, a bull when bugling will have his ears pinned back giving their bugle everything they have; then, when finished, they will pop their ears forward to listen. If you can violate this gentleman's agreement, so to speak, it can drive them over the top. If they feel disrespected, they might stomp in to show you who's boss.

A Wayne Golden Rule is do not overcall. He normally only calls when the bull calls or sometimes Wayne just rakes a tree in response to a bugle. In regard to grunting, one observation he's made is that if a bull grunts 8-10 times, he is almost always going to come in. Wayne feels that such inspired grunting or chuckling is almost always a sign of a nasty attitude, which makes him that much more susceptible to the call. Patience is still the word of the day though.

What I think happens many times when guys get an answer to their bugles is they barrel in toward the bull, which if you're hunting remote, you definitely do not need to do. It seems the public land hunter has a tough time shaking the feeling that they are racing other hunters to that hot bull. This is the nature of the beast and is also why elk hunting success with a bow on big bulls is around 3%. This should be reason enough to hit the backcountry and up your odds with Dr. Wayne's guide to elk relationships.

Solo Elk Calling

By Jody Cyr

Use your calls sparingly. *In my experience, the more you use your calls, the more chance that animal has of pinning down your exact location. When you know he is coming, don't call any more unless he hangs up and you can't see him. If you can see him, wait him out. If he turns to leave, give one call to try to turn him back.*

Try to set up on breaks *in terrain where the bull is forced to come and see where the sound is coming from. In my opinion this is where many people make mistakes. With the exception of lovesick elk, most elk will only come to a point in which they should be able to see the elk making sounds. This is tricky calling by yourself. When you see the elk, he should be in shooting range. Always have at least one shooting lane downwind.*

Be passive/aggressive. *There's a time to move, and a time to hold tight. Just because a bull has gone silent, doesn't mean he's not coming. If you know a bull is working the area, never leave your setup without waiting at least 20 minutes. Many bulls will respond to every call while leaving the area. This happens to be a time to put on your running shoes and get close before calling again.*

Always get close after locating a bull before calling again. *If you want a chance at a herd bull, you have to be close while setting up. After locating a bull, I try to get within 70 yards of where I think he is. The big guys won't travel far from their cows. Why fight or leave for something you already have?*

Don't risk the wind. *If it's not right, leave that bull. It's hard to do, but if you want a real chance at killing him, wait until the wind changes. You might have to travel to another ridge or simply wait until later in the day. Whatever the case may be, don't risk the wind.*

Jim Hamilton

The Roos' vs. The Rock

Different species, same formula for success.

In official terms, there are four subspecies of elk roaming North America. At one time there were six, but the Merriam and Eastern elk subspecies are no longer with us. Of the remaining in order of population numbers, smallest to largest, is the Tule, Manitoban, Roosevelt and Rocky Mountain elk.

Tule and Manitoban elk, with very restricted ranges and limited numbers, are species most of us will never hunt, whereas many can and will hunt both Roosevelt and Rocky Mountain elk as these animals are flourishing. In fact I have hunted Roosevelt one day, driven "over the mountain" as we say here in Oregon and hunted Rocky Mountain elk the next.

Roosevelt elk, which range on the west slope of the Cascade mountain range and throughout the rugged Coast Range of Oregon and Washington, are renowned for having incredibly large bodies and heavy antlers. I can attest to this, but it is generally only the largest bulls that truly stand apart in regard to body size from their cousins to the east, the Rocky Mountain elk. And, in comparing huge Roosevelt elk to huge Rocky Mountain elk, the Roos' will weigh in roughly 100 pounds more, which doesn't seem like much until you're the one packing it out.

So, yes, the legend of their behemoth bodies precedes them. Roosevelt elk range as far north as Vancouver Island, B.C. and have been introduced to Alaska's Afognak Island and as far south as California's Humbolt County. A mature Roosevelt bull will generally have heavy, dark antlers and may sport "crown points" above the royal. Their antlers are typically more massive for their length when compared to the antlers of the Rocky Mountain elk.

So far as the border goes in terms of the record books, Interstate 5, which runs from Washington to California and obviously through Oregon, is the line. West of the highway are Roosevelt elk and east are Rocky Mountain. In regard to the Pope & Young and Boone & Crockett scoring systems (typical), a Roosevelt bull will have to score 225 to make P&Y and 290 to make B&C, whereas a Rocky Mountain bull will need to tally 260 to qualify for P&Y and 375 for B&C.

Rocky Mountain elk are much more numerous than the other subspecies and have by far the largest range. They range from British Columbia and Alberta south to Arizona and New Mexico and from central Washington east to South Dakota. Rocky Mountain elk have been transplanted in Kentucky, Pennsylvania, Michigan, Ontario, Minnesota, North Dakota, Kansas, Oklahoma, Texas, New Mexico, California, and Oregon.

A mature Rocky Mountain bull will stretch the tape to about 7 ½ feet and stand five feet at the shoulder. A true monster bull can weigh in at over 1,000 pounds on the hoof.

Depending on the species of elk one chases, strategies for a lot of hunters can be as different as night from day, but not for me. When chasing behemoth-bodied Roosevelt of western Oregon, the species I grew up bowhunting in my "backyard," or bowhunting the Rocky Mountain elk that call the majestic high alpine meadows home, my strategy isn't altered much.

Regardless of species, my key to success is simply finding areas untainted by other hunters. For Rockys this means wilderness areas that are big and nasty enough to ward off other hunters. When the object of my desire is the dark-horned Roosevelt that call the west coast of California, Oregon, Washington and the southern tip of B.C. home, that means finding remote areas that limit vehicle access.

Remember if it is easy for you to get to, it is easy for everyone else as well. What this typically means is the hunting will be tough and trophy class

Before I was able to afford hunting the backcountry, I hunted close to home, but still was able to get away from the crowds by way of mountain bike. Just 30 minutes from the house, I experienced first rate trophy elk hunting for big Roosevelt bulls.

animals will be rare. Getting away from other hunters to chase unpressured bulls is the only tactic I have found to be effective along the densely populated Interstate 5 corridor that virtually dissects the areas I hunt.

I have had great luck arrowing big bulls on private timber company land here in Oregon. During elk season, it is typically hot and dry. The timber companies, in an effort to reduce the risk of costly fires, restrict their lands to hunting by non-motorized vehicle means only. For me, that means access by way of mountain bike.

It is strange how lying in the middle of a log landing, on a bed of crushed rock, had never felt so good! Perhaps it was because I had just completed my ritualistic weekend morning ride for the eighth time of the season and was in dire need of recoup time. The nine-mile uphill trek on my mountain bike has a way of wreaking havoc on my body. My shorts and T-shirt had been replaced by camo. Face paint had been applied to my face and to the back of my hands. My Leupold 10x40s rested safely on my chest. My bow and pack served its purpose as a makeshift pillow. I stared straight up, going through a mental checklist of equipment and possible animal locations. The skies, enhanced by the presence of ominous clouds, altered from varying degrees of blackness. With more than 30 minutes to first light, there seemed a good chance that this morning's hunt would be accompanied by a little precipitation.

From dawn until 8:00 a.m., it rained in light to moderate waves. This was pleasant enough and a nice change from the recent mid-80 degree weather we had been experiencing. The pleasantness, however, came to an abrupt end as the floodgates opened, dumping buckets of angry rain. The animals that had been up and feeding promptly bedded. From what I have observed, weather conditions such as this render the highly acute senses of elk and deer virtually useless. Being naturally nervous animals, they can become incapacitated when subject to abrupt environmental changes such as this. Twenty to 25 minutes later the storm broke.

During the festivities of the storm I had traveled to a favorite vantage point of mine, and now began glassing in earnest. From this lofty vista, I could effectively glass up to 10 different logging units for elk or deer. I try to implement efficient hunting tactics such as this during each of my hunting forays. This point is accentuated during the early season when we are, as I mentioned, subject to very hot and dry weather conditions, resulting in our target animals spending very little time out in the open. It was from here that something far off in the distance caught my attention. Even though the elk were over two miles away, it is hard to miss 15 very large, lightly-colored animals. The elk were bedded on the edge of a clear cut, just off the point of the ridge. During a herd count, I was pleased to observe the easily distinguishable rack of a big herd bull, bedded on the uppermost corner. The stakes had just increased dramatically!

Fast forward, 45 leg-burning, heart-pumping, go-for-broke minutes...Yes, the elk were only two miles away-as the crow flies. However, as the bike pedals, I was in excess of six miles out, with plenty of ups and downs.

I eased along a rain-soaked game trail, wind in my face, landmarks in sight—holding all the cards. The last thing I wanted to do was get in a hurry. My plan was to come in high on the herd, as the bull had been the highest animal in the configuration of bedded elk. I was praying they had not changed their positions. Carefully peering over the edge of a small slope, the view caused my heart to stall. Only 30 yards away lay a huge, heavy-beamed 6 x 5 bull. He was staring down the hill monitoring his domain.

From my quick estimation, I knew the bull would easily surpass the record book minimum. I must admit I was a bit surprised to see the bull laying in the exact position from which I had glassed him earlier. It is a rare occurrence for a bull to be inactive for this long during the peak of the rut. Usually driven by adrenaline and testosterone, they are always on the move or at the very least standing, serving sentry to the herd.

Pedal to the Metal—I cut my teeth in regard to elk hunting by mountain biking for big Roosevelt bulls like this one.

Regardless of why, I was presented with the opportunity I had practiced all summer for. I'd dreamt about this moment who knows how many times? When I came to full draw, the bull caught movement and swiveled his head, staring in my direction. Usually substantial movement such as that associated with the drawing of a bow will cause a mature elk to send up a red flag. I prepared myself for him to stand. Apparently, with the wind as my ally, and being clad in quality camo, I had enough in my favor to cloud his better judgment and he remained bedded. My 30-yard pin hovered over his chest before I locked onto the precise spot I wanted the broadhead to penetrate. The shot felt good—solid. My arrow flew true, dissecting the exact imaginary spot where I had placed it on the bull's chest. Exploding out of his bed, the bull was immediately affected by the trauma that the arrow produced. He ran 10 yards and stopped. Capitalizing on this unexpected opportunity, I sent another arrow into his vitals before his final frantic sprint.

I sat down to collect my thoughts and relive what had just happened. I felt grateful that I was allowed the time to get two arrows into him; the bull would die quickly—humanely. As if in a time warp, the cows finally spooked. I watched and listened as they crashed down to the creek and ascended the other side in strong powerful leaps. Glassing each and every elk, just to confirm what I already knew, the bull would not join the herd in their dash for safety. I began to search for evidence of my bull's path of travel. The heavy blood trail confirmed my suspicions. Quickly, I covered the 100 yards to where my bull had expired. I sat in awe staring at this magnificent and majestic brute of an animal. This chance of a lifetime experience is something I will never forget.

Hunt Report Card – Hindsight is always 20/20

What I learned on this hunt: I learned that even in the toughest hunting conditions, all it takes is one chance. With one opportunity all those tough days in the field with no animal sightings become fading memories. The area in which I killed this bull is some of the most popular, and thus over-hunted areas near my hometown. I hunted the area for years and years and only took a couple of big bulls, the one killed in the hunt described above being the best. Finally, I accepted the truth and moved on to find more fertile hunting grounds.

What I did wrong: As I mentioned, I spent many tough bow seasons running around the private timber company land that I killed this bull on. I realize now that I should have looked for better hunting earlier on. Yes, my bullheaded perseverance was both good and bad. That being said, I don't regret my time spent working my butt off in this country. The experience without a doubt made me a better hunter, as now I know what tough hunting really is. I have hunted many different places and animals since and can say with confidence that nothing has been as tough.

Grade: Years of sacrifice, fruitless hunts and tough lessons from the field culminated with the harvest of this trophy Roosevelt bull. **A–**

SECTION 6

North Country Adventures

Bear of Alaska

Big Bears in the Red Zone

Depending on your preference, there are three exciting strategies a bowhunter can use to tag a hulking black bear. Spot & stalk, baiting, or running them with dogs are all great ways to get in close on these intimidating predators, and I have used all three methods to arrow many Pope & Young bruins. It would be safe to say that while I love all bowhunting, taking a big public land black bear with a bow and arrow rig has always been one of my favorite bowhunting challenges. And of the three disciplines used to hunt bear, my personal favorite and most used tactic is baiting.

This chapter will cover in detail the hair-raising hunting adventures I've experienced and the baiting methods I've used and refined over nearly 20 years.

THE ART OF BEAR BAITING...

I began baiting in bears nearly 20 years ago with my buddy from home, Roy Roth. Pretty much from the beginning, we considered hauling bait, hanging tree stands and arrowing big bruins a

Roy's 2005 spring grizzly green scores over the Boone & Crockett threshold and should rank in Pope & Young's top 20.

rite of spring. We started out learning the art of bear baiting back in Oregon and had a great time and many great hunts until the use of bait to harvest bear was taken away from hunters in 1994.

That was the year Ballot Measure 18 passed, which outlawed the use of bait and/or dogs to harvest bear and cougar in Oregon. We had developed such a passion for bear hunting that after a couple springs without, Roy and I took our game to Alaska where baiting is still used as one of the most effective management tools for black bear. Since our Oregon days, Roy and I have had more than our share of great Do-It-Yourself bowhunts for monster black bear in southeast Alaska, but for Roy, the spring bear hunting got much more interesting. In April 2005 Alaska Department of Fish & Game, in an effort to ease pressure on the declining moose herd, made it legal to hunt grizzlies with bait in a very remote part of Alaska where officials say the moose population was at the greatest risk.

The Fish & Game began issuing permits the first week of April for a program aimed at thinning out grizzly numbers in a 3,000-square-mile area of brushy terrain and tundra near the Canadian border. The program allows permitted hunters to use bear-attracting food to lure the animals to spots where they could be shot. The practice of baiting grizzlies or coast-dwelling brown bears has never been permitted during the 46 years of Alaskan statehood. As you may have guessed, once this program was announced, Roy fired up his rig and peeled out of his driveway. He simply couldn't get to the Fish & Game office fast enough to get signed up for his grizzly baiting permit. This was such a rare opportunity he even backed out of our traditional Prince of Wales hunt for trophy black bear, which I thought was about as likely as pigs flying.

Roy's brown bear from Kodiak Island was actually his second grizzly of 2004. In Alaska, although I doubt it has been done too many times before Roy, a resident can arrow a grizzly in the spring and then one in the fall. Definitely a "Big Bear Double" for the books.

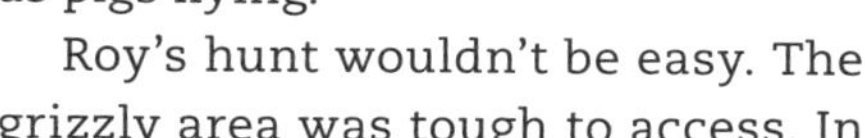

Roy's hunt wouldn't be easy. The grizzly area was tough to access. In order for Roy to get geared up for one of his many baiting excursions for the big bears, he had to load his flatbed with bait and four-wheelers, plus tow his skiff as one bait required a river crossing and just in case he had problems with the skiff, he also threw in an inflatable raft.

Roy also tells me grizzlies are a lot more work than black bear in terms of sheer bait quantity. A little pan full of Bear Crack and dog food isn't going to

In an amazing turn of events, just minutes apart in the fall of 2004, Roy arrowed a hulking Kodiak brown bear and then a handsome Pope & Young Sitka blacktail. Another rare double to be sure.

get it done on these big carnivores. After getting loaded up, Roy would then head northeast on a seven-hour drive from his home in Wasilla to where he would be hunting.

After weeks of working the bait, Roy finally had a couple hitting. He says grizzlies are much different to bait than black bears especially in the spring as they're breeding and the moose calves are dropping. Both these factors meant the big boars would be on the move and not likely to hang out at a bait site for too long. As we all know, hard work pays off and it did in spades for Roy the last week of May.

Sitting on an active bait one afternoon, Roy caught a flash of blonde in the brush just 40 yards out. In the blink of an eye the big grizzly was on the bait but, as Roy relates, was acting like a Tasmanian Devil—in that it was flying all around, thrashing the bait and in general tearing stuff up. Typically, a dominant black bear, knowing he owns the bait, will be more relaxed. On POW the big boars seemingly have no fear and act like it. While the no fear attitude is likely the same, the behavior is apparently much different—at least in terms of Roy's bear.

The grizzly then turned and padded off through the muskeg and didn't return for three anxious hours. When it did, Roy knew he'd have to be ready and act quickly. As the bear moved toward the bait, Roy came to full draw, anchored in and took a deep breath. In a flash of carbon as the hulking mass of muscle turned broadside, Roy buried an arrow tight behind the boar's shoulder. After some tense blood trailing, which fittingly went through the site of a recent calf moose kill, Roy recovered his first ever inland grizzly and what a monster it was.

Roy's bear green scores over the Boone & Crockett Awards threshold of 23" and will probably rank in Pope & Young's top 20. His was the first grizzly taken under the newly initiated grizzly baiting program and the first ever killed by a hunter over bait legally in the state of Alaska.

For Roy, the 2005 spring bear hunting in Alaska took on a new and heart pounding twist. Congratulations Roy, but don't make a habit of it. POW wasn't the same without you.

Note: If Roy Roth doesn't have big bear figured out, I don't know who does. This guy seemingly arrows a monster black bear or grizzly every time he heads into the woods. In regard to grizzlies, he not only arrowed the one chronicled above but in 2004 he also killed two big grizzlies with his bow—one in interior Alaska in the spring, and then a huge bear on Kodiak in the fall. What an amazing run. In addition to the "big nasties," he also killed a number of huge black bear during the same two year period.

Bear Crack Recipe

Ingredients: *Marshmallows, powdered Jell-O mix, syrup and granular sugar*

1• *Fill up a decent-sized pan, one that your wife or girlfriend is not going to need back I might add, about halfway with marshmallows. Dump in a half a package of powdered Jell-O mix; add a quart of syrup and a pound or so of sugar.*

2• *Set pan on a single burner propane stove and bring to a slow boil. Stir occasionally while letting the Bear Crack boil. The sweet smelling smoke emitted from this concoction then wafts through the timber and pulls all those big bear in like they were on a string. This is some good stuff and once the bears are hooked, look out. Sometimes there is very little you can do to keep them from coming to the bait whether you're ready for 'em or not.*

3• *Just for those special occasions, have a separate pan to fry up some bacon while at the bait and then dip it in the Bear Crack. I call this "candied bacon" and oh boy, only do this if there is somebody available to serve sentry. Those big ol' ornery boars can only stand so much before they just up and decide to crash the baiting party.*

4• *After the Bear Crack has boiled for about five minutes or so, dump the liquefied mixture onto dog food, nearby stumps or anything else in the area that you don't mind whether it gets torn up or not.*

Just like Mom used to make!

Bear Camp 2003

By *Cameron R. Hanes*

Originally featured in Eastmans' Bowhunting Journal *issue 19*

Our last trip up to Prince of Wales Island, Alaska had us basking in a very warm glow of bowhunting success. On that trip, Guy Eastman filmed Roy Roth and I arrowing a couple of trophy black bear. Our bears were easy Pope & Young qualifiers and being that this was another public land Do-It-Yourself bow and arrow hunt, we were more than satisfied with our bruins and the accompanying footage of the hunt. This hunt was featured on *Eastmans' Bowhunting Volume 1.*

Roy and I, like many of you, have been doing the D-I-Y thing for years. We were doing all the research, scheduling and putting our plan into action long before Do-It-Yourself had its own acronym. Where we bear hunt can be a tough place to get into and out of at times. There are no roads for miles, no phones, and for us, no other human contact whatsoever. But, bear in mind; it is precisely because of these factors that the hunting is so good.

And while the bear bait game is still the same regardless of where it is played, the players are definitely not. Down in Oregon, where we began baiting some 15 years ago, we were pumped if we had a bear hitting with a four-and-a-half-inch track and it usually took three weeks to get that first strike. On P.O.W., we expect a six-inch track and if we set a bait that doesn't get hit in

This nearly 20" Pope & Young boar fooled me initially as his body didn't scream "big bear."

one day, we are bummed. Undeniably, this is bear baiting heaven.

Heaven, not just because the baits get slammed quickly, but as I alluded to the size of these bears. Make no mistake, this is a trophy hunt. On some bear hunts you go for hides and on some you go for heads. On P.O.W. you are going for oversized skulls that will get you well into the record book. A good hide can't be counted on as the bear here very commonly have the back of their paws and forearms rubbed at the least and sometimes between their eyes on the forehead. Although we have taken a couple from the island that have had flawless hides, this surely can't be counted on.

On this most recent hunt, we had set our sights very high. In my opinion, this is the best trophy black bear region in the world. All of my hunts have to be semi-affordable with a high likelihood of success on trophy animals and P.O.W. is tailor-made for these requirements. This is the best hunt money can buy and to think it will run you right at $2,000, which is quite a bargain for an out-of-state big game hunt.

Once we finally made it to "Roy Island," it was time for the work to begin. Roy had camp set up, but the real work on this hunt comes in the baiting. We had nine baits to tend that were spread over miles of shoreline. The actual killing of a bear is many times easier than getting them locked into a routine first. On this hunt we baited for three days before we even packed a bow. It was tempting to sit before we finally did but as we like to say, "We will kill no bear before its time." We have learned that if you pressure a big bear too early in the game trying to force the issue there is a chance he will leave and not come back.

My good friends from home, Bruce Barker and local contractor, Rick Nation, joined Roy and me on this hunt. Bruce and Rick were real limited on bear hunting experience prior to this hunt. We invited them because they are good guys and I knew they would love the challenge. To say they were green might be an understatement. Bruce was brand new to bowhunting and had never drawn a bow back on anything but a target butt. Rick has experienced pretty commendable success with his rifle, but never on bear. And, his bow experience inspired Roy and I to lump the both of them right into "rookie" status. I had faith in them though as both of them have been around the block so to speak. I believed Bruce and Rick could weather the storm of emotion that accompanies arrowing a bear at spitting distance.

We had been working our tails off baiting and by that fourth day we were all ready to roll. We had a number of baits that were just getting hammered and not one of them had anything less than big, record book boars hitting. My bait selection was an easy one. The track on it was very wide, six inches, and very deep with big, fat toes. He had cleaned out the bait everyday and was bedding right there like a dog protecting its food bowl. This was obviously a monster and he displayed his dominance as big bears often do by tearing up everything around the bait, chewing on roots and ripping up stumps. Also, the day I decided to sit, we went in to give a little teaser bait at 9:30 a.m. and he was there. I stumbled in on him and pushed him off the bait.

That afternoon Roy and I motored back in the skiff to spend the evening over the bait. Roy was perched in a tree to my right about 20 feet off the ground with the video camera at the ready. There weren't many mature trees at this site so I decide to sit on a root wad that got me off the ground

Roy Roth with one of his many big blackies.

a little bit and put me back about 10 yards off the bait. We had good wind so I wasn't too concerned about getting busted and I kind of liked the thrill of a possible close quarter encounter with this bruiser. I would be right in the eye of the storm, which is how I like it.

Rick Nation begins his bear hunting career in a big way.

We hadn't been in the stand even 10 minutes when a loud "crack" echoed from back in the brush behind the bait. That was fast. Roy and I shot sideways glances at one another while nodding with thin knowing smiles. A handful of minutes passed and then I saw a flash of black, and another and then the silhouette of a big bear. He was lifting his nose and tilting his head back as he gulped in air through his nostrils reading the wind. I originally decided to pass on this bear but after watching him clean up the bait for about 20 minutes I came to the conclusion that he was bigger than I had originally estimated.

His body was kind of slender for a magnum boar, but his head was big and I could see his paws were huge. I motioned to Roy that I was going to shoot him the next good chance I had. I had visions of holding out for a 20-incher, and after really getting a good look at him I was confident he would be very close to this threshold. He would rank right up there with my largest black bear if I could make a good shot. Plus, this set-up was perfect and there was ideal lighting for videoing.

As the bear, with a slow deliberate gait, eased around the bait stump and offered me a perfect, slightly quartering away shot opportunity I readied myself. Sitting comfortably on the root wad stand, I pulled my bow back. The red 20-yard pin hovered on his side right at mid-body momentarily before zeroing in on the exact spot I wanted to dissect. With the pin centered in the peep and the bubble level true, I was locked on. As Roy zoomed in tight with the Canon video camera, I slowly squeezed the release. The bright green fletched arrow ate up the 10 yards of distance to the bear quickly and caught him perfectly. My arrow blew clear through him and bounced straight back off of the stump. He was immediately traumatized and only made it a short eight yards before piling up. The afternoon's silence was broken by his eerie "death moan."

This was a good bear and being that it was early in the hunt I was now free to film and photograph. My bear's skull measured nearly 20 inches P&Y as I had judged and his hide stretches the tape 6-foot 11 inches from nose to tail and 6-foot 7 inches front claw to claw. To square a bear hide, as many seasoned bear hunters do to gauge their trophies, you take the two measurements I listed, total them and then divide by 2. This means my bear squares 6-foot 9 inches.

The rookies sat this first hunting evening together, with Bruce hunting and Rick filming. We had them set up on a very hot bait, with a couple of real good bear hitting. Of course they had good action that evening and Bruce ended up passing on a bear I never would have. When we all finally made it back to camp late that evening he said that they had a "little" bear come into the bait. This struck me as odd, as I knew we didn't have any little bear hitting. After reviewing the film I told him that if that bear comes in again, shoot it. It was a big bear and a sure record book boar. Live and learn. Roy and I had told those guys that if they were unsure at all, wait. There was no reason to shoot anything other than a big bear up here. So, all told, Bruce showed discipline and made the right decision, as he wasn't 100 percent certain on the bear's size.

The second night it was Rick's turn to hunt as they decided to take turns filming. Sitting on the same bait as the night before, Rick made like a cagey veteran and put the hammer down on that P&Y boar. Rick killed the bear that Bruce passed on, which ended up being an 18 11/16-inch bear with a very stocky body. Not a bad first bear. Not a bad any bear. Bruce was even able to catch the entire sequence on film. The rookies were making it look too easy.

That same evening a few miles away, I was sitting with Roy and watched him make a perfect shot on a beautiful bear. As we made our way to the stand that afternoon we bumped the bear off the bait, which is a good sign. You gotta like when those bear are in there at the bait in the middle of the day. After getting settled in our stands it didn't take long before bears began to circle. Finally, after about an hour, a big boar made his way to the bait and Roy, in his typical, "cool as the other side of the pillow" bear hunt persona, made an absolutely perfect shot.

He "pinwheeled" it and the bruin went right down after a 100-yard crashing sprint. Of course as is standard operating procedure with Roy, his was the largest bear in camp. He beat me out by an eighth on the skull and his bear squared seven-foot two inches. This was a very big bear, but not Roy's largest by any means. He has killed five that square over 7-foot and most of those have over 20-inch heads. Not everyone knows this, but black bears of this size are actually larger than most grizzlies killed. The average-sized grizzly taken by hunters squares about six-foot six inches. Something else to ponder, the minimum to enter a grizzly in the all-time P&Y record book is an even 19 inches. Proof positive, these are monster black bear.

There was no more killing until I went out to film Bruce a couple of days later. We took the early morning shift as we believed the bears were so programmed and hooked on the crack, they would come in anytime we wanted them to. We climbed into the stand at about 7:30 a.m. and by 9:00 we had a big boar in our laps. Bruce made good on the chance with one very, extremely, drop-in-your-tracks-lethal arrow. I have never seen anything like it. The bear didn't

Bruce Barker with a POW rarity—a big bear and an absolutely perfect hide.

move an inch. Another P&Y bear on the ground. And, for Bruce, he downed this record book animal on his first arrow ever released while bowhunting. That'll work. Congratulations buddy! Bruce's bear had well over an 18-inch skull and a thick, jet black, flawless hide. It was a definite life-size mount candidate.

Four hunters, four record book bear taken with four arrows! We got three of the kills on film to boot and hours of great bear action. This surely was a D-I-Y hunter's dream and I ask, "How could it get any better than this?" Miles of public land and over-the-counter tags make this one heck of an opportunity for guys wanting to hunt trophy black bear. Start planning now for next year.

Bear Down

By Cameron R. Hanes

Originally featured in EBJ 26

Roy turned around to sit down and said, "There's a bear right there."

If there is anything better to do in the spring than bear hunt Alaska I sure don't know about it. I make the long trip north almost every year and can't seem to get enough of those big ol' bears. In fact, this past season I made two trips to The Last Frontier and was lucky enough to bring home two Pope & Young class black bears.

REDEFINED PRIORITIES

Anymore though, arrowing a bear is not what makes the trip for me. I will say that years ago, when I first started bowhunting, the hunt's success hinged solely on whether I brought home a trophy. In other words, there was no way I could have a good hunt without killing a bear. Times have changed a bit.

And, while I am not going to pretend that I wouldn't like to kill a good bear every year, nowadays what I cherish more than anything is exposing new friends, old buddies or my own family to the tradition that is spring bear hunting. There is nothing like watching a fellow hunter's eyes light up when they get that first glimpse of a ghosting black shadow as a big-headed bear snakes through the underbrush. It's similar to seeing the excitement on their face when you've unraveled a heavy blood trail and recover one of bowhunting's ultimate trophies, a trophy black bear.

GETTING THERE FROM HERE

As with many good hunts, accessing the country your quarry calls home is one of the biggest challenges you'll face. It is no secret that Alaska is loaded with black bear. Getting to them can be difficult, but not impossible. This is where boats, jet sleds and bush planes fit into the equation.

I am lucky in that Roy lives in Alaska. This is huge, but even if you don't have a best friend that calls Alaska home, setting up a D-I-Y hunt is still very realistic. In fact, many of the hunts Roy and I team up on in Alaska require him to travel almost as far as I do. For instance, our annual Prince of Wales bear hunt is probably closer to me down here in Oregon than to his home north of Anchorage.

The other prime spring bear hunt we like takes place in the Yetna River country of interior Alaska. This area is absolutely loaded with black bear and is all public land. In fact there are so many blackies, you can kill two a year in the unit we hunt. While the bears aren't quite as big as those on P.O.W., there are more of them. Wild thru and thru this area also has quite a population of grizzlies, which can make checking baits along this brush-choked river interesting at times. We usually see a handful of moose each year adding to the Alaska experience.

A handful of years back, Roy and his dad Ray built a cabin some 65 miles up this river. They hauled all the building material up in the winter with snow machines pulling trailers. This small but homey cabin serves as our base camp for this hunt. To complete the stunning scene, Mount McKinley can be seen in all its majestic grandeur not too far in the distance. Incidentally, there

Alaska offers incredible black bear bowhunting opportunities for guys hungry for adventure.

are a number of lodges up and down the Yetna that cater to the bear hunters and/or salmon fishermen.

THE HUNTING PARTY

This year, I had invited Ben Maki of Mossy Oak Apparel and Lannie Wallace of Mossy Oak to join Roy and me on our hunt at the cabin. Also, at the last minute I decided to bring along Tanner, my oldest son, as an 11th birthday present. This was Tanner's second trip to the cabin as he came up with us when he was eight and this would be Lannie's first ever trip to Alaska from his home in the deep south—West Point, Mississippi to be exact. Ben, who now lives in Atlanta, Georgia, where MOA is based, still considers Alaska home. He went to high school in Alaska and his parents still live in Anchorage, so hunting the Alaskan backcountry was nothing new to him.

LET'S GO BEAR HUNTING

The first night out was kind of slow. Lannie, who was rifle hunting because he hadn't had a chance to get his "Bowhunting Certification" which is required to hunt bear over bait in this unit, did not see a bear. Ben did not see a bear either. The weather had as much to do with this as anything though. Roy and Ray had the baits slamming, but bears just don't like coming in when the rain is falling in buckets like it was that night.

Now, Tanner, he fared a little better. I got him set up in a tree stand right beside mine with Roy about five yards behind us in another tree stand. Roy was supposed to be filming but he forgot to change the battery and forgot to put a tape in the camera. As a hunting partner he is first rate. As a cameraman, he has a little room for improvement.

Finally after about an hour and a half in the stand I spied a good bear coming in behind the bait. Tanner who was wet, cold and tired as it was about midnight Oregon time (but still plenty light in Alaska) was fading fast. The bear came in perfect but was nervous,

Steve Sims, inventor of the LimbSaver, and I have become great friends since first bumping into each other waiting for a plane on Prince of Wales Island in 1999.

likely because of the blowing rain. Tanner put a twinkle in my eye as he made like a veteran bear hunter and broke the bear down with a perfect shoulder shot from his 20 gauge firing big old bear killing slugs.

The next night Lannie saw his first bear ever in the wild and killed it. It was a good day in Alaska for Lannie as earlier that morning he caught his first king. It was also a good day to bear hunt in general as I arrowed a beautiful bear that night myself, which sported the best hide of any bear I have ever killed.

Filming Roy Roth arrow this bruiser was as rewarding as if I had killed it myself. Roy was born to hunt big bears. He is the master.

Roy and I went way upriver to a bait he hadn't checked in quite some time. Because of this, we really didn't have too high of hopes as we burned our "Bear Crack." The situation turned around quickly. Roy climbed up to join me in a neighboring stand and as he turned around to sit down he looked down at the base of the ladder and said, "There's a bear right there." That'll work. I shot it through the heart and he made it about four long strides before dying. Again, Roy was supposed to be filming, which can be hard to do when you forget the camera!

Ben did not end up killing a bear unfortunately but I think it bothered Roy and me more than it did him. We really wanted everyone to kill a bear. We could have extended the hunt and would have with no reservations, but on Ben's insistence we headed out with plenty of time to get back to the airport, have a nice meal and not be rushed. This was very unselfish of Ben, and it probably has something to do with the fact that he has killed more animals than I probably ever will in my lifetime, including a big Alaskan brown bear.

Still though, other than wishing Ben had tagged a big bear, I wouldn't change anything about our hunt. We had a great camp and those guys, Lannie and Ben, are sure to be friends for life as a bond built hunting bear is a tough one to break.

CHRISTENING THE EL DORADO

I first met Steve Sims, founder and CEO of LimbSaver Inc. back in 1999 on a remote dock in southeast Alaska as we waited on a bush plane. It was the middle of May and we had both been bear hunting, not together, but apparently not too far from one another either. Incidentally, we had both tagged out on good bears, so sprits were high and a friendly conversation ensued. I noticed he had a LimbSaver jacket on and commented while nodding to his jacket, "I have those on my bow and they really seemed to make a difference." Of course I didn't know who I was talking to until he filled me in that he was the inventor the LimbSaver and manufactures them near his home in Shelton, Washington.

Well it wasn't too long after that, not only did I have them on my bow, but everyone I knew had them on their bow and very likely everyone since that meeting some five years ago has LimbSavers on their bow.

This year at the Archery Trade Association get-together Steve let on that he had just purchased a 60′ fishing boat, completely remodeled the thing, with bunks for nine, a kitchen, a shower, a TV with VCR, the whole nine yards. He also had a 20′ aluminum skiff that they kept with the big boat. Steve told me that the plans were to christen his new hunting and fishing vessel, The Eldorado, starting in the spring and graciously offered up the boat to serve as a base camp if we would like to team up on a bear hunt in our tried, true and remote monster bear area. I quickly accepted as it made perfect sense and I knew Roy and I could expose Steve to some incredible bear hunting, which would be fun for everyone.

PRINCE OF WALES – HOME OF THE BIG BEAR

Roy and I met Steve's brother Mike, the El Dorado's skipper, in Craig, Alaska two days before the rest of the guys were to get in. I set it up this way because I wanted a day or two to get the baits fired up before everyone showed up to start hunting. To say this strategy worked well would be an understatement. Roy and I tooled around in the skiff and set eight baits in one day, which is a ton of work in itself. The next day we checked them and freshened them up. To our pleasant surprise all but one of them were slammed and we saw bears at three sites.

In fact at one of the sites as we approached with our bait buckets after tying off the skiff, we walked right up on a 19″ Pope & Young class bear. We didn't have a bow with us since we just planned on baiting so we set the buckets down and ran back to the boat to get a bow and the camera. Roy and I headed back in, sneaking along the soft wet trail wondering if in fact the bear would still be there, and it was.

While this bear wouldn't break any "Big Bear" camp records for us, I thought that if one of us could get a kill out of the way, then we could concentrate on filming and helping the other guys when they arrived. Roy agreed and went so far as to say I should be the shooter. Part of his reasoning no doubt is that he has probably lost count of how many

Gary Sims set the standard for us on this hunt. His big boar taped out at close to 21″ P & Y.

six foot, 19" black bears he has killed. At this stage of his bear hunting life, he seldom shoots anything that isn't near 21".

With the shooter/cameraman decision out of the way, I walked up to within about 10 yards of this bear, which apparently had no fear of humans, and dotted it with a perfectly placed arrow. We knew this bear was aggressive based on all the head high bite marks we noticed on nearby trees. This is a common behavior of a dominant bear. The situation was a little unsettling as we didn't know what the bear would do after I shot and a bear can cover 30 feet in the blink of an eye. Luckily for us, the big bear took the arrow like a champ before crashing off through the brush a short 25 yards before going down.

With that stroke of luck, we had one bear down a day before we even planned on hunting. The next day, I filmed Steve arrowing a giant bear with perfect hide as it hesitated only eight yards from our treestand. That same night, Roy filmed Steve's younger brother Gary kill an absolute monster. The bruin only made it about 20 yards after Gary made a great shot in fading light. Gary's bear ended up being the biggest of the trip, taping out at 20 10/16 Pope & Young, which is not too far off from that magical Boone & Crockett threshold.

When I filmed Roy shoot an old scarfaced bear a couple days later, we were all tagged out and The El Dorado was christened in style. We had a fantastic hunt to say the least. The inaugural "LimbSavers Bear Camp" crew ended up arrowing four record book bears in four days with four arrows. That might be the most productive four days in the history of bowhunting for a handful of guys out doing it on their own in the wilds of Alaska.

During the week I had the chance to really get to know Steve Sims. While he is a true pioneer in the archery world who will no doubt go down as a guy who turned the archery industry on its ear back in 1999 and has pushed the envelope ever since, in camp he just seemed like one of my ol' hunting buddies from Oregon. Now to me, that says a lot about him.

A SPECIAL THANKS

The Sims' oldest brother, Mike Sims, was the man that proved to be unflappable in guiding our floating 'bear camp' through some pretty interesting challenges. Kevin and Billy, who alternated between cooking and doing anything and everything else that needed to be done, joined us on the boat. These guys are both not only handy at a multitude of tasks, but they have an "open water" savvy about them that proved to be priceless so far as skiff operation goes. Without a doubt, these men really added to the hunt.

CONCLUSION

When it was all said and done, the highlight of my spring was not arrowing two record class bears in Alaska. My kills are more of a footnote to the real story. First kills, new friends, teamwork, dull overworked skinning knives, big bear and beautifully wild Alaska are some of the vivid memories that stand out from the 2004 spring bear season and I'll carry them with me for a lifetime.

The Big Picture

"It is only as we develop others that we permanently succeed."
–Harvey Firestone

I wanted to mention Tanner's bear kill here, even though it was not a bow kill, because of the importance I think we should all place on teaching our children, the next generation of hunters, about our cherished pastime. Spring bear hunts are perfect for bowhunters and ideal for kids who I think can really shine in a controlled hunting set up like this. Kids can learn many of life's most valuable lessons in the woods. Heck, we all can. Many of us are well aware of the challenges that accompany backcountry hunting. Personally, I think it is okay for kids to be wet, cold, fatigued or in general challenged every once in a while. Any discomfort they may encounter on a hunt like this is only temporary. Nowadays, a big dilemma for most of Tanner's friends back home are if the TV quits working or if their Gameboy runs out of batteries. Tough to develop much resolve in such an environment. It is not just kids though. In today's society, life is really almost too good. Too easy I think. Personally, I like the being miserable sometimes as it makes you really appreciate how good we really have it back at home.

In this regard, Roy's kids are off the charts tough. They spend pretty much all summer at the cabin, catching king salmon and killing bears. Amazingly, Roy's youngest son, Justin, who is only six years old, has killed four bears. Roy's middle child Taylor, who is 11 like Tanner, has killed a handful of bears, including his first with a bow this year as well as caribou. Ellen, Roy's oldest and only daughter, has also killed a number of bears.

North Country Caribou

The Perfect Hunt for the Adventuresome D-I-Y Bowhunter

"Feast or famine," might most appropriately describe bowhunting for caribou in wild Alaska. I have heard many a story of hunters facing a parade of animals in which the biggest challenge is trying to choose just one to arrow. And, conversely I have witnessed firsthand, times where the expansive tundra seems oh so desolate—void of animals or for that matter, all forms of life.

If you are in prime caribou country, the latter situation probably won't last long, as this nomadic species is always on the move. Just when you believe there is no hope, here comes a set of bobbing antlers over a nearby hill, popping out of a river cut, or you will glass a handful of animals that have seemingly materialized from thin air.

The fact is that Alaska has almost twice as many caribou as people. Alaska's human population numbers around 600,000 while there are over one million caribou in the state. The largest herd is the Western Arctic herd with almost half the total caribou in Alaska. Other big herds are the Porcupine and the Mulchatna herds.

There are 28 smaller wild herds ranging from the North Slope to the Canadian border, northeast of Tok, and a few herds of domesticated caribou—or reindeer as they're called—on the Seward Peninsula.

Caribou numbers are somewhat cyclic, but the timing of declines and gains is as tough to predict as the weather. Although, overhunting caused some herds to remain low in the past, today, varying weather patterns (climate), overpopulation, predation by wolves and grizzly bears, and disease outbreaks determine the number of animals and quality in the herds.

Alaska offers both the best and worst for the traveling Do-It-Yourself bowhunter. So far as animals go, the sheer numbers and variety of species makes the Last Frontier your best bet this side of Africa.

Despite all of its beautiful splendor, the harsh reality of the Alaskan backcountry is just one quick hitting storm away. Weather can hit hard at any time of the year, which makes adequate preparation paramount. One must expect the worst, and consider yourself lucky if all of that cold weather gear and rain-proof clothing goes unused. However, odds are, you will need it.

THE HUNT

I've made the long trip up north with the goal of harvesting trophy class bull caribou that call the rolling tundra on the Brooks Range's north side home a couple times now. I have been lucky on many previous trips to Alaska for a variety of animals, having returned home with a boatload of Pope & Young trophies and a whole magazine full of memories. On my last caribou adventure, just as in all of my hunts in the North Country, longtime hunting partner Roy Roth was my camp mate. Roy's cousin, Walter, who was 16 years old, joined us in our pursuit of trophy bulls.

The feeling was that we should be good to go weather-wise given the timing of this hunt. We hunted the last week of July, just days after the nearly four-month season opened, as our plan was to get a crack at good bulls right out of the gate and have comfortable conditions—the swarming mosquitoes notwithstanding. Given my thinly veiled foreshadowing, you can probably guess what ol' Mother Nature had in store for us. We were pummeled mercilessly for days on end. Ice-cold winds, blowing rain, sleet and snow definitely made this a trip to remember.

This was young Walter's first ever hunt in Alaska and I can tell you, the whitetail hunting back on the farm in Wisconsin didn't prepare him much for this Artic storm. The middle of nowhere feelings of isolation and the fact that all we had for shelter was a four-man tent didn't help matters much. I have a feeling that many from the "Lower 48" experiencing Alaska for the first time would have shared Walter's angst. At times he wondered if he would even survive the trip, let alone kill anything. This proved to be a pretty good source of entertainment for Roy and myself. He did make it out of the bush and I can say with certainty that on the heels of this trip, those cool mornings spent in the tree stand back home probably won't seem quite so bad. As they say, "It is all about perspective."

Roy with a great Haul Road bull. The hard hunting bowhunter could expect to tag two bulls on this hunt with a little luck.

We had been dropped at the head of a river not too awfully far from the Arctic Ocean. The plan was to hunt the snowfields (the caribou would bed on these in an effort to find some relief from the relentless mosquitoes) the Supercub dropped us off near for a couple days, kill a bull or two and then begin our 40-mile float on our inflatable raft back to the Haul Road.

Once we began our float, we envisioned camping where we found caribou and filling our six tags, two bulls apiece, by the time we hit civilization. Our way out, to civilization and eventually home, was the Haul Road. The Haul Road has a more formal name, The Dalton Highway. This highway parallels the Alaska Oil Pipeline for many miles and really, nearly dissects this huge state. We drove north from where Roy lives near Anchorage for over 15 hours until we finally arrived at our pilot's residence. This put us about 80 miles from the legendary town of Deadhorse on Prudhoe Bay, which also marks the end of the Haul Road.

I will cut to the chase and tell you that we had exactly two days of hunting before a big storm came in and completely shut down the caribou activity. The first morning, Roy and I took off together and let Walter roam the hills near camp to "get his feet wet," we reasoned. We found caribou, but in sparse numbers. After hiking in hip waders, which because of the many river crossings was mandatory, for about 10 miles, we finally found a bull

We hired a bush plane to fly us up river some 40 miles to a predetermined drop off point. From there we hunted for a couple days, killed a couple bulls and then floated down to the Haul Road. This was a classic Alaskan adventure.

that was in a stalk-friendly position. I eased up in stocking feet on the young bull in his icefield bed and arrowed him through the heart. My thinking was that since we hadn't seen a ton of caribou, I just wanted to get on the board with my first tag, and have some meat to take home. Mission accomplished. After photos and boning out my bull, we buried the meat in the snow and forged on to find Roy an animal.

We didn't go too far before we glassed up a big bull bedded on the edge of another ice field. The bull would intermittently get up from his bed and take off running through the brush and over the tundra in an effort to find relief from the mosquitoes. On one of his mad dashes, we headed him off and had him right in our laps. As we stood in the middle of a small river that cut through the icefield, the bull broke through the brush and stopped broadside at about 20 yards. Filming over Roy's shoulder I got some great footage of his arrow flying cleanly over the bull's back. That one hurt, as this was a great bull with double shovels and would have scored very well in P&Y. I can tell you this is a shot Roy seldom misses, but as we all are well aware, "bowhunting ain't easy."

It took us most of the night to get back to camp where we found Walter, how should I say, "Anxiously awaiting our return." Not a bad first day in the field. Not exactly the 'feast' I spoke of to kick off this piece but it wasn't a 'famine' either. We had decent action, especially for what I am used to in the bowhunting woods back home, and garnered lots of nice video footage.

The next day we spent moving camp down river, as we wanted to get closer to where we had my bull stashed. This move saved us about six miles of packing, but still left us with a round trip that tallied 14 miles to the meat and back to the river. This is quite a pack over tundra, but luckily the days are long up here in July and in Alaska you do what you have to do.

Well, so far as bowhunting opportunities go, that was it. We didn't even see a caribou for the entire rest of the hunt. That evening the weather moved in and stayed. In fact, even though we were floating down the river, we still had to row the entire 40 miles. The bloody wind was so strong that it would blow us to a stop or over into the riverbank if we were not rowing. What was frustrating was that the year prior, Roy had made this exact same float with two other guys and they each killed two good bulls with their bows. But, that was last year and this was this year. Things change. Now the hunt was taking on a very definite 'famine-like' feel.

Regardless of the outcome of this trip, I would do it again in a heartbeat. I mean chances are that one would not have back to back years like we had, so the odds would strongly indicate that next year would be a big bull bonanza. Nevertheless, chasing incredible animals around tough country, with a backdrop of some of the most amazing scenery in the world, made for a first rate hunt in my humble opinion. As most know, when hunting Alaska there are no guarantees and whether you are on a guided hunt or a Do-It-Yourself trip you are at the mercy of the weather. It is the allure of the unknown that makes Alaska so appealing to the adventuresome bowhunter.

GEAR FOR THE CARIBOU HUNTER

Hunting caribou in Alaska will almost assuredly be a spot and stalk affair or a variety of this approach that might be best referred to as spot and ambush. Either way, high quality camouflage that will effectively break up the human silhouette is a must. I wore Realtree Advantage Timber on this hunt with good results. I would suggest that all your clothing be weather-proof, waterproof, rainproof or whatever you want to call it. And with the terrific quality of jackets and pants available from a multitude of sources, I would go ahead and throw in windproof too. A good insulated set will run you about $280.

Bottom line is that your clothing needs to keep you dry. I don't even waste space or weight, which you will find are both critical when hunting the Alaskan backcountry, on clothing that is not waterproof. Under no circumstances pack anything made of cotton. This includes socks, of which mine are Ultimax from Cabela's and go for about $9 a pair. All undergarments absolutely have to be made of some sort of a synthetic blend that will wick moisture away from your skin. You can get a good top and bottom for about $60.

In keeping with the waterproof theme, I also have quite a selection of nylon-reinforced PVC bags that ensure my food, clothing and equipment stay dry. I have a variety of these in different sizes, which enable me to pack my gear in smaller, more manageable amounts. While the total mass of my gear is the same, these smaller sums that make up the whole are a bush pilot's dream. Those Super Cubs are quite tiny and big duffel bags of equipment and clothes simply will not work. In fact, on all of my Super Cub flights, I have had to hold my bow, as there was simply no other place to stash it. When at camp, the waterproof bags, which I ordered from Cabela's for between $35 and $70 depending on the size, also allow the option of keeping gear outside in the elements as opposed to in the typically confined space of a tent where real estate is a premium.

On my caribou hunt, and most others I have heard and read about, much of the hunt was spent wearing waders. These animals live in notoriously soggy, river riddled land and as much as they like to travel, you could be faced with the prospect of logging many miles in ill-fitting waders. This is why an exact fit and top-notch quality is of such importance when choosing waders. They also need to be tough, as ripped waders aren't much use. I paid $120 for mine and they have held up for years.

IN CONCLUSION

For more information on hunting off of Alaska's "Haul Road" please refer to Section 7 for my Top 5 D-I-Y Public Land Backcountry Bowhunts. This one makes the list, as I believe bowhunting along the Haul Road offers a great chance for the nonresident, D-I-Y public land guy to experience some unbelievable caribou hunting at a great price.

The Legacy Lives On

By Cameron R. Hanes

Editor, EBJ NWT 2005

I have to be honest, while I look forward to and get fired up for all bowhunting adventures, my recent hunt for big central barren ground bulls in Northwest Territories took "getting fired up" to new heights. Firstly, I would be hunting side by side with Mike and Guy Eastman, which always puts a little extra pressure on. Guy and I have shared some memorable hunts together but Mike and I have only really hunted together once, and it was a brief stint. He filmed me arrowing a good four-point mule deer in Montana a

It was an honor for me to hunt side by side with Mike Eastman.

handful of seasons ago and since then, I'd been doing my bowhunting thing and his schedule's been packed with rifle hunts, filming and producing TV shows. On this hunt, we would boat the same waters, walk the same trails, glass the same country and scrutinize the same bulls as we looked for a trophy. I was excited, mostly with the opportunity to learn from a couple of North Country veterans.

Mike has filmed and hunted Canada many, many times over his long and storied career. Her expanse and rugged beauty has been a special and momentous place in building the Eastman legacy. Gordon Eastman, Mike's father, captured some of the most powerful footage of his time in the mountains and tundra of the North while producing the classic documentaries High, Wild and Free (1968) and the Savage Wild (1970). Mike has carried on this legacy by producing countless TV shows and hunting films that chronicle hunting "The Eastman Way" from the artic tundra to the Maasai of Africa and of course all over the West.

For all you longtime Eastman's fans this is old news, as for decades Mike has been making movies that have educated and entertained legions of hunters and their families. As a bowhunter, one filmed adventure that's been burned in my memory was Guy's hunt with Jim Peterson of Peterson's Point Lake Lodge back in 2002. On that trip both he and his brother, Ike Eastman, took a couple great bulls including Guy's #7 Pope & Young bull of all-time. This remarkable animal still grossed right at 400 inches nearly a year and a half after he made a perfect shot on the bull on film at 40 yards.

On this trip Mike, Guy and I would again be hunting with Jim Peterson, who runs a first class operation if there ever was one, and guided by the same man who helped Guy and Ike in 2002, Paul Jones.

IN THE FIELD

Our first day in the field was one I will never forget. It was a little different than I expected, as there were definitely not caribou streaming by like I had visions of. We had to work a little to find them, which for me is nothing new. We didn't see thousands or even hundreds of animals but you don't need to, do you? All I wanted was one good bull to have a crack at.

Given I would be hunting with my bow and arrow rig only, Mike and Guy graciously gave me first opportunity, as our primary goal was to get some killer bowhunting footage. Mike also had visions of arrowing a bull as he was packing his trusty custom recurve. He has downed a number of good animals with stick and string over the years including one beautiful antelope back home in Wyoming. If everything was perfect Mike wanted to get one with a bow, but if it didn't work out he'd have no problem shooting a good bull with a rifle. Guy was packing his .30-378 magnum so after I either blew it or came through, he would pull out his sweet shooting Weatherby if an animal he was interested in presented itself.

After a cold, 20-mile boat ride down the 75-mile long lake, we tied our 16-foot skiff up in a protected cove and headed into the hills. Topping the first ridge we glassed up a handful of bulls, but nothing extraordinary. Hiking deeper, a few ridges and a few miles farther, we saw a bull that caught our attention. He looked to be about a 320 bull and he was headed our direction, likely in an attempt to outrun the black flies. Unbelievably, he kept coming right toward us. Paul, Guy, Mike and I collapsed onto the tundra as he topped a slight rise only 100 yards out. At about 60 yards I got up on my knees as Guy ran the camera just off of my shoulder. I had been ranging him in, but when he closed to 35 yards the rangefinder was put away for good. Finally, he saw us hunkered down and stopped, quartering hard to us. I was at full draw and had him right where I wanted him, other than the angle of the shot. I anchored hard, patiently waiting for him to open up a little. The bull trotted another 30 yards parallel to us, staying right at 35 yards out. Still on my knees I swung with him, the 30-yard pin hovered high lungs waiting to lock on. He stopped again and quartered away hard, too hard. Not the shot I wanted. Again, he was off and didn't stop again until he was about 100 yards out.

I was beside myself. I couldn't believe that a bull I wanted to shoot could come into 35 yards and leave without an arrow in his lungs. There was little doubt I was going to kill that bull when he came into less than 40 yards. I had so many thoughts racing through my mind now that the opportunity was gone; one being, "What if that was the last good chance I was going to get on a big bull during the hunt?" In some respects I felt like I let the guys down. With a rifle that bull was dead a hundred times over. Were they thinking, "Dang bowhunters, gotta have everything perfect?" It was a long walk back to the boat.

We slid down the lake another couple of miles and went through the same "beach the boat, hike inland from the lake" routine. After about a two-mile hike, we topped out and immediately glassed up an enormous bull snaking through the brush toward us. He was still a ways out and we contemplated setting up the spotting scope, but there was little doubt this bull was one anyone would love to tag. The tough part was trying to guess where in the heck he was going.

We quickly dropped down and hustled between two small ponds, making our way to the other side of the basin. Once there we angled upwards toward where we lost the bull in the trees. About thirty minutes after last seeing the big caribou we crested a finger ridge and I spotted him in the bottom, standing in some fairly high brush right on the creek. It is strange; at times these animals just run around, nonstop, with no rhyme or reason, then as in the case of this bull, they stop and hold tight for an extended period.

SHOWTIME

Paul and Mike would stay put just off the top of the ridge as Guy and I tried to close on the bull. This would give them a bird's eye view of the action from about 300 yards away. With Guy on my heels, I dropped down to the creek and made my way toward the bull. Now, we just needed that bull to hold tight a little longer. The stalk went quickly as even in the thick brush there were some good trails to follow. With perfect wind we closed to about 60 yards, and by using the brush and the contour of the land, never exposed ourselves to the bull. This was key as the caribou keep a watchful eye out for the many grizzlies and wolves that call the tundra home. In fact, as a sidenote, we saw five grizzlies over the course of the hunt and one day kicked a sow and cub off a fresh kill of a pretty darn good bull. This finding inspired me to come up with the phrase, "Life on the artic tundra is hard and final." At that time, little did I know that my catch phrase also nearly served as an omen on a more personal level.

With the camera rolling and Guy capturing some great "crunch time" footage I eased into the red zone. I could see the enormous tops of the bull's antlers as I picked each footfall carefully in making my way up the creek. He had his head down slightly and almost seemed to be sleeping. Every once in a while he would shake his head in an attempt to discourage the black flies.

At about 30 yards Guy sidestepped off the trail to a place where he could video the bull. I moved forward, painstakingly slow as the artic wind rustled through the brush and grass. With an arrow nocked, at 20 yards I bent my bow back and anchored in. Stepping up on a slightly higher piece of tundra that gave me just enough elevation to sneak an arrow over the brush, I nestled my red 20-yard pin behind the bull's shoulder just as he snapped to attention. He saw me, but it was too late. My green fletched arrow covered the distance separating us in a fraction of a second and before he knew what had happened he was basically dead on his feet. After a short 50 or 60 yard burst he crashed down on the spongy ground.

Neither Guy nor I could see him fall as we were in the creek and he ran up and over a small ridge, but Mike and Paul from their vantage point watched the entire episode. Too bad they weren't outfitted with a camera as well.

The insanely palmated tops on this bull are what help to push his Pope & Young score up to over 380. He will end up in the top 10 for P&Y's velvet category of the Central Canada caribou species.

With emotions peaking, Guy and I scampered up the ridge where we could see his antler sticking up above the tundra. That is a great feeling and I felt even better after I ran up to the monster bull and pulled his head up off the ground where I could look at it. I inspected his beautiful double shovels and insanely palmated tops, which incidentally really pile on the inches in regard to the record book. We taped him out green at over 380 P&Y, which should put him right in near the top of the listings in the velvet category. What an awesome animal.

With meat in my pack and those antlers draped over my shoulders, the walk back to the boat was one I will cherish. I am so glad Guy was there to film everything and Mike was there to share in the experience and pose with me for a few memorable photos.

THE HUNT CONTINUES

Caribou hunting can be a bit like rolling the dice, as you never really know what you're going to get. Finally, toward the end of the trip we got a real hint of what this area has to offer. Some unseasonably warm weather had slowed the caribou activity down substantially from the time I killed my bull until now. In fact one day, we only saw one single caribou, a bull. This was a rare occurrence and a first for our guide Paul, but it wouldn't be the last "first" of the hunt for Paul.

On the ride down the lake that fateful morning it became apparent a little weather system was moving in. The water was rough and the wind was stiff. My Suunto wrist computer confirmed this as it indicated a plummeting barometer. Bursts of water came over the bow in regular succession, which made for slow going and some nervous sideways looks when a particularly hard wave would slam into the boat. I secretly thought that maybe this would finally get the caribou moving. It did.

Soon after beaching the boat, shouldering our packs and heading up the hill, caribou were spotted. We kept sidehilling up and deeper in to the next vantage point. At each setup we'd pull out the big glass and scrutinize which bulls were worthy of going after. Without divulging too much (we will save that for the video) I can say that both Mike and Guy killed a couple great bulls on film with their rifle. It was a special day no doubt.

Isn't that something? After a week of fighting tooth and nail for any and every opportunity, we got into 'em thick on the last day of the hunt. We must have seen 30 to 50 bulls just that one morning.

After getting the bulls loaded up into our packframes, we got started on the two-mile hike down the hill and across the tundra to where the boat waited. We wanted to get both the animals and all the gear out in one trip. This meant the going may be a little slower and heavier, but we'd avoid the two trips scenario. The weight of our packs wasn't too bad, but the weather seemed ominous, which was a big distraction. We got the bulls to the boat and sat down on the bank to eat lunch before the boat ride home. The lodge was going to be a welcome sight tonight. A full day of hunting and packing, on top of the rough ride out and a sure to be rougher ride back in, would leave us beat and ready for a hot meal, a shower and a comfortable bed.

Rounding the bend out of the cove to the "open water" was distressing for lack of a better word. It was like flipping a switch as the water and wind went from relatively calm to angry and violent in nature. With whitecaps shooting skyward, our boat rocked and creaked under the strain of the powerful water. "Would the rivets in that aluminum boat stay put given we were fully loaded and beyond? " I wondered while staring at one particularly vulnerable looking fixture.

THE PERFECT STORM?

Normal winds, even when accompanying storms, come from a direction in which their impact is minimized on the lake. Typically, the ridges serve as protection or a barrier from the frigid blasts of air that routinely come in perpendicular to Point Lake. On this day, the winds shifted and came directly out of the north, which meant it was running lengthwise down the huge body of water. This can be bad, especially when, as in our case, we were 25 miles from the lodge and were fully loaded down. We had four guys, gear and two big caribou in the 16-foot aluminum boat, and to get back, we were going to have to go headlong into the wind.

I never would have fathomed that a lake could get as nasty as Point Lake was that night. It acted ocean-like and the problem was once we had committed, the frequency of the 6, 7 and 8-foot waves in the stretch of open water we were taking on made turning back impossible. At a minimum we had two miles to go as the crow flies until reaching the safety of a protected cove, which meant we would be covering the equivalent of about eight boat miles as our skiff would be climbing up and falling down those waves at a turtle slow pace. Under normal conditions we would cover the two miles in about ten minutes; tonight it would take us an hour and a half. In the cove was an empty grain bin set up as an emergency shelter. They called this the Outpost. We called it heaven.

Amid the uneven and strained drone of the 30HP motor we slowly forged into the rising and falling walls of water. When the timing was right, or more accurately, wrong, we would jump off the top of one of the rollers and land as hard as if we were landing on concrete. I expected to spit fillings in my teeth out at any moment. Or, if we weren't airborne and Paul didn't time it perfectly, the flip side was water would boil in over the back of the boat, at which time Guy would scamper back and with one hand latched on for dear life, with the other he would bail water like there was no tomorrow. Guy admitted later that the water bailing duty was a welcomed distraction from watching the angry waters boil all around us. Mike and I manned the seats toward the bow of the boat where we felt more like saddle bronc riders than hunters. White knuckle excitement if there ever was.

Not wanting to sensationalize our "situation" on the water, I can tell you that everyone who was there and experienced the harrowing boat ride on the water will attest to its intensity. To put it in perspective, Paul has guided on Point Lake for 20 years now and has never had to stay out even once before that night. That is 20 years, five hunts a year, five days a hunt and in the boat every one of those days. So in 500 trips, he had always made it back to camp. There was little doubt this streak would end tonight.

The boat experience is really part of the deal when you sign on for such adventures. There are no guarantees in the field, in the NWT or anywhere else and that is why up here, you sign a release. No one can control or harness Mother Nature, the grizzlies and any other miscellaneous and very real risks we face in the field. Life is fragile, but really it is just a numbers game. In the boat that night, crashing into the waves I simply hoped that the dynamics of the water did not come together in such a way that a huge wave was created that would either land on top of the boat and fill it up with one fell swoop or flip the boat over like it was a bathtub toy.

All I can say, and I know I am speaking for Mike and Guy too, is thank goodness we had a good captain at the wheel out there. Paul did a great job and got us to a place where we could spend the night out of the weather. Hitting the beach and slowly making our way up to the Outpost with stiff legs and bodies, cold and racked with shivers inspired yet another catchy and timely phrase, "Any day above water is a good day." We wondered if we had just lived through the Point Lake version of "The Perfect Storm."

In the end, three of the five boats did not make it back to the lodge that night. They too felt it was too dangerous to challenge the venomous water. The next day, the winds had shifted just enough that we were able to make it back to camp. On the way back in, through the bucks and jumps of the skiff and the spray of water, Paul admitted that he had never been on water like that in a boat the size of ours.

IN CONCLUSION

The final night of the hunt, we all were once again assembled for dinner and with lively chatter the one thing that stands out in my mind is Jim's relieved look on his face. All the boats were in and all the hunters were safe. For us the only thing that could have topped it off was if Mike would have somehow had a chance at a good bull with his recurve. Given the addicting nature of the pedal to the metal adventure that comes with hunting the Canadian artic, something tells me we will be back taking on those big bulls with stick and string only.

In the end, we had logged yet another successful chapter in the Eastmans' storied hunting saga north of the border. Thank you very much for the gracious invite Guy and Mike; glad I could do my part to ensure that the legacy lives on...

Peterson's Point Lake Lodge

Jim & Amanda Peterson

PO Box 447, Yellowknife, Northwest Territories Canada X1A-2N4

Phone: 867-920-4654, email: peterson@ssimicro.com

Adrenaline Overload in Alaska

By Cameron R. Hanes

Originally appeared in Eastmans' Bowhunting Journal *issue 7.*

What on earth could possibly rival the adrenaline rush one experiences when arrowing one of Pope & Young's highest scoring Barren Ground Caribou? How about facing the prospects of stopping a charging grizzly, mere feet from engulfing a loved one. Now, either one of these experiences would cause most of us to suffer an adrenaline overload, but couple these incredible happenings together on the same hunt and one would be measuring adrenaline levels on a Richter scale!

When my hunting partner Roy Roth left for his first caribou hunt since moving to Alaska four years ago, I had no doubt that he would return with many memorable and noteworthy experiences.

You see, Roy and I were inseparable hunting partners prior to his big move to Alaska and if I don't know anything, I do know that when Roy goes afield, he gets results. I respect no one else like I do Roy, for his toughness, woodsmanship and consistent archery success. Roy has been there from the beginning as he was the one to get me started in the wonderful world of archery. I reciprocated by prodding him into the extraordinary world of photography. I was there when he arrowed his first bull elk, and he helped me trail my first bear. You get the picture; if anyone has ever had a "hunting partner," Roy was mine and I was his.

Sure we have shared hunts since. There was the Sitka blacktail hunt on Kodiak Island, spring bear hunts in the Chugach Mountains and Prince of Wales Island of Alaska, wild boar in California, mule deer in Arizona, but now it is more the exception than the rule when we share a hunting camp. As a result, I now live Roy's hunts vicariously through his stories and photos. I believe the story of Roy's caribou hunt is one for the ages, which has inspired me to put his narrative into written prose.

On the inauguration of this hunt, Roy was accompanied by his father Ray and nephew Chris, whom would help pack camp in, stay a night or two, then leave Roy for the remainder of his two-week vigil before returning to help him pack out.

Roy did a considerable amount of homework searching for an area that held a good number of P&Y bulls and received little or no hunting pressure. Eventually, Roy did find a region on the Kenai Peninsula that fulfilled his predetermined mandates. And although this territory was renowned for producing trophy class caribou, it would also require a ridiculous amount of effort to get gear and pack animals into this isolated area. Ah, but this is what sets Roy apart from every other Tom, Dick and Harry packing a bow. For Roy, no effort is too great.

The trip began with a four-hour drive from Roy's home in Palmer, then there were the three separate trips with gear and pack llamas, in Ray's jet sled, 25-miles across a large glacier-fed lake that had all the qualities and appearance of the ocean itself. From there, if that wasn't enough, the region Roy planned on hunting was eight miles inland.

The pack trail that led across the tundra was very wooded with tall grass providing most of the ground cover. This trail paralleled a small stream that was so full of salmon it appeared as though one could walk from bank to bank without getting their feet wet. As unique of a sight as this salmon stream was, it was also a bit unnerving, as anyone who has spent time in Alaska knows that where there are salmon, there are bears. However, Roy, Ray and Chris were reassured by an Alaska Fish & Game biologist for this area before embarking on this excursion that this area held a low number of resident grizzlies and in all likelihood the only bears they would potentially have to contend with were black bears. And heck, everyone knows that even if there are a few grizzlies around, they are more afraid of you than you are of them, um, *right*?

After packing for approximately eight miles, the trio found an old moose-hunting campsite, which they decided to use as their base camp. Caribou season had commenced a couple days prior, so Roy and Chris decided to go afield for a quick evening hunt to familiarize themselves with the area as Ray set up camp. Roy and Chris had scarcely begun their trek when they spotted a caribou sporting extraordinary headgear. The bull's position could not have been any more perfect for Roy to try and sneak into bow range. This caribou was behaving in an atypical manner compared to others of his lineage. By that I mean, he was by himself, whereas they are historically herd animals; he was slowly plodding along nibbling on browse, while

Ray turned to Chris and asked if his gun holster was unsnapped.

conversely, they usually feed with the 'cruise control' locked on about a seven-minute mile pace. Not to mention, the terrain he was in consisted of small patches of alders and rolling hills, which was very conducive to a close quarters approach.

While Chris served sentry from afar, Roy quickly closed to within about 60 yards, thanks in large part to the idealistic conditions. From there he switched to super slo-mo, as he inched on his butt toward the unsuspecting monarch.

By using the crest of a hill as a shield, Roy closed in, all the while keeping his eye on the bobbing crown points of the bull, as it nibbled on bunch grass. Finally, time seemed to stand still as Roy rose from his half crouch, and while he cleared the uppermost tentacles of brush and grass, his line of sight ever changing, the bull's vitals became increasingly exposed, until Roy had the opportunity he needed. Reaching full draw, Roy's middle finger settled firmly into the corner of his mouth as he visualized his "money spot" behind the bull's shoulder.

Concentration was the word of the moment as the adrenaline surging through Roy had reached a deafening crescendo, making mental focus all the more difficult. Roy's arrow cut through the 30 yards of air that separated hunter from hunted, in a beautiful arc that only an archer could appreciate and instantly disappeared into caribou's slate gray hide. And, just like that history was made. Roy had just taken his first caribou - an animal that would rank as the #2 Pope & Young Barren Ground Caribou – velvet category. (Additionally - the bull also qualifies for the Boone & Crockett record book). Not bad for a beginner, but as I keep telling him, "Roy, how do you ever expect to take a World Record animal if you keep shooting the first thing you see?"

As Roy approached the fallen caribou, he quickly realized what an awesome trophy he had downed. This was by far the biggest caribou he had ever even laid eyes on. It was well after sundown by the time Roy and Chris completed the skinning and boning of the bull, so understandably Ray was waiting up, anxious to learn about the cause of their tardiness. Spirits were high as they filled Ray in on the hunt over dinner, and made plans for their premature departure out of regards for the meat, as it had been very warm.

Early the next morning, the trio took the llamas back to the harvest site to load up the

boned out meat that Roy had hung in nearby trees to cool in preparation for the pack out. With the llamas loaded up, they headed back to base camp, where they enjoyed caribou backstrap cooked over the campfire. The mood was one of merriment, as camp was disassembled, llama packs were filled, and finally, Roy, Ray and Chris wrestled their heavy pack frames onto their backs. With one last look around camp, everyone fell in line and the eight-mile pack out began.

The pack out was going according to plan, the llamas performing admirably, and so on. However, there was one disturbing distinction. The trail was full of bear sign and there were salmon carcasses strewn all about. Granted, they expected to see a considerable amount of bear sign and were even prepared for potential bear encounters. This is why they had outfitted the llamas, and themselves, with "bear bells." They also made an all out effort to be noisy on the pack out, so as not to startle any bear.

Ray was in the lead with about 70 pounds of meat and gear on his back, with his grandson Chris, wearing a .45-caliber Colt revolver in a holster on his hip, behind him leading the llamas. Roy brought up the rear, as he struggled with the awkwardness of packing those gigantic caribou antlers along the narrow, brushy trail. The trio continued to see increasing amounts of bear sign, which provoked Ray to turn to Chris and ask him if he had his gun holster unsnapped. Chris dutifully unsnapped his holster, and they continued toward the trailhead, all the while ringing their "bear bells" and singing silly songs for additional noise.

Not long after Ray queried Chris about his holster, they entered an area with very tall grass and the aroma of fresh fish in the air. This caused the trio a considerable amount of apprehension and over-the-shoulder glances, as they steadily forged forward. And, then they went from the uninspired rhythmic gait one gets into on a long pack, to sheer wide-eyed panic in a matter

of seconds, as a living nightmare unfolded before their eyes - a scene all hunters dread: A large sow grizzly stood up above the tall grass a mere 25 feet in front of Ray, and unleashed a half roar, half bellow that shook the woods.

The bear zeroed in on Ray, emitted another roar with a few extra decibels just for good measure and shook her head furiously, saliva flying all about her muzzle. The bear, with clear intent, then charged full-bore. Ray's first instinctive thought was to run, but he was simply packing too much weight to react. As the sow charged, Ray realized his only option was to dive out of Chris' potential line of fire and assume a defensive position.

With catlike reflexes, Chris responded immediately to the charging bear. His first shot with the .45 missed, but Chris, slipping into his "cool as the other side of the pillow mode" connected with his second shot. The bullet hit the bear directly above the left eye and exited behind the right shoulder. The grizzly died instantly and dropped a miniscule five feet from Ray. It probably seemed closer. Chris was only 10 feet away. The whole episode lasted no more than a few seconds, and Roy being behind the llamas, never even saw the grizzly. He heard a roar and then the two shots almost simultaneously. As Roy sprinted past the llamas toward the commotion, his mind raced a thousand miles a minute.

Roy figured that Chris and Ray had run into a black bear and being ever the cautious ones, fired a couple of warning shots to spook the animal. Needless to say, he was very surprised as he stared incredulously at the sight before him. Ray splayed out in the tall grass to the side of the trail, virtually pinned by the weight of his pack, Chris standing slack-jawed, the .45 still spewing a thin line of white smoke from the end of the barrel, and an eight-foot grizzly sprawled out in the trail. And then, amid the ringing in their ears from the booming pistol shots, their full attention went to the crisp sound of brush popping and grass rustling in close proximity. A partial explanation for the big bear's aggressive behavior became evident as two full-grown grizzly cubs tore off through the thick Alaskan foliage.

Sitting in the wet grass, they all stared blankly more than they spoke. Understandably shell-shocked, they tried to put the whole thing into context amid the musty smell of the grizzly and strong stench of salmon. In my mind's eye, I see Roy, Ray and Chris using this window of time to unknowingly take the advice of noted philosopher Rainer Maria Rilke who encouraged us to, "Go into yourself and see how deep the place is from which your life flows." A sobering experience like this puts the frailty of life into stark focus, which is why the quiet conversation among these men kept returning to the unbelievably fortunate outcome of this horrific confrontation.

Philosopher Rainer Maria Rilke's words seemed appropriate. If Chris' shot would have done anything but dropped the bear in its tracks, at the very least Ray would have been mauled. And, anyone who knows anything about this, one of the world's most fierce carnivores, knows that to stop a grizzly in its tracks is truly a rare feat.

"Little Chrissy" as his grandpa calls him during lighter times, deserves a lot of credit for single-handedly averting a sure disaster. Obviously, the sow wasn't bluffing her charge and in one cataclysmic moment, Chris at 16 years of age excelled in a situation where many grown men would have fled, failed or folded like a cheap suit. Chris, ever the humble hero, tells me matter-of-factly that, "I did what I had to do."

Being a man of strong Christian faith, Ray is convinced that the Lord directed Chris' shot, and he thanks and praises him for protecting him and his family. He is also thankful that he has a grandson with a cool head and a brave heart. By having this inconceivable grizzly experience inserted into an Alaskan wilderness hunt that had already made a resounding impact on the record books, one has got to believe they have truly been blessed with the often clichéd, "hunt of a lifetime."

Note – Given the fact that the big grizzly Chris was forced to kill was not taken during an open bear season, he underwent quite a process in order to take possession of the hide.

In what is termed as a 'Defense of Life & Property' type instance like this one, which is perfectly legal, the Alaska Department of Fish and Game holds an auction for such things as bear hides, with the proceeds going back to ADFG. What makes this a crapshoot is they will not announce where the auction will be held and in this case, Chris could not even find out whether or not his bear would even be there to be bid on. The reason for this is ADFG does not want people intentionally shooting animals and then simply going to an auction and buying their 'trophy.' As it turns out, Chris was able to learn of a nearby auction, which he and Roy attended. In going through the bear hides, Roy was able to recognize the hide, based on appearance, size and in part, on the way he had skinned it out. Chris successfully bid on the hide and for $450 took his cherished prize home. The bear in now preserved in a life size mount.

Note from CRH: I want to give my respects here to a good man who died recently at the young age of 22. Chris Stringer tragically lost his life in a boating mishap on the remote Yetna River in Alaska. In this story, Chris, who was my best friend Roy Roth's nephew, heroically killed a charging grizzly at 10 feet with a .45 caliber handgun as it was about to engulf his grandpa, Ray Roth. The bear died at their feet as Chris' actions averted sure disaster. Chris, who leaves behind a wife and daughter, was loved by many and will be missed.

Bowhunting in the Land of the Big Bear

Contemplating Claw and Fang

Black and brown/grizzly bears live almost everywhere in Alaska, but for most bowhunters, it is not the blackies that are of concern. It is the 'Big Bear,' the Alaskan brown bear or the grizzly that psych out many guys before they even get into the woods. Once ghastly thoughts of marauding grizzlies get into one's head, they can be difficult to purge and truthfully can have a great impact on the hunt's success or lack thereof.

In most cases, bears usually either avoid people or try to bluff their way out of an uncomfortable situation. Generally, the only time they attack is when they feel threatened. The threat could be to their cubs, food source or cache, or their personal space—especially if they are injured.

When threatened they will continue to fight until they feel a threat is neutralized, or they see a way to escape. Most bear attacks occur when a hunter surprises a bear at close range. A couple of the most common hunter/bear issues arise when the bear finds a hunter-killed animal carcass before the hunter or when the bear comes up on the hunter while they're breaking down their harvest. Either one of these close range examples seemingly puts your heart in your throat.

The vast majority of charges are ones in which the bear stops before making contact. The intensity of the charge or associated vocalizations may vary, but it is distinct in that it is an aggressive or defensive act clearly directed at another bear or human. Bears may charge immediately, as a sow fearing for her cubs, or may exhibit stressed or erratic behavior before charging.

There is no guaranteed lifesaving method for reacting to an aggressive bear. Being hunters, who make split-second decisions in the field all the time, we probably have an edge over the non-hunting population in the frantic environment created by a charging grizzly (Please refer to the story, 'Adrenaline Overload in Alaska' for a firsthand account of such an incident). Some behavior patterns have proven more successful in close encounters than others. What is recommended is to take a calm assured posture. A firm voice and gradual departure are better than a retreat in panic. But, there may be a time when one must need to protect himself. Before the adventure begins, you should decide whether you'll pack a firearm or bear spray for protection, or are you simply going to roll the dice and hope for the best.

If worse comes to worst and you find yourself on the losing end of a bear attack, lie face down, protect your neck with your hands and arms, and don't move. This requires considerable courage, but resistance would be futile. Numerous incidents exist where a bear has sniffed and departed without serious injury.

Rules for Hunting in Bear Country

The best way to avoid conflicts with bears when hunting is to remember a few simple rules.

- *Learn about bears and their behavior.*
- *Educate yourself about bears. Learn about where they live and what they like to eat during the time you will be in the field. When you are hunting, keep alert for fresh bear tracks and droppings. Try to stay away from obvious bear feeding trails and areas, such as near streams and lakes when fish are abundant.*
- *Let your presence be known to possible bears in the area.*
- *If a bear hears or sees you coming in their direction, they will almost always move away from you. You will likely never see or hear the bear. When you are stalking game, be very alert to the possibility of surprising a bear. If you do surprise a bear, talk loudly and wave your arms above your head. If you have a hunting partner, stand side-by-side to make yourselves look larger. Don't turn your back and run; this may cause the bear to think you are an animal to be chased and caught.*

Section 7

Top 5
Hardcore Hunts that Rock

D-I-Y Public Land Backcountry Bowhunts

I will discuss in detail each of the following hunts, which I deem the Top 5 public land bowhunts for the Do-It-Yourselfer—Wyoming & Idaho elk, Alaska black bear, Nevada mule deer, Sitka blacktail and Alaska caribou. In this chapter I'll fill you in on trophy potential for these adventures, likely odds of success for the hardcore hunter if you follow the guidelines in this book (no money back guarantees on this one—sorry), cost, which will included everything from travel to tags, and give each hunt my own personal Loss of Life or Limb rating:

Cameron's Loss of Life or Limb Rating System

☠☠☠☠☠ Might make sense financially to save a little money by buying a one-way plane ticket when you're booking the travel arrangements for one of these hunts, 'cause the over and under is even that you might not need that return flight. Oh, and it's probably a good idea to ensure your life insurance policy is paid up. The five-skull rating is saved for brown bear bowhunts and the like.

☠☠☠☠ If you do make it back from this hunt and really you probably will, it will be an adventure unlike any you've ever experienced, and may include seeing the face of God. On a four-skull hunt, big bear issues are almost guaranteed for the backcountry bowhunter. You could be stranded for a day or two by the pilot and very likely will be dealing with some very nasty weather.

☠☠☠ You may think you'll never see your loved ones again, but you'd be overreacting. While there will be many risks, you should make it home just fine unless you lose it and panic during times of high stress. You very well could see a few big bears, but chances are they will leave you alone. The most dangerous part of the hunt will be related to access, i.e. packstring rodeos, the bush plane flight or the big water boat trips in small crafts.

☠☠ This will be just your typical backcountry adventure—no bears, no big water. The hardest thing on the hunt will be dealing with the solitude and withstanding the physical abuse doled out by the country you'll be hunting. The chances of dying are remote unless you get struck down with appendicitis, stab your leg with a broadhead or somehow cut your aorta while breaking down your animal. Self-inflicted injuries aren't considered in this rating.

☠ The only way a hunt rated at one skull will cause you problems is if you are/were not committed to the challenge of the backcountry to begin with. To hunt for long periods in the wilderness has to start in one's heart. Tough to fake it back here. If you're not into it, you can be distracted or bored which both can lead to getting lost while you wander half-hearted through the mountains. A lackadaisical approach could be dangerous but because it is self-inflicted, the sympathy factor is low.

Why These Hunts Rock

It doesn't take a math genius to look at the following figures and know why these hunts rock if, and this is key, you do your part. Of my Top 5 they average a 73% success rate with a median cost of $2,140, which is what makes them so appealing for the blue-collar bowhunter. I have done all of these hunts at least once and been successful every time.

This is key for me. If I am going to save my pennies to hunt out of state, I sure the heck want a better than average chance of bringing something home. I mean, I can get shut out at home for far less money. On that note, let's get into the breakdown.

I killed this 6x7 bull in country I had never seen prior to pulling up to the trailhead.

Wyoming & Idaho Elk

A great blue-collar bowhunt for big bulls

For guys who are after a good six-point bull, this is the hunt for you. You probably won't kill the new World Record on either of these public land hunts, or see many 350-class bulls, although it is much more possible in Wyoming, but the chances of taking a Pope & Young bull are real for the hardcore Do-It-Yourselfer.

The odds of drawing a general Wyoming elk tag really aren't that bad (40%) and will only get better with the implementation of a preference

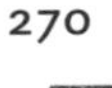

In one memorable season, Nate Simmons arrowed three six-point bulls, two in Idaho and one in Wyoming.

points system in 2006. For Idaho elk, they run a first come, first served over-the-counter system and you can pretty much count on getting a tag if you plan ahead and buy before the quota is filled.

In fact, my buddy Nate Simmons has killed two bulls in Idaho in one season. How this works is if you tag an animal and there are still licenses left (i.e. the quota hasn't been filled), you can buy a second nonresident tag and keep hunting. In 2004, Nate killed a decent six-point bull right out of the gate on his weeklong hunt, packed it out and processed it. He then

Simmons was able to kill a second bull in Idaho by taking advantage of extra nonresident elk tags.

ran down and bought another tag, went out and killed another six-point. Now that is maximizing your opportunities! Oh, and incidentally, he then drove over to Wyoming where he had drawn a tag and killed another great six-point immediately following his Idaho adventure. Do you need more proof on the quality of my recommendations? I can do that.

I have known quite a few guys besides Nate who have hit it hard in Idaho and Wyoming and killed good bulls. In 2004 I drew a Wyoming general season elk tag and killed a 6x7 bull on the 8th day of a great backcountry National Forest public land hunt. (Note: As a nonresident you must hire a professional guide or hunt with a Wyoming resident to hunt designated wilderness areas—check the regs.) While on my Wyoming hunt I wasn't hunting a true designated wilderness area and you couldn't tell the difference. I was miles from any road, hunting a beautiful and rugged mountain range and didn't see another hunter. It was awesome.

Idaho is much the same in regard to backcountry hunting opportunities,

World-class elk hunting on a budget best describes the backcountry of Idaho & Wyoming.

the biggest difference being you can hunt the wildernesses on your own without a guide, which I think is how it should be.

LIKELY ODDS OF SUCCESS

I think if you get in shape, get outfitted with high quality gear, hunt hard for an entire week, and do what you need to do during crunch time, your odds of success on a P&Y six-point bull should be right at about 50%.

LOSS OF LIFE OR LIMB RATING

Other than the rouge grizzly, the risks are pretty minimal for the seasoned backcountry guy. Relatively speaking, there won't be too many crazy happenings on this hunt, just the usual stuff that comes up in the wilderness. In regard to bears, some areas are worse than others. I didn't see any, but then again I wasn't in a big bear area. Check it out before you go and if the Game & Fish says you are in a bear area, I would suggest packing a can of bear spray on the waist belt of your pack frame just in case. ☠☠☠

COST OF THE HUNT: $1,700

Alaska Black Bear

Big bears and lots of them

For the traveling bowhunter, southeast Alaska has got to be the #1 place for the D-I-Y, public land guy to arrow a Pope & Young animal. If it is not #1 outright, it is tied with another hunt on my list, Kodiak Island Sitka blacktail.

For SE black bear, a guy can buy his license and tag over the counter, but if you plan on baiting, you'll need to set aside a little time for registering your bait sites and getting permits. I would call Alaska Fish & Game plenty in advance to give you enough time to do it right. I have experienced some great spot and stalk action as well up there if that is something you have an interest in.

Since securing tags is not a problem and the country is full of big bears, you're probably asking what's the catch, right? Well, there is also some vital logistics work you will need to do before this hunt works out. What we've done is fly from home into Ketchikan, then to Craig and from there, we hire a fishing vessel to haul us to our hunting grounds and leave us with a couple skiffs. The big boat powers out through some open water (believe me it can get nasty and we've seen it very nasty) for about a half a day to get us to the

Good friend Ben Maki snapped this photo of me leaning on my oldest son Tanner's first bear as we headed back to camp after a long wet day in the Alaska backcountry.

drop off. We have actually stayed on the fishing boat itself before when their schedule was open and they could stay. A couple of different years we set up an elk hunter's type camp on a small chunk of rock in the bay we call, "Roy Island." When camping out, we outfit Roy Island with a wood stove, a canvas cook tent and four man sleeping quarters.

From main camp on Roy Island, we use the 16' skiffs to motor to and fro setting our baits and/or looking for bears to stalk. Besides dealing with nasty water and fighting the hugely fluctuating tides, making sure to have enough bait up there is always a lot of work. If we have a couple of friends joining us and set up our normal bait site routine, we will need at least 1,000 lbs of dog food, not to mention an ample supply of Jell-O, bacon, marshmallows, and so on. Having this huge stash of bait is one reason we either camp on a small island or the boat. Bears would love to get in our stash and while they can swim very well, we haven't had any issues on Roy Island.

If you do your homework, nail your logistics, get into remote bear country and break out the "Bear Crack" you can experience success like Roy and I have up north. We have spent many weeks in Alaska "Bear Country" over the years beginning in 1999 and have both taken big Pope & Young boars every year. Sometimes Roy takes two as he is allowed a second bear because he is a resident of Alaska. As a testament to our system and the area, every person who has gone with us on our cherished spring hunt has also arrowed trophy bear. We are over 100%, thanks to Roy's extra resident bear, on public land on our own with bows. I don't know how it could get any better than that. This has become one of our favorite "can't miss" hunts.

Roy Roth has proven his mettle many times in the angry ocean waters off the Prince of Wales Island.

LIKELY ODDS OF SUCCESS

If you pull out the maps to find remote shorelines that bears will cruise looking for crabs and eating grass and get on the phone to secure travel arrangements, line up access to boats and finally, plan on giving yourself at least 8-9 days (it does take time to get those baits going) your odds of success on a P&Y bruin should be right at about 80%.

LOSS OF LIFE OR LIMB RATING

No big bear (grizzly) in the country, but there are still plenty of things to watch out for. The big water I mentioned is very dangerous. Any time you are crossing open water (which means the ocean) in a skiff, you're at risk. The weather can be brutal sometimes and other times it is beautiful. The month of May can be dicey up there in this regard. Other than the bush plane rides, the only other issues that come up happen when dealing with big black bear. If you don't hit those hulking beasts with a good arrow you can have some drama. We have had a number of interesting experiences up there in regard to wounded bears, but thankfully we haven't been chewed on yet. Be careful. ☠☠☠☠

COST OF THE HUNT: $2,500

Nevada Mule Deer

Big bucks, big country and big adventure

I don't have a ton of personal history to base my review on, but when considering the one year I have hunted the Nevada backcountry and the feedback from those I trust like South Cox, I can say with confidence this is one of the best public land mule deer hunts out there. There might be some naysayers who are partial to Colorado or Utah and it would be hard to disagree too much, as there are some great mule deer hunts in those states as well. I just think that given the healthy deer herd, thanks to some great and easily accessible winter range and tough to access backcountry, all the elements are in place for the deer hunt of a D-I-Y bowhunter's lifetime.

Both the Jarbidge Wilderness and the Ruby Mountains produce many good bucks. The adventuresome bowhunter should see a handful of Pope & Young bucks every single hard hunting day. In 2005, South and I had an incredible hunt. We both killed the first bucks we stalked; mine on the first day of season (170+ P&Y) and his on the third day of season (180+ P&Y). Thanks to Shon Simpson we captured it all on film to boot. We couldn't have scripted a better hunt, but don't think the hunt was all gravy. Those mountains are very rugged, very high and the country we were hunting was very remote. Plan on hiring a packer to do it right, if you don't own your own pack animals.

You'll have to draw a tag to hunt Nevada, but it is not too tough. I put in for three years before drawing and South has pulled four tags in the last eight years.

LIKELY ODDS OF SUCCESS

The bottom line is bowhunting trophy mule deer is never easy. I don't care where you are hunting and how many deer there are. Throw in some tough country, and well, you know where I am headed. While South has gone 100% on good bucks, his best hunting buddy and bowhunting pro Lon Lauber has been shut out in Nevada a few different times. I will tell you, if Lon can get shut out, anyone can. He successfully hunted the Alaska wilderness for years and is definitely right at home in the mountains. That being said, if you give yourself enough time (at least a week) and prepare like I've instructed in this book, I would put the odds of arrowing a 160+ P&Y buck at 60% for the hard working backcountry guy.

LOSS OF LIFE OR LIMB RATING

Just as the rating chart indicates this is your typical backcountry adventure. A good enough hunt to make my Top 5 but tough enough to keep most guys out of the mountains. Except for a freak accident and dealing with the solitude, the most risky part of this hunt will be the horse ride in if you hire a packer or own stock. A lot of up and down to this country and what those horses or mules are going to do is anyone's guess. One misstep or untimely bee sting and you could have a rodeo on your hands on trails that are not real conducive to rodeos. This is all part of the deal though. Game on.

☠☠

COST OF THE HUNT: $1,500

South Cox' 2000 Nevada buck.

Kodiak Island is home to big bears, big country and trophy bucks. It is one of the D-I-Y bowhunter's best bets.

Sitka Blacktail

Multiple harvest potential for the hardcore bowhunter

This is an awesome hunt for the D-I-Y guy wanting to experience Alaska. If it wasn't for first tier type hunts (reasonably priced) like this, I would have never had the chance to take on the Alaskan backcountry. Throw in the fact that you can buy multiple tags (four in most years) and for the nonresident bowhunter the price per Pope & Young animal is real attractive. When considering an out-of-state hunt I don't really like the thought of getting shut out, so I look for hunts like this where I think I'll see lots of animals and won't drop a bunch of money. All I am after is a realistic chance of bringing a trophy home. What I do with that chance is up to me.

I captured this memorable photo during our first trip to the island in 1997. We were as happy to get this photo "in the can" as we were with any buck either of us killed. Incidentally we both killed multiple P&Y bucks on the maiden adventure.

The toughest part of going after a P&Y Sitka blacktail is getting into the country and living there unscathed once you make it. I have always hunted Kodiak Island the first week of November, which is the peak of the rut, and always killed record book animals. Sounds good so far right? The problem is on each trip there have been times when I've honestly wondered if I'd make it home alive. This is what keeps a lot of guys out of Kodiak's backcountry despite the fact that I've seen on average 20 bucks a day while bivouacking out.

Looking at the big picture though, if you set up the logistics right, get off the beach, which is where the rifle hunters hammer, and head to the island's interior, this can be one of the most memorable hunts you'll ever experience. A mature Sitka blacktail, with its contrasting coloring and

After getting pummeled by a nasty November storm I was rewarded with a beautiful break in the weather the day after I arrowed this Pope & Young buck.

double throat patch, is one of the most handsome animals I've ever bowhunted, period.

Roy Roth and me with a great 4x4, my best buck of that first memorable Kodiak hunt.

LIKELY ODDS OF SUCCESS

Okay, there are a lot of factors that will go into whether or not you'll be successful on this hunt. Namely, your comfort level concerning, well, comfort or lack there of. I have done the bivy thing on all my hunts and don't think I have ever been more miserable. In November up there you can pretty much count on rain or snow every day. I would figure on rain as you'll typically hunt the rutting bucks fairly low on the hill. Even the best raingear after days and days in the wet will soak through. If you can deal with the wet weather and the bears, either the thought of them causing havoc or the real thing, I would say your odds of bowhunting success on at least one record book buck is 100%.

LOSS OF LIFE OR LIMB RATING

Here is where this hunt gets dicey. Every time I have made this trip it has been with my buddy Roy Roth and while we haven't had too many big bear problems when we've been together, he has had plenty on his own. One time an ornery ol' boar crashed his party on the first day of a 14-day hunt. The bear showed absolutely no fear while staring Roy down at 25 yards despite a couple warning shots from Roy's pistol. Then the big brown bear proceed to eat all of Roy's food and tear up his tent. He had to shoot deer just to have something to eat. That was a long two weeks.

In 2005 Roy was hunting with Dwight Schuh, and as expected, they too had their share of drama. They were scheduled for a 12-day hunt and while that went well (Roy killed five P&Y bucks and Dwight killed three),

Tony Graziadei

The best hunting on Kodiak is in remote areas. This means access by boat or plane, which in November, the time I suggest going to take advantage of the rut, can be dicey because of notoriously nasty weather.

Tony Graziadei

Dealing with the hulking brown bears of Kodiak is serious business, especially figuring out a way to keep them off your trophy after the kill.

the problem came about when they were scheduled to be picked up by the bush plane. They had planned on floating down the river from the lake they were dropped off on deep in the backcountry, but a cold streak moved through, freezing everything.

The lake was a solid block of ice, which meant the plane couldn't land and also meant they couldn't float the river. They were in such a remote spot they couldn't walk to a place the plane could get to. Plus they had 1,200 lbs. of gear to haul wherever they went, so they waited and waited and waited. Thank God for satellite phones or their wives would have been even more worried than they already were and Roy would have lost even more than 20 pounds on the hunt. While the pilot couldn't land he was able to fly over a couple times and drop food and propane for their stove. Finally, after nine days of waiting it warmed up and thawed out enough for the plane to get in to them. After 21 days in the bush they were headed home. They lost one deer to a bear but other than that, no real big bear issues.

Probably the most frightening time Roy and I ever had hunting Kodiak took place on the water. A huge storm was moving through and we made a bad decision to try to use a small inflatable raft with an outboard to get over to some good deer country we wanted to check out. That was nearly our last boat ride ever. I'll never forget the sight of Roy bending over and kissing the sandy beach when we finally did hit land after getting pummeled and soaked by the angry ocean water for about an hour. It didn't get much better as after the boat trip with all our gear sopping wet, we bivouacked out on the hill for four wet and cold days. Moral to the story though, I arrowed a great P&Y buck on day two; oh, and we lived.

Kodiak Island = Great hunting at the risk of paying the ultimate price and I am not talking money. ☠☠☠☠

COST OF THE HUNT: $2,800 WITH THREE DEER TAGS

There are many bear that call the Haul Road area home.
Good hunting for us means good hunting for them, too.

Alaska Caribou

Great hunting at a great price

For a guy just wanting to get his feet wet in the Alaska hunting scene, this is the hunt for you. For the Land of the Midnight Sun, going after trophy Barren Ground caribou off of the "Haul Road" in northern Alaska is a relatively mild hunt but still a great experience.

The Haul Road has a more formal name, The Dalton Highway. This highway parallels the Alaska Oil Pipeline for many miles and really, nearly bisects this huge state.

Our first time doing this hunt Roy and I drove north from Anchorage for over 15 hours until we finally arrived at our pilot's residence, (we did a slight variation of the typical Haul Road hunt as we wanted to get into the backcountry) who flew us some 40 miles into the hills. We floated from the base of some remote Brooks Range sheep mountains back to the Haul Road a few days after getting dropped Where we came out was about 80 miles from the legendary town of Deadhorse on Prudhoe Bay, which also marks the end of the Haul Road.

I will cut to the chase and tell you that we had exactly two days of hunting before a big storm came in and completely shut down the caribou activity. Hunting this far north, weather is always going to be a concern. Even so, we did bring two bulls out of the backcountry. Incidentally, you can buy two caribou tags if so inclined. This is something I would suggest because if you

Roy with a trophy bull from one of our recent Haul Road adventures.

go that far to bowhunt you might as well make the most of it.

The type of bush plane add-on we did is not required, as for five miles on either side of the Haul Road it is bowhunting only. This means that even by car camping you can experience a great Alaska caribou hunt, as there are a huge number of animals that call the tundra along the gravel Haul Road home. Because it is bowhunting only, you will need to pass a Bowhunter Certification course to hunt the bow zone. This is the case in all bowhunting only areas of Alaska, not just along the Haul Road.

LIKELY ODDS OF SUCCESS

The tundra the caribou call home is open of course, which can make getting to within bow range a little bit of a challenge. There is enough contour though that you will be able to attempt to close in most of the time. Some bulls will simply be unstalkable and you'd be advised to hold off and wait for a better opportunity before pushing the animals. This is a good philosophy no matter where you're hunting. Before making this trip, I would get comfortable shooting out to at least 40 yards. If this is within your effective range and you give yourself at least a week of hunting time, I will put the chances of successfully arrowing one Pope & Young (325 inches) bull at 75%.

LOSS OF LIFE OR LIMB RATING

There are grizzlies that call this country home so there is always the issue of coexisting with these big bears. The last time I went up there I was chased back to the road by a very aggressive boar and woofed and huffed at by an agitated sow with two cubs. If you have a phobia of grizzlies, this might not be the hunt for you. You have to understand, the caribou hunting is not only good for you, it is for them too.

Ray, Roy and Chris: Some bowhunters choose to set up a tent and camp out off the Haul Road. Keep in mind for 5 miles on either side of the Haul Road it is a bowhunting only zone, which means you must pass the bowhunter's education course to hunt this area. Check with Alaska Game & Fish for details.

If you opt to do the bush plane fly out and float back, well of course this opens up a whole gamut of additional risks. On the water as we know anything can happen and flying in the mountains is always an adventure. The pilot we used, who was one of Alaska's best, died in a plane crash a couple of years after our hunt. Life is oh so fragile, especially in the harsh and unforgiving country of northern Alaska. ☠☠☠

THE COST

This hunt was a handful of years back, but actually the prices haven't changed much. Back then, I spent under $2,000 total on this hunt. That includes: $650 ($325 x 2) for nonresident caribou tags, $85 for a nonresident hunting license, $350 for my portion of the bush plane airfare, $200 for my portion of the gas to travel from Anchorage to Deadhorse, $250 for airfare from Portland, Oregon to Anchorage, $150 for food and miscellaneous gear, $100 to get the meat air freighted home and $200 for eating along the way and staying a night in Deadhorse after the hunt.

This is still a fair bit of money, but this type of unguided adventure is the only way it has been possible for me to hunt Alaska. Consider that to make a guided caribou hunt you will easily spend double my $2,000. For some, the guided hunt might seem more appealing; to others, maybe the D-I-Y deal works. All I know is that the difference between $2,000 on a hunt and $4,000 on a hunt is the difference between me going and me not going. Plus, the feeling of self-satisfaction that comes with bringing out your trophy on a hunt that you are 100% responsible for is, to steal a catch phrase, "Priceless."

COST OF THE HUNT: $2,200 WITH TWO TAGS

END NOTE

The timeless and honorable tradition of bowhunting has given me so much; my goal with this book is to try and give something back. Years of surviving and thriving in the backcountry seem to have given me a heightened sense of life. Without a doubt, I've learned more about myself during one season in "deep" than I could in 10 years on the "outside." Those tough hunts in the mountains have made me who I am. My hope is that maybe this book will make "the" difference for a bowhunter who has been hungry for adventure. After reading my manual, maybe they will have the confidence to dive off into the wild with just the gear they can pack on their back. If this book motivates, educates or inspires even one person and they too experience the unrivaled feeling of hunting on their own in the mountains and end up bringing home a trophy, I will consider my work a success.

If nothing else, I want this book to prove how much is possible for the Average Joe. I didn't come from money nor did I have incredible hunting opportunities thrown my way when I first began bowhunting in the hills just outside of Springfield, Oregon. Coming up, I was just like any other guy out there with a bow and a dream. Back in the early years, if I wanted to arrow a trophy, there were no shortcuts to success. I had to work my tail off on public land to find a wallhanger, earn a little luck and make a good shot, period. No special draws that limited the number of hunters or private ranches that ensured quality animals, just good old fashioned, over-the-counter, blue-collar bowhunting. And, honestly, this is the way I like it. Pure bowhunting.

One thing I have learned from my exploits is success will be rare for a bowhunter who lacks passion and drive. Because the backcountry bowhunter must be so dedicated to this discipline, the pain of failing can be excruciating. The backcountry bowhunter will be hardened by the test because of this pain but in a perfect example of bowhunting justice, they will also appreciate success more. I wouldn't trade the day I arrowed my first wilderness 6x6 bull on a solo hunt for anything. The moment that arrow buried in his side will be etched in my mind for eternity because it meant I had finely achieved a goal that for years I had long thought impossible.

Rich, life-defining experiences that run the full gamut of emotions are there for the taking. That is, if you are you ready for the next level. If you are, good luck and maybe I'll see you on the mountain.

Cameron R. Hanes
March 2006

Hunt hard. Pick a spot.
Cameron R. Hanes